Geocriticism

ALSO BY BERTRAND WESTPHAL

Le monde plausible. Espace, lieu, carte

Austro-fictions. Une géographie de l'intime

L'œil de la Méditerranée. Une odyssée littéraire

Roman et Évangile

Littérature et espaces (with Juliette Vion-Drury and Jean-Marie Grassin)

La géocritique mode d'emploi (editor)

Geocriticism

Real and Fictional Spaces

Bertrand Westphal

Translated by Robert T. Tally Jr.

palgrave
macmillan

GEOCRITICISM

First published in France as *La Géocritique: Réel, Fiction, Espace* by Les Éditions de Minuit

First published in English in 2011 by PALGRAVE MACMILLAN® in the United States—a division of St. Martin's Press LLC, 175 Fifth Avenue, New York, NY 10010.

Where this book is distributed in the United Kingdom, Europe, and the rest of the world, this is by Palgrave Macmillan, a division of Macmillan Publishers Limited, registered in England, company number 785998, of Houndmills, Basingstoke, Hampshire RG21 6XS.

Palgrave Macmillan is the global academic imprint of the above companies and has companies and representatives throughout the world.
Palgrave® and Macmillan® are registered trademarks in the United States, the United Kingdom, Europe and other countries.

ISBN: 978-0-230-11021-2

Library of Congress Cataloging-in-Publication Data

Westphal, Bertrand.
[Géocritique. English]
Geocriticism : real and fictional spaces / Bertrand Westphal ; translated by Robert T. Tally Jr.
p. cm.
Originally published in French as La géocritique: réel, fiction, espace.
ISBN 978-0-230-11021-2
1. Space in literature. 2. Geography in literature. 3. Geographical perception in literature. 4. Geography and literature. 5. Geocriticism. 6. Literature, Modern—History and criticism—Theory, etc. I. Tally, Robert T. II. Title.

PN56.S667W4713 2011
809'.9332—dc22 2010043637

Design by Scribe Inc.

First edition: May 2011

10 9 8 7 6 5 4 3 2 1

Printed in the United States of America.

À Titti

Contents

TRANSLATOR'S PREFACE

The Timely Emergence of Geocriticism

In recent years, *space*—along with such related concepts or practices as spatiality, mapping, topography, deterritorialization, and so forth—has become a key term for literary and cultural studies. The nineteenth century had been dominated by a discourse of time, history, and teleological development (following in the Hegelian tradition) and by a modernist aesthetic that enshrined the temporal, especially with respect to individual psychology (à la Marcel Proust's *In Search of Lost Time*). But after the Second World War, space began to reassert itself in critical theory, rivaling if not overtaking time. The "spatial turn"[1] was aided by a new aesthetic sensibility that came to be understood as postmodernism, with a strong theoretical critique provided by poststructuralism, especially in French philosophy, but quickly extending into various countries and disciplines. Moreover, the transformational effects of postcolonialism, globalization, and the rise of ever more advanced information technologies helped to push space into the foreground, as traditional spatial or geographic limits were blurred, erased, or redrawn. In this context, critics and theorists had to develop novel interpretive and critical models to address what Fredric Jameson, referring specifically to Edward Soja's illuminating study, has called the "new spatiality implicit in the postmodern."[2] In the churning wake of the postmodern condition—or perhaps, now, post-postmodern condition—we are understandably interested in making, reading, and revising our maps. Space is, well, *timely*.

Thus, it is also timely that Bertrand Westphal's *Geocriticism: Real and Fictional Spaces* appears (now in English). Westphal, who directs the research team devoted to "Espaces Humains et Interactions Culturelles" at the Université de Limoges, has long advocated a "geocentered" approach to literature and cultural studies, which would allow a particular place to serve as the focal point for a variety of critical practices. Thus, Westphal's edited collection on the Mediterranean[3] looked at the various depictions of that multifaceted zone—whether using classical myth, modern fiction, historical works, tourist brochures, or something else—to form a pluralistic image of the place. After all, a *place* is only a place because of the ways in which we, individually and collectively, organize space in such a way as to mark the topos as special, to set it apart from the spaces surrounding and infusing it. Our understanding of a particular place is determined by our personal experiences with it, but also by our reading about others' experiences, by our point of view, including our biases and our wishful thinking. (For instance, on my first trip to London, I remember being disappointed at landing at Heathrow on a bright and sunny summer's morning; steeped as I had been in Dickens and others, I felt that it was somehow wrong that London wasn't rainy and foggy—happily, the rain and fog soon came.) Drawing on interdisciplinary methods and a diverse range of sources, geocriticism attempts to understand the real and fictional spaces that we inhabit, cross through, imagine, survey, modify, celebrate, disparage, and on and on in an infinite variety.

Geocriticism allows us to emphasize the ways that literature interacts with the world, but also to explore how all ways of dealing with the world are somewhat literary. The geographer—and not just Borges's famous mapmakers who tried to create a map coextensive with the territorial empire it purported to represent—is a kind of writer ("earth-writing" being what geography is, literally), and the representational techniques used in such sciences are often analogous, if not identical, to those used in so-called imaginary writing. In my brief review of Westphal's *La géocritique*, I noted that "all writing partakes in a form of cartography, since even the most realistic map does not truly depict the space, but, like literature, figures it forth in a complex skein of imaginary relations."[4] Indeed, the realistic London of Dickens or Paris of Balzac are part of what I call the *literary cartography* of the world, but so is Amaurotum, capital city of Thomas More's Utopia, or Minas Tirith, capital of Gondor in J. R. R. Tolkien's Middle-earth. So is William Faulkner's Yoknapatawpha County, which would seem to combine the referential space of Faulkner's own Oxford, Mississippi, with the imaginary spaces traversed by fictional Compsons, Bundrens, and Snopeses. But really, all places are like Yoknapatawpha, combining the real and the imaginary. As Westphal points out, the referentiality of fiction (and other mimetic arts) allows it to point to a recognizable place, real or imaginary or a bit of both at once, while also transforming that place, making it part of a fictional world. In this sense, geocriticism allows us to understand "real" places by understanding their fundamental fictionality. And vice-versa, of course. We understand "fictional" spaces by grasping their own levels of reality as they become part of our world.

Westphal draws heavily upon the insights of poststructuralism and postmodernism, among other nonscholastic "schools" of thought, but Westphal insists on a kind of referentiality that a Baudrillardian hyperreality was to have permanently done away with. Westphal takes such an argument seriously, and he certainly does not attempt to return to an unsophisticated notion that fiction is able to offer a mirror reflection of the "real" referent out there. Rather, Westphal understands that the referentiality operating between fiction and the "real" world is characterized by constant movement, or *oscillation*, as he puts it, whereby one can never really fix or pin down the referent—only the text of God could purport to do such a thing—but neither does one simply abandon the effort. Indeed, the inability to fix a referent in a literary text makes the project of geocriticism all the more worthwhile, as the critic may look at the multiple, well nigh infinite, variety of texts that refer to a place in order to shape the vision (an ever-shifting image) of the "real-and-imagined" place, as Soja has dubbed it.[5] This also encourages further explorations. As Westphal elaborates in more detail in Chapter 4, geocriticism will involve what he calls *multifocalization* and *polysensoriality*, among other things, insofar as the approach moves beyond merely a single author's perspective (e.g., Joyce's Dublin or Dostoevsky's Saint Petersburg) and engages all five senses. By bringing together multiple authors, including multiple genres and disciplines (e.g., reading tourist brochures alongside Homer in examining Mediterranean spaces), the geocritic orchestrates a number of different points of view, allowing diverse perspectives to flesh out, to round out, and perhaps to overcome the stereotyping or otherwise limiting images of a given place. By taking time to focus on senses other than merely the visual, the geocritic can register the sensuous plenum of a place, where the fragrance of jasmine commingles with the flavor of some Proustian tea-soaked cookie, or the texture of the cobblestones echoes the bone-rattling clamor of horse-drawn hearses (in a nursery rhyme exhumed and reiterated for the epigraph of Neil Gaiman's *The Graveyard Book*). These senses do not overthrow, but rather supplement, the kingdom of the visual, of *le regard* (which, out of deference to the tradition of Sartre and Foucault, among many others, I have for the most part translated as "the gaze"), rendering the polysensorial place more completely "realized" in our fictional interactions. Of course, the idea of *completing* the geocritical analysis of a place is as false as the idea of fixing it in a permanent, unchanging, and static image. If failure is inevitable, then the goal must be to fail in interesting ways. And geocriticism presents interesting ways to engage with the spaces of fiction and reality.

The title of this book, here and in the original French edition, is deceptively categorical. This book does not once and forever provide a definitive answer to the question, "What is geocriticism?" *Geocriticism* surveys a territory, speculates about others, suggests possible paths to take, and argues in favor of certain practices and against others, all while peregrinating around multiple discourses of space, place, and literature. In a world in which fiction may be as reliable as any form of understanding the world, what grounds do we have for analysis?

What methods can we use to make sense of things? Indeed, in his introduction, Westphal indicates his paradoxically tentative and yet bold project: this book is "an attempt—one trial, among many other possible ones—to answer these questions, to capture if only fleetingly the mobile environment in a cautious, humble way." *Geocriticism* is an *essay*, in the strongest and broadest sense of the word, an "attempt" to make sense of things, to make sense of the ways we make sense of things, which is after all the role of the critic. As Frank Kermode has said, in a book dedicated to the study of temporality rather than to spatiality, but no less apt, "It is not expected of critics as it is of poets that they should help us to make sense of our lives; they are bound only to attempt the lesser feat of making sense of the ways we try to make sense of our lives."[6] So too with geocritics. *Geocriticism* offers Westphal's attempt, one among many he has made and will make, and one among the many being made or to be made by other critics (whether they would embrace the term *geocriticism* or not) working with real and fictional spaces, to make sense of the ways we make sense of our world, of our places in the world, and of our various and complex mappings of those worldly and otherworldly spaces. The final word in *Geocriticism* is quite fittingly the verb *explore*, for, notwithstanding the seemingly categorical title, Westphal intends for geocriticism to be an exploratory critical practice, or set of practices, whereby readers, scholars, and critics engage with the spaces that make life, through lived experience and through imaginary projections, meaningful. As is apparent by the rapidly growing library of books and articles devoted to such projects,[7] this is a timely moment for the emergence, and proliferation, of geocriticism.

* * *

In translating a book on geocriticism, I am made especially aware of the spatial significance of such a project. As most know, *translation* refers to a crossing over, much akin to what Westphal refers to as transgressivity in chapter 2. The Latin *translatio* means "to carry over," which certainly implies border crossing, in more ways than one. In transporting Westphal's prose, I have endeavored to allow his style and language to come through as much as possible, while inevitably making a lot of changes in order to do justice to Westphal's thoughts now rendered in English. I have also modified the original by citing the English versions, where available, of the eclectic and wide-ranging array of texts that Westphal enlists in making his argument. Every translation is a mistranslation, of course, and just as no representation of a place can be a perfectly mimetic copy of the "real" location, no translation can "really" bring the original across the linguistic and cultural divides. I am painfully reminded that the Romance languages, over time, allowed the "carrying across" of *translatio* to become the "leading across" of *traduco*, such that the French word for translation is a cognate for an English word (*traduce*) that suggests betrayal. Hence, the perfidy of translation, of transgression, which is a good enough reason for travelers and readers to explore the originals . . . not because they are pure or authentic, but in order to makes one's own translations, betrayals, and interpretations. In the meantime, I hope that this effort to carry Westphal's geocriticism across to other zones is a fruitful step in a larger movement conducted—like geocriticism itself—by multiple authors.

I am grateful to Bertrand Westphal for his support at every stage of this project. I also want to thank Irène Lindon of Les Éditions de Minuit and Georges Borchardt Inc. Brigitte Shull of Palgrave Macmillan has been an extremely patient and helpful editor, and I gratefully acknowledge her support. I have benefited immensely from the collegiality of my many colleagues at Texas State University, particularly Michael Hennessy and Ann Marie Ellis. I am especially thankful for the support of Reiko Graham, who has to put up with far too many questions, interruptions, non sequiturs, general complaints, and occasional rants, but who always manages to do so with love.

Introduction

The perception of space and the representation of space do not involve the same things. There is no mere apprehension of unchanging spatial criteria and no static reading of topological data. Western culture's views of space and time are still beholden to models inherited from the Enlightenment or, more directly, from positivism. Just as time is not reducible to a river metaphor that would enshrine it as a gradual and horizontal unfolding or to a sagittal metaphor that establishes its reversibility, space is not the empty container of a Euclidean geometry adapted for the use of the positivists. The Einsteinian revolution broke through these metaphors. Everything is now relative, even the absolute. Since the early twentieth century, Euclid is no longer the man he was, or *what* he was. Where are the benchmarks, which are the stable coordinates of space?

In fact, space may have already escaped from this caricature, even at the beginning of the Euclidean order. Historically, space has always been subject to symbolic readings. The concrete details of geography often relate to a spiritual hermeneutic rather than to immediate observation. Speaking of geographical space in medieval Russian texts, Yuri Lotman noted, "Geography becomes a kind of ethics. So any movement in geographical space is significant in the religious and moral sense."[1] Of course, the Middle Ages leaned in this direction. Whereas medieval *time*—defined early on by Saint Augustine—punctuates the journey of man toward God, who monopolizes his spirit and conditions his soul, medieval *space* is, as Giuseppe Tardiola puts it, "eminently ontological, psychological, conclusive; like time, it becomes the sphere of activity of the symbol and the liturgy."[2] When Saint Brendan, legendary Irish monk, leaves the coast of Kerry to undertake a *navigatio* toward paradise, he adopts a liturgical calendar and a course marked out by his memory of the Bible. Euclid is forgotten; he was never taken into account by such monks and the scholastics. Space and the world in which it unfolds are the fruits of a symbolic system, of a speculative movement, which is also a glimmer of the beyond, and (let us venture the word) of the *imaginary*. This imaginary is not entirely cut off from reality. The one and the other interpenetrate according to a principle of nonexclusion that is regulated within the religious canon.

All things being created by God, they partake of the same transcendental reality, eluding in advance the cleavage that will emerge later between reality and fiction, between an affirmed verisimilitude and the supposedly unrealistic. Dante conceived his *Divine Comedy* according to this panoptic (and vertical) orientation, enabling him to comprehend three dimensions of the afterlife: hell, purgatory, and paradise. With Dante, the Middle Ages ideally posed a holistic unity, in what Mikhail Bakhtin called "the coexistence of everything in eternity."[3] Space was inherently a speculation on the supernatural and a reflection of creation. If the conception of time was static, as a measure of material action, that of space was more dynamic. In the *Divine Comedy*, the character of Dante is placed in the visceral spatial environment that he describes and must confront, whereas time hardly passes (and would not pass at all if the protagonist did not maintain the characteristics of the living in a context in which only those in purgatory escape the strict timelessness of eternity).

The concept of space-time has emerged and evolved since the Renaissance. Bakhtin has commented on this transformation in "Forms of Time and Chronotope in the Novel," in which he stressed the importance of a major shift from the verticality of time to its horizontality, which resulted in "a general striving ahead."[4] Indeed, a *flight* ahead. Bakhtin might have also added that the perception of space becomes vertical with the introduction of perspective in painting and mapping, and with the alignment of the planet's sidereal depth in the solar system. This shift has strengthened over the centuries, and it still holds true today. But something suggests that our space and our time have recovered some of the salient features of the framework in place before the Renaissance. Perhaps it may be that God is dead, who knows? Nietzsche is dead, anyway. In any case, whatever the fate of God, he is no longer at the heart of these debates. Our society does not aspire to transcendence. The plan of space-time has not returned to the vertical, but space-time is no longer quite horizontal either. The benchmarks have lost much of their former validity. The postmodern condition has cast doubt on the certitudes of modernity and has reconciled the contemporary with a certain protomodernity—the one that proclaimed the coherence of a world under the sign of nonexclusion and coexistence of all things. The postmodern also strives to establish a holistic coherence . . . but of heterogeneity. "Coherence" and "heterogeneity"—this unlikely alliance of words also registers the chaos of the new space-time. This study of geocriticism is situated in the labyrinthine space of the postmodern.

It is much easier to trace the history of postmodernism than that of representations of space: sixty years at most for the one against the entire span of humanity for the other! But it remains that postmodernism is readily defined by its lack of definition. This absence of a clear, agreed-upon definition has led to a multiplicity of approaches. I am not interested here in conducting a tour of them, or even in embarking on the quest myself, but my presentation of geocriticism in this book will follow from encounters with postmodernism. In *The Spaces of Postmodernity: Readings in Human Geography*, Michael J. Dear and Steven Flusty set out several principles worth noting. In their view, postmodernism supplies an ontology of radical uncertainty. Postmodernism emerges from the ruins of the twentieth century: the smoking remains left by conflicts (especially by the Second World War), but also the cacophonous ruins of the former unity of language and representation, whose crisis had been detected and analyzed by Ludwig Wittgenstein and his successors. The former harmony, thought to be "objective" (by positivism), was in fact ideological, and was seen at the moment of its collapse to be a scattered collection of multiple subjectivities. Discourses multiplied in a beautiful *profusion* . . . and a not-so-beautiful *confusion*. "Hence," Dear and Flusty argue, "we must inevitably fail in the task of representation (i.e., the 'objective' reporting of our research 'findings'), and in attempts to reconcile conflicting interpretations."[5] As Dear and Flusty conclude, in the wake of Jean-François Lyotard and many others, "In sum, postmodernism undermines the modernist belief that theory can mirror reality, and replaces it with a partial, relativistic viewpoint emphasizing the contingent, mediated nature of theory building. Metatheories and foundational thoughts are rejected in favor of microexplanations and undecidability. More than most thinkers, postmodernists learn to contextualize, to tolerate relativism, and to be conscious always of difference."[6] In this environment, in which we admit that reality has been relativized, if it is not entirely relativistic, *reality* itself has become "a plural word."[7] And the reality here referred to is "objective" reality, "real spaces" of which we might have expected geographers such as Dear and Flusty to be the fiercest defenders.

In this context, the role of those arts that have a mimetic relationship to the world is transformed and achieves greater significance: literature, cinema, painting, photography, music, sculpture, and so on. Are these aesthetically confined to the task of reintegrating this world? A difficult question, which calls for a response, albeit one that is provisional and subject to change. Without anticipating the discussion in what follows, I would postulate at the outset that if the perception of spatiotemporal referentiality fades, then the fictional discourse conveyed through the arts is ipso facto also transformed from its original vocation. Less clearly on the margins of reality than it was in the prewar era, fictional discourse has gained the force of persuasion. And if credibility in fiction has always been measured in terms of the reference to the "real" world, in the postmodern era one can no longer say that the world of cement, concrete, or steel is more real than the world of paper and ink. I mentioned earlier the postmodern labyrinth, and each hierarchical, spatial labyrinth has a monster in the center. In ancient teratology, the Minotaur was half man, half bull. And what about today? What would happen if the Minotaur had survived? It would have been a monster, a composite being, but like many monsters it would be rehabilitated. Just think of the empathy and romance woven around the various King Kong films and of all the Beasts that have been encountered and sometimes loved by the Beauties. It is because times are heterogeneous. At the heart of the labyrinth, the Minotaur constitutes a tangible sign of a new alliance between a normative reality ("normality," in a word) and that which would no longer be separated from fiction, placed outside of the norm. Today there would be no need for Theseus to slay the Minotaur, for the monster no longer devours that human part of its nature (embodied in the myth by the seven young Athenians). Theseus no longer gets to decide, and there is no bright line between the real and the fictional.

Moreover, today, is there any point of view that can claim primacy? When colonial rule ended, many other things were discredited along with it: the domination of one civilization, one color, and one religion over all others and, in the same way, the domination of one sex over another or of one sexuality over others. The hour has come of the copresence of diversity, but now in the silence of God. The analogy is thus related to the medieval perception of existence, but the difference is absolute. The lack of a unitary and comprehensive norm points to what Douglas Hofstadter has called the "heterarchical," a desecrated hierarchy in which all ideas of priority have evanesced.[8] What happens to space-time in an anomic context in which fiction, among other forms, becomes key to a reasonable reading of the world? What methodology can we use to understand that which seems to escape our understanding? In the face of this paradox, the pages that follow are an attempt—one trial, among many other possible ones—to answer these questions, to capture if only fleetingly the mobile environment in a cautious, humble way.

Another question remains unanswered. What do we mean by *space*? A priori, space is a concept that encompasses the universe; it is oriented toward the infinitely large or reduced to the infinitely small, which is itself infinitely and infinitesimally vast. Moreover, ignoring for the moment the distinction between macrocosmic and microcosmic space, specialists seem hardly more advanced, at least from the perspective of the stars, *sub specie aeternitatis*. According to geographer Hervé Regnauld, "we do not know if it [i.e., space] is infinite or not, we do not know if it moves toward contraction or infinite dilation, we do not know what form it has . . . We just know that it has little to do with the psychological experience we have of it, and it calls for more intellect than perception."[9] It is not this absolute, totalizing space that I am most interested in, although it certainly occupies a significant place in literature and film. This space is indeed the primary material for science fiction and for all of those possible worlds projected beyond the visible, but not beyond the conceivable. However, I will focus on the visible areas, which themselves are quite resistant to definition, because, as Regnauld puts it, "there is no global space that contains all the geographical problems, even if reduced to theoretical laws."[10] And what is true for geography is, a fortiori, true for literature and other mimetic arts.

At the risk of oversimplification, one could propose two basic approaches to visible spaces, one rather abstract, the other more concrete: the first would encompass conceptual *space* and the second factual *place*. However, these are not mutually exclusive, if only because the line between space and place is always shifting. In *Space and Place: The Perspective of Experience*, Yi-Fu Tuan viewed space as an area of freedom and mobility, while place would be an enclosed and humanized space: "Compared to space, place is a calm center of established values."[11] This is a common view in the United States. For Tuan, space turns into place when it gains definition and becomes meaningful: "All people undertake to transform amorphous space into articulated geography."[12] Place is a landmark upon which the eye pauses when it surveys a general scene, "a point of rest."[13] This distinction between space and place has been studied by geographers, sociologists, and others who endeavor to add practical application to theoretical reflections.

Given the uncertainty that marks the boundary between space and place, some have preferred to explore other avenues. After having endorsed a moderate and critical use of the term *space*, urban planner Flavia Schiavo has simply proposed to substitute the notion of *context*, which brings together the material and immaterial valences of the two words (space and place). According to Schiavo, context includes social and cultural areas, among others, that "organize overall architecture of an inhabited place."[14] In short, context connects the space and place by establishing meaningful space in the constitution of a place. Phenomenology has focused a great deal of its energy on this question. For its part, phenomenology separates the *Lebenswelt* (à la Edmund Husserl and Alfred Schütz), which is the locus of intentional activities of man (and woman), from the *Umwelt*, which is the framework within which these activities are accomplished. Again, the challenge is to identify a typology of interactions between human space itself (*Lebenswelt*) and the space that surrounds man (*Umwelt*). Moreover, if one agrees with Maria de Fanis, subjects are understood as "entities that, in giving shape to *space*, take actions and form ideas, with individual and collective values, in order to convert space into *place*."[15] Not everything fits easily into the dichotomy of space and place. Hans Robert Jauss, the reception theorist, has also contributed to the debate. Based on the work of sociologist Alfred Schütz and his pupil Thomas Luckmann, Jauss has argued that space-time is inscribed in everyday life: "I experience the reality of the everyday world as an intersubjective world which I share with others (*Mitwelt*). The 'here-there' situation organizes the life world as surrounding world, the 'face-to-face' situation organizes it as a world in which I engage with others."[16] If the *Umwelt* is the realm of simple existence, the *Mitwelt* requires action, or rather interaction, which gives meaning to the existence of the individual. Like the phenomenologists who inspired him, Jauss evokes "the 'here-there' situation beginning with which the reality of the everyday or life world organizes itself as surrounding world."[17]

In fact, the study of this relationship motivates the entire project of geocriticism. Geocriticism probes the human spaces that the mimetic arts arrange through, and in, texts, the image, and cultural interactions related to them. Before arriving at a tentative outline of a geocritical methodology, three stops are planned. These allow me to identify the theoretical underpinnings of geocriticism. First, in Chapter 1, a reflection on *spatiotemporality* will enable us to see how temporal metaphors tend to spatialize time, and how, especially in the aftermath of World War II, the critical attention to space has increased relative to time, which had previously held nearly unchallenged supremacy in literary criticism and theory. Then, in Chapter 2, I will focus on a characteristic element of contemporary space: its capacity for mobility or movement. Is there now a permanent state of transgression, of boundary crossing—a *transgressivity* that would make space fundamentally fluid? The peregrinations through spatiality make for a grand odyssey. Chapter 3 is devoted to theoretical speculation about links between the world and the text (or image), or between the referent and its representation. *Referentiality* refers to the relations between reality and fiction, between the spaces of the world and the spaces in the text. A special place is reserved for the theory of possible worlds, illustrated in Europe by a number of thinkers following in the line of Alexius Meinong and Ludwig Wittgenstein, who had drawn an analogy between the "objective" world of reality and the abstract worlds of texts.

If we reverted to the traditional distinction between space and place, we would note that the first three chapters privilege space, as spatiotemporality, transgressivity, and referentiality delineate the conceptual framework that geocriticism establishes. But although the dichotomy is cast aside in the developments that follow (space and place are deliberately conflated by me in the concept of "human space"), we must recognize that geocriticism gives priority to place. Chapter 4 describes the geocritical methodology, which I hope can complete the portrait that I had initially sketched in an earlier article published in the book that launched my own geocritical adventures.[18] In a final chapter, which is nonetheless meant to be more provisional than conclusive, I will examine the importance of the text in the construction of a place, which will take me from the spatiality of the text to the *legibility* of places. Deferring the question of referentiality to the end, I ask what the text and the place are doing . . . and doing to each other. In the twilight of structuralism, the fictional text returns to the world and settles in comfortably. Perhaps, even, it may create the world?

One of my goals throughout is to begin to establish a "spatiological" inventory (*à propos* Henri Lefebvre's call in *The Production of Space*),[19] beyond the national borders of a critical field of study, beyond the linguistic confines of fictional works, and also beyond disciplinary limits, since literature is here recontextualized in an environment that gives due respect to geography, urban planning, and many other disciplines. It may seem obvious that literature, as well as other mimetic arts—precisely *because* they are mimetic—may no longer be isolated from the world in this new millennium. Everything is in everything, and vice versa? Maybe. And that's the problem. But just as we embrace heterogeneity of views and voices in our freedom of speech, criticism itself benefits from the increased diversity in its theory and practice.

CHAPTER 1

Spatiotemporality

History: The End of the Line?

The passage of time has often been conveyed through spatial metaphors. In the nineteenth century, time was compared to a tranquil, flowing river. To be sure, unfortunate events could disturb its course, but nothing could interrupt its flow. In *Gone with the Wind*, Scarlett O'Hara could witness houses burning under the Georgia skies, lovers separated, corpses piled by the hundreds, and yet she could aver, "Tomorrow is another day." For her, the progression of time accorded with progress itself, a view codified by a form of positivism. Progress and progression were virtually synonymous in the time of the Industrial Revolution. And a demon straight out of the imagination of the physicist Pierre-Simon Laplace, no doubt with a sardonic smile at the corners of its mouth, could direct the mechanical and rectilinear trajectory of all events. This anonymous demon was formidable, at least as much as Goethe's Mephistopheles or Mikhail Bulgakov's Woland, and more so in some respects. What was his strength? According to Ilya Prigogine and Isabelle Stengers, Laplace's demon was "capable at any given instant of observing the position and velocity of each mass that forms part of the universe and of inferring its evolution, both toward the past and toward the future."[1] Time, which we had begun to consider controllable and even programmable, became a simple configuration. As Prigogine and Stengers put it, "The qualitative diversity of changes in nature is reduced to the study of the relative displacement of material bodies. Time is a parameter in terms of which these displacements may be described."[2] Such homogeneity was possible due to the application of reason, but also and above all it was due to a consciousness endowed with reason, an entity with a God's-eye view of everything. The hierarchy that such a vision imposed seemed unbreakable. Time contained progress, and time was enslaved to progress. Consequently, space became an empty container, merely a backdrop for time, through which the god Progress would reveal himself. And this scene was used to support the scenario that positivism (without much imagination) imagined: a space subjugated to the programmatic materiality of time. Space only mattered insofar as the "homogeneous flow" of time had to happen *somewhere*.

The history of the relations between time and space has long produced fascinating narratives. For example, it has transcribed minutes onto parallels and meridians in order to constitute colonial spaces. Even today, my heart skips a beat to think of the manicured lawns surrounding the Royal Observatory in Greenwich. The experience of time zero, fixed in a specific place a few kilometers from London, once the capital of a vast colonial empire, will not leave anyone indifferent. This famous model of spatiotemporal intersection has inspired a number of contemporary novels, such as *The Greenwich Meridian* by Jean Echenoz, *Waterland* by Graham Swift, and *The Island of the Day Before* by Umberto Eco. But these imaginary circles of longitude, although quite important, do not prove to be isolated examples, limited to the concerns of maritime navigation. When the railways developed and flourished in concert with the telegraph, it created new kinds of work for geography. It was not only the task of locating the stations on the map of the wide world but also that of recognizing the uniform schedule of departures and arrivals. Space was captured in a universal time. The challenge of this complex process was concrete: by harmonizing timetables, we reduced the number of rail crashes due to incompatibility of temporal markers. Consider that a station in Pittsburgh once used as many as five clocks to indicate the specific schedule for each railroad company in order to make this work!

Space falls prey to time, and the construction of a universal timetable can become a life's work. In *Garden, Ashes*, a novel by the great Serbian writer Danilo Kiš, the protagonist's father has worked for several years to develop a comprehensive railway guide. In his desire to answer a compelling question—"How does one get to Nicaragua?"—he eventually covers eight hundred pages with signs, annotations, and ideograms of all sorts: "This magnificent manuscript had absorbed all cities, all land areas and all the seas, all the skies, all climates, all meridians. The most remote cities and islands were joined together in this manuscript in a mosaic, in an ideal line. Siberia, Kamchatka, Celebes, Ceylon, Mexico, New Orleans were all represented with as much weight as Vienna, Paris, or Budapest. This was an apocryphal, sacred bible, in which the miracle of genesis was repeated, and yet in which all divine injustices and the impotence of man were rectified."[3] For this hero of modern times, the apostle *ante litteram* of spatiotemporal compression, the correction of these injustices involved reestablishing the balance between the coordinates that allow the living to situate themselves within creation. Perhaps the same concern was guiding those who introduced standardized time to North America in the mid-nineteenth century. In any case, at noon on November 18, 1883, standard time was extended throughout the northern part of the continent, thanks to the pressure of the American Railway Association. This operation preceded the division of the globe into time zones of 15 degrees each. The European countries joined in this reform in the 1890s, with the exception of France, which waited until 1911 to bend its time to that of Greenwich. Then there was the growth of civil aviation that helped popularize time zones and their inevitable corollary, jet lag.

Secure, stable in appearance, time was used to understand a space that one feared in an era when mankind and the great powers made it a top priority to survey the world. But once space was mastered, subjected to increasing compression by the development of enhanced communication (material and immaterial), time itself finally became unhinged, ruptured, and lost. This theft of time is certainly evident in jet lag, but the first blows against the supremacy of the temporal dimension of human existence were not the result of the Wright brothers, Bleriot, and other aviation pioneers. It was first attacked by several geniuses in physics and mathematics, who conceived space in four dimensions, the fourth being time. This temporalized space became "space-time." The decisive contributions of Henri Poincaré, Hermann Minkowski, and Albert Einstein with his theory of space-time were all published in 1905. In September of that year, Einstein formulated a special theory of relativity, which he completed in 1916 with the addition of a general theory. After the space-time continuum had been formulated, the dimensions of time and of space decisively escaped from the realm of false impressions; it stopped in its tracks the sun's "course" around the earth. As Jean-Paul Auffray explains, "In ordinary space, where the distance between two points is zero, we say that these two points coincide. It is not the same in space-time: the interval between two points can be zero without the two points coinciding."[4] The year 1905 is a significant milepost, representing the moment of the theory of relativity, which undermined the foundations of so many certainties. But have the theories of Einstein and his immediate successors really changed the worldview of ordinary mortals? That's less certain. Relativity remained the exclusive preserve of scientists and the very rare person of letters. Franz Kafka would attend to Einstein, as would Robert Musil, who would make use of his discoveries in *The Man Without Qualities*. Today, it is Einstein's remarkable personality, more than his theories, that captures the public's imagination.

In sum, neither the theory of relativity nor the theory of space-time revolutionized the relationship of space to time or of time to space. And it is worth recalling that though Einstein promoted relativity, he strongly objected to the quantum physics developed by some of his heirs, starting with Niels Bohr. For many, Einstein was indeed the last great classical physicist. But for a new reading of time, and hence a different perception of space, there needed to occur an event powerful enough to engage all the people in the world, from Nobel

Prize-winning physicists to anonymous citizens. This event, of course, was the Second World War. After that, in 1945, was it still possible, or even imaginable, to conflate chronological progression and the progress of mankind? If the gradual and progressive river of time led to Auschwitz, Mauthausen, Stutthof, or Jasenovac, sites of the abomination that drained the color off the map of Europe, or if that same river of time led to Hiroshima and Nagasaki and also to Dresden, where fire-bombing transformed a city into a lunar landscape, then it is better to dam the river entirely. The stream of time had allowed an unwelcome guest: perverse progress. The lesson should have been learned after the First World War, but perhaps the painful spectacle of the trenches had been minimized. There were so few who wished to recall the extent of the damage. The atrocities of war, after a time of reticence, are slow to make a noticeable impact on the minds of men, but then the breakthrough is inevitable. What happened in 1945? We signed an armistice, several armistices. We began to rebuild the world, too. Most of the great colonial powers were in the camp of the victors, if they had not remained neutral (such as Spain and Portugal), but they had lost their pride in the fact. Their guiding alibi—the civilizing mission—had collapsed. Moreover, new matters arose that literally and figuratively altered the world map. At Yalta, Churchill was the only representative of a colonial empire that had survived for centuries. France was absent, as were Belgium and the Netherlands, not to mention Spain or Portugal. The United States and the Soviet Union, lacking the tradition of large-scale colonialism, were still novices. Decolonization thus accelerated in the Crimea. Postcolonialism was to follow, and neocolonialism as well.

At the end of the war, the two coordinates of the plane of existence were in crisis, and with them all that exists. Time was deprived of its structuring metaphor. Space, dangerously concentrated, got lost between the barbed wire of the camps and the rapid fire over the trenches. The straight line was dead. Decolonization shattered the legitimacy of entire organizations of the world, organizations that had been carefully developed over decades and centuries and had been supported by an entire system of morality. Time and space suffered irreparable harm, a chronic and topical disruption. They at last found themselves in shared metaphors associating them with the point, the fragment, and the splinter: a kind of geometry of the vestige accompanied by a sense of vertigo in which one hovers over the depths of chaos rather than gazing down from the lofty heights of the Enlightenment worldview. At the height of this global crisis, postmodernism (as an aesthetic) and postmodernity (as a condition) found their epistemological and ontological foundations, if they may be so called. In *The Postmodern Explained*, Jean-François Lyotard posed again the question others had set out before him: "What kind of thought is capable of 'relieving' Auschwitz—relieving (*relever*) in the sense of *aufheben*—capable of situating it in a general, empirical, or even speculative process directed toward universal emancipation? There is a sort of grief in the *Zeitgeist*. It can find expression in reactive, or even reactionary, attitudes or in utopias—but not in a positive orientation that would open up a new perspective."[5] If, after Auschwitz, poetry is no longer possible (per Paul Celan and Theodor W. Adorno), the ideas of unity, teleology, and a clear hierarchy of values are no longer conceivable as well. It comes down to the disconnect between progress and progression.

The disenchanted vision of Lyotard is not really characteristic of a generation that has been marked less by postwar reconstruction than by the theory of deconstruction. In his 1955 essay on literary temporality, *Time in Literature*, Hans Meyerhoff noted, "There is no doubt that the belief in progress has sharply declined within our own generation, and no doubt that this decline has added another brick to the burden of time as it weighs upon human lives."[6] Meyerhoff then advocated the Nietzschean idea of eternal return because it did not introduce an axiological perspective of time. For him, this was the only temporal format still acceptable. Two decades later, Gianni Vattimo's idea of *pensiero debole*, or "weak thought," followed along the same lines. But to stay with Meyerhoff for the moment, his view of "grand narratives," whether dialectical (Hegel, Marx, and Comte), evolutionary (Darwin, Huxley, and Spencer), or cyclical (Vico, Nietzsche, and Spengler), is not motivated by a postmodernist orientation but is fascinating in itself. While each is distinct, the views of time that Meyerhoff inventoried had one thing in common: they were supposed to be universally and eternally valid. Thanks to their rigid ideological, ethical, and conceptual frameworks, these grand narratives (code, history, doctrine, etc.) place the individual subject in a larger totality, a universe under his control or at least logically able to be mastered. This assumption, however, had been delegitimized by the developments of history between 1939 and 1945 or between 1914 and 1945. Consequently, for Meyerhoff, the vision of history became plural. History is fragmented; it is unintelligible or meaningless as a whole. It is thus not really necessary to credit or blame the postmodernists for their decanonization of grand historical narratives and the weakening of the concept of historicity. Indeed, already in 1947's *Dialectic of Enlightenment*, Adorno and Horkheimer had made clear how the rhetoric of human emancipation could lead to a universal system of oppression (as shown in literature by often-prophetic counterutopias like those in *Brave New World* and *Nineteen-Eighty-Four*).

Hence, one might say that the spatiotemporal revolution took place around 1945. After the Second World War, time and space became less ambitious, more tentative: the instants do not flow together at the same duration; in the absence of hierarchy, durations multiply; the line is split into lines; time is hereafter superficial. The perception of historical time was overtaken by the relative laws of space-time. After 1945, this view of time and space was brought home to people everywhere. The concept of temporality that had dominated the prewar period had lost much of its legitimacy. There emerged a weak ontology (*ontologia debole*) that, in Vattimo's analysis, does not serve the quest for emancipation but is well adapted to the oscillations between image and reality, simulacrum and referent—a context where experience is always mediated. The *pensiero debole* then becomes a "declension of difference," a "heterology" that repositions the "progressive and the cumulative" in ways not easily reconciled with the unitary Logos of traditional historiography. In this volatile environment, there is a weakening of historicity, which does not mean the end of history (e.g., in the vision of Francis Fukuyama) or even the weakening of the historical. History continues its march, as with Walter Benjamin's *Angelus Novus*. The wind rushes under the wings of the angel of history and carries him onward, inevitably, despite the overwhelming sadness caused by the spectacle unfolding before his eyes. But this movement no longer signifies an unswerving and progressive straight line; blown by such unpredictable winds, history can go forward, turn in circles, or cross and recross its own paths. This is a secularization of progress, freed from the single trajectory that the progressivists celebrated with such euphoria not so long ago. Synchrony seems to take precedence over diachrony. Events are crammed into the present, a process that Hermann Lübbe has called "musealization," in which every temporal moment is frozen and preserved as if in a museum: "Never before has the actual been attached to the past in such a way. The intensity of our efforts to safeguard the actuality of the past has reached a level unprecedented in history."[7] According to many theorists, this is the dominant characteristic of the era. And it is not only postmodernism that typifies this trend. Postcolonial criticism has also contributed to the decanonization of this vision of history. For instance, as Homi Bhabha puts it, "Our existence today is marked by a tenebrous sense of survival, living on the borderlines of the 'present,' for which there seems to be no proper name other than the current and controversial shiftiness of the prefix 'post': *postmodernism, postcolonialism, postfeminism*."[8] It is true that for the first time in the history of our culture, an epoch has arrived that is not defined autonomously or in relation to a renewal (*neo-*), but is defined in the context of an inclusive passing away (*post-*). This terminology registers that uncertainty principle that has paradoxically ruled over the last decades.

The Semantics of Tempuscules

The fragmented view of time has decisively affected the image of space as well. The principle that structures the representation of postmodern (or simply modern) temporality is the same as that which governs all existence. It leads to the multiplication of the unitary and therefore to the plurality, causing transition from homogeneity to heterogeneity. Prigogine and Stengers, in one of their many parallels between human time and scientific time, in which they attempt to demonstrate the absolute compatibility of the two, confirm this view: "Every complex being is constituted by a plurality of times connected to each other by subtle and multiple links. History, whether that of a living being or a society, can never be reduced to the monotonous simplicity of a unique time that is invariable or that traces the paths of progress or of degradation."[9] Whether postmodern, postcolonial, neohumanist, or some other designation, contemporary epistemology and aesthetics can agree that the river metaphor is no longer apt and a new age of exploration has opened up. Enlivened, new metaphors embrace several new forms. A certain number designate the crisis of temporality and its strongly familiar images (depth, thickness, etc.). Others replace the relationship between the instant and duration with a relation between a point and a line, and thus contribute to the translation of the temporal regime into an order dominated by spatiality. The most elaborate metaphors popularize certain schemata or diagrams, which enable more complex readings of the world and its coordinates.

I do not wish to dwell on the disqualification of former spatial metaphors of temporality, of which "depth" (or sometimes "thickness") was the most powerful. These figures were described and denounced by almost all those associated with the *nouveau roman*. In 1953, Roland Barthes dismissed this metaphor in *Writing Degree Zero*. Shortly after, in *For a New Novel*, Alain Robbe-Grillet sketched "a novel of the future" by announcing "the destitution of the old myths of 'depth,'" which he called a "trap in which the writer captured the universe in order to hand it over to society."[10] Depth is reflected by the use of past tense, third person, and other markers of alienation that accompany a "bourgeois" writing intended for bourgeois society. A generation later, Fredric Jameson returned to this metaphor. In *Postmodernism; or, The Cultural Logic of Late Capitalism*, Jameson correlated the weakening of the concept of historicity to a lack of depth, which is the primary dimension (or nondimension) of a culture of the image and of the simulacrum. Comparing Vincent Van Gogh's *Pair of Shoes* (1886) with Andy Warhol's *Diamond Dust Shoes* (1980), Jameson marked the characteristic decline in modern concepts of time and duration and, as a corollary, the emergence of a pure synchrony. Thus the metaphor of depth gave way to metaphors of the surface.

Photography and the television screen thus begin to take over the traditional functions of literature. While television has long been regarded as the enemy of the book, it has nonetheless inspired many literary figures. It is true that the TV is a perfect metaphor for the spatial dimension of the expanding present of the postmodern era. It combines the pure superficiality of its flat surface with a geometry of the line and point in the seemingly infinite number of luminous pixels. In his novel *Television*, Jean-Philippe Toussaint provides a good example. Fittingly, the cover of the novel (in its French paperback edition, at least) is a blank screen sizzling with confused, colorless, and evanescent points that refer to a flat surface. Becoming both chaotic and cathodic, the story emerges, requiring color or contrast in order to give meaning and order to these pixels; from the flat image, the story is brought to life on the screen. Ultimately, the story is a diagram drawn at the heart of a luminescence of glowing dots and lines. It arises from a simple, subjective impression of a totality whose existence is based on the juxtaposition of images lasting tenths of a second on our retinas. This impression relates to the narrative process that Paul Ricoeur, in the third volume of *Time and Narrative*, refers to as *retention*, which is "the adhering of the retained past to now–point within the present that continues even while fading away."[11] History is also the result of a retinal impression, establishing an oscillating relationship between what was and what is. There was a time when history was child's play: it was through the points (events) that were connected through a series of increasing numbers (dates) that meaning and order were achieved. Once it was completed, we would have a superb schematic that could be filled with whichever ideological coloring we deemed fit. As Georges Poulet noted in his introduction to volume 3 of his *Studies in Human Time*, "The specific objective of history is to put in place a continuity among different moments of time, to show some rational principle according to which they relate to one another. But a string of discrete moments cannot form a history."[12] A little further, Poulet states that the individual does not apprehend time itself, but rather the moment: "With a given moment, it is for us to make time."[13] This seems unfair! But the new game consists in grasping those points or moments in a way that eliminates any hierarchical arrangement, so that the linear model disappears and, with it, the meaning and unity it afforded. The way is now free, but labyrinthine. From a given moment in time—or rather, in history—the straight line becomes a tortuous path.

In the 1960s, the point and the line received a great deal of interest from formal logicians, especially logicians of time (e.g., Arthur Prior and Georg von Wright). Among these logicians, Maria Luisa Dalla Chiara Scabia (in a remarkable article published in 1973 in *Rivista di filosofia*) argued that it was conceivable that the *moment* would give way to the *tempuscule*. While the moment is a homogeneous and indivisible point, the tempuscule is "understood as an interval of time (a given Δt) 'brief enough' in relation to a theoretical context for reference."[14] The tempuscule corresponds to the threshold at which one may determine "the truth value of propositions in a theoretical frame of reference that remains indeterminate."[15] Under this theory, the "moment" is no longer a point (sensu stricto) in an autonomous ensemble with limited meanings. In developing this theory, Dalla Chiara Scabia elaborated the principle of biographical lines, which rely on different tempuscules. Each of these lines would fit into a family of biographical lines in an overall system of individuals who participate in analogous, if not shared, histories. I believe we can venture further in this direction and consider that these temporal ensembles also disrupt the hierarchy, which is determined by a higher authority (i.e., by one who draws the biographical line). The idea of the tempuscule reveals that the classic relationship between the moment and duration in time, between the point and the line, may be superseded beneficially, to interconnect infinitely variable sets of tiny series or intervals endowed with a modicum of meaning. Such semantics requires a free circulation of tempuscules in a sort of erratic coasting across an archipelago of the possible. The interaction between tempuscules is much like the *event* in Gilles Deleuze's definition, "a vibration with an infinity of harmonics or submultiples, such as an audible wave, a luminous wave, or even an increasingly smaller part of space over the course of an increasingly shorter duration,"[16] which, to remain perceptible, unfolds beyond the threshold of intelligibility.

Could a semantics of tempuscules make sense of the archipelagic logic of postmodern time? It would mean at least a further expression of the spatialization of this temporality, because these distant groups, these tempuscules that break apart from the line, are necessarily disseminated in a temporalized field containing multiple paths or options. Illustrations of the semantics of tempuscules are numerous. When Karlheinz Stockhausen, the famous German composer, imagined a situation in which classical scores were replaced by groups of scattered notes on paper, he fought his way against the continuity of a line, the quintuple line of the musical score, to construct a alternative route. In a sense (but which one?), the only line conceivable in this anomic environment would be that which Deleuze and Guattari find in Glenn Gould: "When Glenn Gould speeds up the performance of a piece, he is not just displaying virtuosity, he is transforming the musical points into lines, he is making the whole piece proliferate."[17] The proliferating line tends to be reduced to a series of points just waiting to escape. This is the line of flight.

In literature, the variability of spatiotemporal relations has been the subject of theories, some of them postmodern, but many established well before the advent of postmodernity. We know that in "Discourse in the Novel," Bakhtin applied the musical principle of polyphony to literature; in the novel, polyphony becomes a kind of ensemble of voices and parties. One moves from the strictly linear logic of traditional historiography to a multilinear logic. Also, according to Bakhtin, in the novel multiple lines cross each other, hybridize, and interact. In the modern novel, the polyphonic genre par excellence, this may be seen in examples of antonomasia; one can see a certain line in the chivalric romance (e.g., *Parzival* or *Amadis*) crossing another distinct line in the age of the baroque (*Don Quixote*), resulting in great pathos. These lines can coexist, allowing for a reencounter with the various characters in stories later. They are based on the principle of intertextuality. Bakhtinian polyphony transforms the novel into "a microcosm of heteroglossia."[18] But with Bakhtin, one retains the metaphor of the line. Certainly, there are now more than one or two, as in the European novel, or perhaps five, as in the musical staves, but in any case there remains linear progression. The texts collected in *The Dialogic Imagination* were largely written between 1924 and 1941, and the original publication of the essays was hampered by the vagaries of the life of the author, who was subjected to Stalinist purges and forced into internal exile in Kazakhstan. Bakhtin seems to be inscribed within a modernist regime, and he is one of its most accomplished theorists. But I believe that his theory is somewhat less operative when dealing with the postmodern. For postmodernism has ensured the movement from the line and lines to a semantics of tempuscules, a semantics where points escape any linear dynamic in a context of hybridity and absolute dialogism. The hypothesis that applies to temporality and weakened historicity can be extended to space.

At least implicitly, this semantics has been supported by a broad metaphorical apparatus in the twentieth century. "Bifurcation" and "entropy" became some of the most common tropes of the new perception of space-time. Anticipating the decades to come, in his usual way, Jorge Luis Borges in 1941 designed a garden of forking paths, a garden that gave its name to one of the most famous stories collected in *Ficciones*. The garden in question was a Chinese labyrinth made of ivory and built by Ts'ui Pen, and this garden is the manifestation of Ts'ui Pen's vision of time: "He believed in an infinite series of times, in a dizzily growing, ever spreading network of diverging, converging, and parallel times. This web of time—the strands of which approach one another, bifurcate, intersect or ignore each other through the centuries—embraces *every* possibility. We do not exist in most of them. In some you exist and not I, while in others I do, and you do not, and in yet others both of us exist."[19] Although this is a fork in time, not in space, one cannot help thinking that this temporal network cannot be accommodated except in a spatial pattern. To my knowledge, Borges here provided the first explicit example of spatiotemporal belief generated by a profusion of timelines. Again, we see that the breakdown of the timeline leads to a spatialization of time. In his *Dialogues* with Claire Parnet, in the heart of a long section devoted to psychoanalysis, Deleuze returned to this issue of multilinearity to draw this spatializing conclusion: "At each moment, we are made up of lines which are variable at each instant, which may be combined in different ways, packets of lines, longitudes and latitudes, tropics and meridians, etc. There are no mono-fluxes. The analysis of the unconscious should be a geography rather than history."[20] In fact, it is perhaps not just the unconscious that is concerned with the spatiotemporal context in which the individual operates;

perception itself is now a matter of geography, while in an earlier epoch, historical discourse reigned.

In any case, the metaphor of the garden of forking paths continues to deal mainly with the line. We are moving toward an organization that undermines crude deterministic fancies or, better yet, that transforms determinism itself. Nevertheless, the semantics of tempuscules should proceed from the dynamic of the point and not from the dynamic of the line, albeit a labyrinthine line. The figure of entropy is undoubtedly more appropriate to express this "pointillism" because it relies on a logic of particles. As we know, the second law of thermodynamics, or entropy, is a function that defines the state of disorder in a system—the increasing disorder as the system evolves to a new state. The corollary of this progression is the loss of energy. Prigogine and Stengers explain that entropy, described in 1826 by Nicolas Léonard Sadi Carnot, emanates either from the outside world or from a production inherent in the observed system. In the second case, entropy is irreversible. Thus the future becomes definable: it is "the direction in which entropy increases."[21] But it is also the time when stable equilibrium is reached and, with it, the ultimate loss of energy in the system. Whenever it is considered as entropy, time is returned to its spatial dimension: it is inscribed in a spatial scheme. Furthermore, in entropy, two dialectical elements are invariably linked: the creative elements of disorder and of order. Prigogine says that, at one time, equilibrium was associated with order (crystal) and nonequilibrium with chaos (turbulence), before adding, "We now know that this is incorrect: the turbulence is a highly structured phenomenon in which millions and millions of particles follow their course in a very coherent movement."[22] Nonequilibrium is coherent and, ultimately, more interesting than equilibrium, since the latter is deprived of history. "It can only persist in this state, where the fluctuations are zero."[23] In sum, equilibrium is equivalent to a nonstory, which is why change is not compatible with it. Through nonequilibrium, it is possible to have a very complex story, which corresponds to a garden of forking paths, of points (not lines!) of instability. In this regard, Prigogine notes, "In the presence of equilibrium it is always possible to linearize, while far from equilibrium we have a nonlinear behavior of matter. Nonequilibrium and nonlinearity are affiliated concepts."[24]

On the metaphorical level, the principle of entropy has animated several literary works of the last century, especially from the 1960s. This is true of Thomas Pynchon's early novels, *V.* and *The Crying of Lot 49*, as well as his short story "Entropy," written in 1959 (republished in *Slow Learner*). Through his work, Pynchon was instrumental in popularizing the concept of entropy in literature, and others have followed. Entropy "structures" novels by Jean-Philippe Toussaint, such as *Bathroom* and *Monsieur*, as well as a number of American novels, like Bernard Malamud's *God's Grace* and Kurt Vonnegut's *Galápagos*.

This list could go on and on. I only observe that most of the stories narrated according to the second law of thermodynamics are rather complex. This is not surprising if one considers that the bifurcation point is the key to their organization. A deconstructed temporality corresponds to an explosion of spatiality, often resulting in a massive investment of geography. The semantics of tempuscules leads to an archipelagic perception of time and space. Its ideal metaphor is certainly entropy. Its universe is isotropic: the dynamic behind it does not favor any direction or configuration. Its progression defies hierarchy.

The Spatialization of Time in Postmodernity

Several theorists have observed the temporal and spatial effects of the act of writing. Similarly, several writers have expressed their amazement at the spatiotemporal implications of their art. In *Mon Europe*, an essay cowritten with the Ukrainian author Yuri Andrukhovych, the Polish novelist Andrzej Stasiuk begins a meditation on European identities. But in a detour from his quest that leads him to explore the border regions of Poland and Ukraine, Stasiuk begins to interrogate his own status as a writer. Writing reveals its lability, the fragility of its spatiotemporal anchor: "I describe circles, detours, I digress as the good soldier Švejk on the road to Budějovice and, like him, I cannot follow along a straight, linear path to a story told properly. I keep drifting, my eyes are regularly arrested, and obsessive vision assails me, as this or that geographical sketch sticks to my retina . . . Life is ultimately the search for excuses that allow us to exist in time or in space."[25] For if writing is a creeping forward in time, it also spreads itself out on the space of the page. Pierre Ouellet, a specialist in the aesthetics of perception, compared the book to a *Flatland* that would highlight the rhythm of reading.[26] The theories that spatialize writing, however, are not universal . . . or timeless. As Brian McHale noted in *Postmodernist Fiction*, the book has not always been viewed in its materiality: "While a manuscript could still be regarded as the record of an oral performance, which unfolds in time, a book was a *thing*, and its material qualities and physical dimensions inevitably interacted with the world. Far from exploiting this interaction, however, fiction in the realist tradition has sought to suppress or neutralize it."[27] Basing his remarks on a generic and secular distinction, McHale said that the critic's attention to the spatial was confined to poetry, as one noted the placement of words on the page and the arrangement of lines and verses according to a logic of separation, while the novel (with its standardized left-justified print, broken occasionally by paragraph indentations) was defined by its nonspatiality (*spacelessness*). By the early twentieth century, poetry had accentuated its spatiality. One thinks of Guillaume Apollinaire's inescapable *Calligrammes*, deconstructing the order of the verses and making them conform to the shape of a drawing, a calligram, which exalts that iconic spatiality with which writing is imbued. Toward the end of the twentieth century, poetry has reached a new level, using hypertextual resources that computers and information technology have made available. Poems can now be electronic compositions on a computer screen. Electronic poetry can exploit all the potentialities of the mobile and fluid space as it invests its multidimensional words with avant-garde synesthetic processes, which may include music, photography, and extremely inventive iconicity. But the postmodern *novel* is no exception, resorting to methods more consistent with the nature of its material, paper.

While the river of time overflows its bed to form a swamp, the line of the novel has abandoned the anonymity of pure rectilinearity. The dislocation of the traditional sense of time has caused a relocation of the text in space. In a way, the *locutus* has moved toward the locus, the *tropos* toward the topos. Of course, there are many variations of this process. Generally much longer than a poem, the novel is not adaptable to formal designs or animated graphics. This has not prevented innovative novelists from emphasizing points of bifurcation, confusion, or vagary. The postmodern novel is, like poetry, about "space." In this regard, one often speaks of an aesthetic of the fragment, an aesthetic that mobilizes the blank spaces between paragraphs and operates on the real, material space of the page. In *Mobile*, originally subtitled *Study for the Representation of the United States*, Michel Butor has organized his text to reproduce experimentally what McHale calls the American zone, "a kind of between-worlds space."[28] Besides Butor, McHale cites Monique Wittig's *Les guérillères*, in which the apparently linear text winds around a capital *O*, thoroughly polysemic, referring to the female menstrual cycle and to the cosmic revolution and political revolution (or circle); to that new beginning, the starting point of zero (0) after the flood waters (the French *eaux*, a homonym of *O*); or again, to *The Story of O*. The feminine circle combats the male line: feminist "guerilla" writing moves by dislocation and relocation, as opposed to the linear continuity that represents (for Wittig) phallocratic thought. In *Le pique-nique sur l'Acropole*, Louky Bersianik creates an adaptation of Plato's *Symposium*, one that again uses the entire space of the page to establish a *place* of feminist discourse, or simply a feminine space that banishes the alienating rectilinear space. Incidentally, Bersianik seems to give her own definition of Wittig's uterine *O*: it is the "geographical speaking place for the whole environment."[29] An Omni-comprehensive place?

Texts that delinearize their narratives by underscoring the iconic, physical space of the book have become quite common. But there are many other strategies, more subtle perhaps, to challenge the predominance of the straight line, to dechronologize and relocate the text in space. From this point of view, the fate of the river metaphor of time in some contemporary novels is significant. In *Lexikon Roman*, Andreas Okopenko depicts a portion of the Danube, in the Wachau region of Austria, to better break up the linear progression of his narrative. The line of the river, which should serve as a stable benchmark, is methodically deconstructed, and scattered parts are reclassified according to a system that replicates the lexical items alphabetically, as arbitrary as any criterion. In this way, a semantics of tempuscules spectacularly replaces the order of time, symbolized by the river. Following Okopenko, the Hungarian novelist Péter Esterházy provides the same type of manipulation in *The Glance of Countess Hahn-Hahn (down the Danube)*, but without adopting an alphabetical taxonomy. Again it is the Danube that serves as the zone for experimentation. The struggle against the constraints of the straight line appears to be one of the defining elements of the postmodern. The spatializing modes of this deconstruction are numerous, infinitely mutable, and almost always ingenious. We remember that Julio Cortázar forced his readers to hop around from one chapter to another in *Hopscotch*; others have preferred to zigzag on a checkerboard or, as in Georges Perec's *Life: A User's Manual*, on a simulated chessboard of a Parisian city block. Another, Italo Calvino in *The Castle of Crossed Destinies*, lays tarot cards down on the table in a medieval tavern to narrate the stories of the world (Oedipus, Percival, Hamlet, Faust, Justine, etc.). The most obstinate in this virtuoso performance is certainly Milorad Pavić, whose works include the novel passing as a lexicon (*Dictionary of the Khazars*), a crossword novel (*Landscape Painted with Tea*), and a tarot novel (*Last Love in Constantinople: A Tarot Novel for Divination*).

To put a different spin on this quick overview, we might mention a few novels that offer the reader the opportunity to choose his or her own route through a text. The best known of these, perhaps, is *Pale Fire*, in which Nabokov organizes a clever play of references between the main text (a poem) and an artifact made up of endnotes. A similar solution is proposed in *The Great Fire of London*, in which Jacques Roubaud advances a series of interpolations and bifurcations, giving a hypertextual density to the narrative. In a rather different genre, Alina Reyes's *Behind Closed Doors* encourages the reader to decide for himself which doors to open in chapters of shifting numbers with many erotic delights. It is "an adventure in which you are the hero": "It is up to you to enter the labyrinth, to choose the doors you want to open, so as to trace your own route, your own book, your own destiny."[30] Returning to Roubaud, we see the sometimes humorous challenge facing the writer who is captive to the straight line: Hortense, the heroine of the cycle beginning with *Our Beautiful Heroine*, hesitates at the foot of a flight of stairs that could lead either to the right or to the left. Depending on the narrator's conscious choice, the story will change direction: turning left rather than right (or vice versa) could affect the fate of the heroine! The narrative becomes subject to the reader's choice, which will impose a monologic principle of linearity upon it. The problem then lies in making the two options compatible, reducing the gap created by linear temporality. Confronted by this dilemma, Milorad Pavić moves toward hyperfiction in *Damascene: A Tale for Computers and Compasses*, in which the reader makes choices by clicking options on the computer screen, forming a garden of forking paths set up by the author and reader together. The Spanish novelist Lorenzo Silva has created an even more democratic hypertextual experience. During the ten weeks he took to write *La isla del fin de la suerte*, he invited the public over the Internet to choose between narrative sequences. So, in the end, the story followed the path suggested by his ereaders. Iconic representations of delinearization, playful journeys that disturb the traditional story line, the staging of points and bifurcations, and the use of hypertextual structure—all of these processes tend to spatialize narrative time.

Space Strikes Back

The relations between those theorists who prioritized time or history and those for whom space or geography was the principal coordinate for writing in the world were irregular and sometimes heated. To the chagrin of the geography theorists, history has strongly monopolized attention. As Marc Brosseau summarized the situation, "It is true, literary criticism has long privileged the question of time to the detriment of an inquiry into space . . . Even if we now look at space in the novel, some remain faithful to the teachings of Kantian philosophy, and accord precedence to time over space as an a priori category of sensibility."[31] We may count Joseph Brodsky, the winner of the 1987 Nobel Prize in Literature, among those faithful to a view of time's priority. In "Flight from Byzantium," Brodsky reserves a few pages for Istanbul and the emperor Constantine, and his wanderings in that city's streets inspired some thoughts on the relationship between space and time: "space to me is, indeed, both lesser and less dear than time. Not because it is lesser but because it is a thing, while time is an idea about a thing. In choosing between a thing and an idea, the latter is to be preferred, say I."[32] We are plunged right into Kant's wake. But, as I have suggested, the situation eventually began to change in the 1960s. The spatialization of time was one of the means of "counterattack" or "striking back" of space against time, or of geography against history. In certain cases, at issue was not the balance between the two coordinates of time and space, but the assertion of temporal rule without giving space its fair share. Among those who first proclaimed the supremacy of space over time, we might mention Karl Haushofer, a founding father of geopolitics between the First and Second World Wars. It is not my intention here to examine Haushofer's geopolitical doctrine, which has, in any event, remained somewhat controversial. Note, though, that when he was interned in Germany during the Second World War and conceived the idea of *geohistory*, Fernand Braudel remembered an assertion of Haushofer's—"Space is more important than time"—and the gloss given by Haushofer, from memory: "Can we say more? Years and centuries pass, he explained, but the stage remains the same one on which humanity plays its endless, but always recommencing, comedy."[33] But does space attain its status because, unlike time, it is immutable? Years and centuries pass, of course, but the scene changes too. Braudel himself has demonstrated this in his work.

It took three more decades for the most ardent defenders of space to come forward. As John Berger noted, originally in *The Look of Things*, "Prophecy now involves a geographical rather than historical projection; it is space not time that hides consequences from us . . . Any contemporary narrative which ignores the urgency of this dimension is incomplete and acquires the oversimplified character of a fable."[34] This sentiment was soon echoed by sociologist Daniel Bell in *The Cultural Contradictions of Capitalism*.[35] For him, the organization of space presented the main aesthetic problem for culture during the second half of the twentieth century. Meanwhile, in *Postmodernism; or, The Cultural Logic of Late Capitalism*, Jameson said that the cultural discourse of daily life was now dominated by spatial, rather than temporal, categories. Space has emerged alongside, or well in advance of, time in recent years, as some of the most important figures in contemporary literature, sociology, and geography have acknowledged a "spatial turn," as Edward Soja has put it,[36] that is no mere fad of a few American thinkers. Deleuze has said repeatedly that "becoming is geographical." Like others, Deleuze has noted that this geographical becoming is illustrated in American literature but would not quite be possible in French literature: "There is no equivalent in France. The French are too human, too historical, too concerned with the future and the past. They spend their time in in-depth analysis. They do not know how to become, they think only in terms of historical past and future." One could retort that this is an overstatement, resorting to a stereotype, but for Deleuze "what counts is the present-becoming: geography and not history, the middle and not the beginning or the end, grass which is in the middle and which grows from the middle, and not trees which have a top and roots."[37] Happiness lies in the meadowlands? Deleuze, sometimes assisted by Guattari, has embraced the spatial in all its forms and nonshapes, establishing the concepts of the *line of flight* and the contrasts between *smooth space* and *striated space*. Michel Foucault, although not quite so passionate as Deleuze in his embrace of spatiality, nevertheless has contributed to that discourse in such texts as "Of Other Spaces," in which Foucault notes that, if the nineteenth century was dominated by a grand obsession with history, the contemporary epoch of the late twentieth century is an era of spatiality.

Why? Why has space been reevaluated at this point, after being relegated to the rank of a mere *thing* engulfed by time? If today the word *space* is experiencing "inflation,"[38] it is for several reasons. Of course, nature abhors a vacuum, and the weakening of traditional historicity, alongside the decoupling of time and progress, has made possible the valorizing rereading of space. But this does not explain everything. We might note first that throughout the long twentieth century, massive population movements have occurred over the entire surface of the planet. The "cosmopolitan diaspora," as Caren Kaplan has put it, is motivated by several causes, not all of which are complementary. There are grand migrations occasioned by economic or political exigencies specific to the industrial, and especially the postindustrial, era. One also sees this mobility triggered by the process of decolonization. An unusual view of space has emerged as a result of planetary air travel and so on. Space has become caught between a logic of partition and a culture of the border. In other circumstances, this mobility emerges not as a negative condition but as creative, spontaneous activity. The individual today has the awesome power to move around the world. The twentieth-century voyager takes the train, then cars and airplanes, moving ever more frequently, rapidly, and cheaply. Often, by the way, the traveler is transformed into a tourist, thereby producing a flourishing industry. One nevertheless continues to write and describe these other spaces. Despite the growing relativization of what counts as exotic, travel narrative continues to be a beloved genre. The travel writer takes part in the only meaningful image of the world, reflecting the abstract spaces through which he or she moves and forming representations of human spaces. Ultimately, space appears as heterogeneous as time. Taking note of such spaces, every migrant, every traveler, and everyone who has eyes to see will inscribe a geographical experience of land, water, air, and sometimes fire.

Perec is not an ordinary traveler; he is thrust into the space between the world and the text while walking in Paris. *Life: A User's Manual* reveals this double displacement both by the modesty of its geographical deployment and by the ambitious absence of physical barriers that its title implies. In *Species of Spaces*, Perec tries to reconcile Paris and the text in an attempt to decipher "a bit of the town, deduce the obvious facts."[39] But the effort is doomed in advance. Piece by piece, we discover that the facts are misleading, that space is fragmented, fleeting, and elusive. "In short," writes Perec, "spaces have multiplied, been broken up and have diversified. There are spaces today of every kind and every size, for every use and every function. To live is to pass from one space to another, while doing your very best not to bump yourself."[40] Thus the surface of places shares the fate of the timeline: the one and the other fall apart to leave room for ad hoc arrangements—in both the spatial and temporal senses of the word.

Space is involved in the same disintegrating dynamic as time. Both find their impulse in the crisis of dimension, as elaborated by one of the major figures of French postmodernism, Paul Virilio: "The crisis in the conceptualization of dimension becomes the crisis of the whole. In other words, the substantial, homogeneous space derived from classical Greek geometry gives way to an accidental, heterogeneous space in which sections and fractions become essential once more."[41] To demonstrate the increasing discontinuity of space, Virilio uses terminology eerily similar to that used to express the fragmentation of the timeline after 1945. Space strikes back, but this counteroffensive remains unfinished. The temporal and spatial dimensions are rebalanced; in recent decades in literature as in other mimetic arts, they have finally come together . . . for better or for worse. The worst is easy to imagine. In *Order out of Chaos*, Prigogine and Stengers recall a line from Hegel's *Philosophy of Nature*, in which Hegel discusses the fate of the individual hit on the head with a brick: "A brick does not kill not a man merely because it is a brick, but solely because of its acquired velocity; this means that the man is killed by space and time."[42] Hegel's quip remains timely, as objects more dangerous than bricks today fall from the skies (in Iraq, in Afghanistan, etc.). It is apparently difficult to divorce time from space, space from time.

New Arrangements of Time and Space

At the beginning of the twenty-first century, the coordinates of time and space must be correlated; certainly, they are inextricably meshed. While it is still conceivable to isolate time from space, or history from geography, it seems intransigent or unwise to deliberately keep the two dimensions separate. It would appear a dissimulation, with time lurking behind space; as Ouellet would have it, "*Chronos* advances masked, disguised as *topos*, place being the veil of time, which hides that which you would not see."[43] On the other hand, it will be objected that space "appears as a notional hybrid, incorporating whatever is discerned in it—time, subject, movement."[44] But in any event, we associate one with the other. The reign of a sovereign and autonomous temporality is completed, and the "counterattack" of space has led to a reweighing. It is now necessary to bury time and space in order to make room for space-time. Even leaving aside the world of the hard sciences and its various postulates about space-time, there are several theories oriented toward the joint study of spatiotemporality in literature as well as in geography and philosophy.

Among other areas of the humanities and social sciences, literary theory has registered the largest deficit in spatiotemporal approaches. I mention again Bakhtin's theory of the chronotope. Developed in the late 1930s, the definition of the chronotope is inspired, as the author himself points out, by Einstein's theory of relativity. It is very concise. This is "the intrinsic connectedness of temporal and spatial relationships that are artistically expressed in literature."[45] The chronotope is primarily a structuring element of the theory of genres. At each period in history, the dominant literary forms, subsumed under a given genre, are determined by spatial and temporal coordinates in which they are *situated.* The emergence of a generic category occurs at a specific point in space-time. For example, in examining the ancient Greek adventure narrative, Bakhtin notes that the chronotope of this genre is characterized by a "*technical, abstract connection between space and time*, by the *reversibility* of moments in a temporal sequence, by their *interchangeability* in space."[46] According to Bakhtin, the sequence of events and episodes in the Greek novel takes place in a framework in which temporal and spatial information is arranged in an almost accidental way.

As a formalist, Bakhtin analyzes the space of the text without taking into account referential space. This is understandable in the context of the ancient Greek novel (e.g., of Heliodorus, Xenophon of Ephesus, Longus, Achilles Tatius, and others); such formalism continues but is no longer necessary in studying the modern novel. Failing to take into account the referential space, Bakhtin marked social space in a spatiotemporal context of tension between the simple, centripetal monologism and the complex, centrifugal dialogism. Favoring the dialogism of the multiple over the monologism of the single, Bakhtin promoted systematic, or systemic, transgression. According to Julian Holloway and James Kneale, Bakhtin delivered "a carnivalesque geography,"[47] but this geography still gave precedence to time. Bakhtin was a modernist, and the Bakhtinian chronotope has been a great asset, however late in arriving. It has been used not only in literary studies but also in architecture, urban planning, and geography. In its travels through these other disciplines, it has been transformed to become more applicable to sensible reality rather than formal fictions. Thus Evelina Calvi, in a brief essay on the temporality of architectural projects, has deliberately relied on the chronotope to define lived space as place, and "place is nothing other than the product of the articulation, interconnection, and therefore the reciprocal relativization of space and time."[48]

After being banished to Kazakhstan between 1930 and 1936, Bakhtin served another sentence of exile in Savelovo, north of Moscow, where Braudel was captured in June 1940 and interned in prisoner of war camps in Mainz and Lübeck. Bakhtin and Braudel shared the painful experience of captivity, and they also shared the desire to put history and geography, temporality and spatiality, into proper perspective. The Bakhtinian chronotope echoes the Braudelian geohistory, each concept developed through discussions with other detained inmates. How can one discount that the experience of imprisonment, of carceral space, influences the overall reading of one's coordinates of existence? For Braudel, *geohistory* had two complementary meanings. First, "geohistory is history that the milieu constantly imposes on humans." In other words, geohistory requires one to factor in the geographical environment in studies of the *longue durée*, which one can quickly see in Braudel's study of the Mediterranean. Space is what remains after the historical event. The event must be superseded because, like the fireflies in the state of Bahia, where Braudel stayed in better days, it illuminates, but not enough for us to reconstruct the surrounding countryside. But "geohistory is also the story of man struggling with his space, fighting against it throughout his hard life of toil and effort." Geohistory relates the event in the context of space and understands history in terms of the relations of man to the spatial arrangements. As Braudel puts it, "geohistory is the study of a double-bind, of nature to man and of man to nature, the study of action and reaction, mixed, confused, repeated endlessly in the reality of each day."[49] Like the chronotope, geohistory provides a methodological foundation for a number of spatiotemporal or geohistorical studies. It has raised hopes in the literary sector. Referring to this concept, Daniel-Henri Pageaux has asked, "Would there be a place for literature or literary history on this quite broad and interdisciplinary platform?"[50] But unlike the Bakhtinian chronotope, Braudelian geohistory has not yet won many converts. According to Emmanuelle Tricoire, Braudel "fails to create specific conceptual tools appropriate to a discipline that would become autonomous and that would ensure that 'geohistory' does not remain a marginal curiosity, little known to students, not much better known to historians, and instituted as a mere side project of geographers."[51]

The field of cultural geography has made many new attempts at connecting time and space. Cultural geography might be said to trace its roots to *tidsgeografi*, developed by Torsten Hägerstrand in the 1960s and early 1970s. *Tidsgeografi* translates as "temporal geography," but we could also say "chronogeography." Chronogeography could then be said to complete geohistory, as Braudel would be supplemented by Hägerstrand and his successors, who have formulated a completed and operational theory. Hägerstrand seems more like Foucault, Michel de Certeau, and Pierre Bourdieu, inasmuch as they associate the rhetoric of displacement with a reflection on the locations of bodies within a social space regulated by an authority.[52] Hägerstrand's model incorporates the effects of individual attitudes in dealing with space-time. He pays particular attention to the pathways selected and used by the individual to accomplish his or her goals in urban space-time. Spatial progression over time is subject to several constraints. The first of these lies in biological vectors (nonubiquity, noninstantaneous displacement, and relative means of transportation); a second derives from interpersonal relationships of the individual whose lingering in one place may be dictated by an entourage (by, say, the length of a conversation or a certain job to do, etc.); and a third relates to the injunctions of an authority that can determine access to certain places or prohibit it altogether. Hägerstrand's theory has had a significant impact in areas such as urban planning and studies on social equity (e.g., adjusting the spatial requirements of doors for disabled people, modulation of space according to gender, and so on). Adapted to literature, the achievements of *tidsgeografi* might be quite useful. It would be easy to design a spatiotemporal analysis of a fictional character's route through the city using some of the criteria developed by Hägerstrand, but so far as I know, no one has done so. Yet, had they known of Hägerstrand's innovative work, many critics could have benefited from his research. For instance, in his *Atlas of the European Novel, 1800–1900*, Franco Moretti meticulously examines the movements of several protagonists from nineteenth-century literature through major cities like London and Paris. Could one imagine a *tidsgeografi* in which the guinea pigs were Rastignac or Sherlock Holmes?

Beginning in the early 1990s, David Harvey's Marxist analyses of the postmodern condition (in, e.g., *The Condition of Postmodernity*) have been widely influential, completing the analysis of spatiotemporal compression. According to Harvey, this spatiotemporal compression is characteristic of any period subsequent to the European crises of 1848. It was then augmented at two moments: around 1910, with the advent of modernism (along with Taylorism and Fordism), and around the crisis of 1973, during the transition to a postmodern system of flexible, post-Fordist accumulation. Harvey describes the spatiotemporal compression as follows: "As space begins to shrink to a 'global village' of telecommunications and a 'spaceship earth' of economic and ecological interdependencies—to use just two familiar and everyday images—and as time horizons to the point where the present is all there is (the world of the schizophrenic), so we have to learn to cope with an overwhelming sense of *compression* of our spatial and temporal worlds. The experience of time-space compression is challenging, exciting, stressful, and sometimes deeply troubling."[53] This compression is similar to the beginnings of globalization, and *The Condition of Postmodernity* is roughly contemporaneous with the fall of the Berlin Wall. At a social level, in drawing attention to the consequences for the individual in dealing with the crisis of intelligibility in a space-time continuum, Harvey follows Virilio's lead when the latter denounces the dematerialization of the human environment. Harvey—like Virilio and many others—confronts that luminous prediction made by Braudel in the prison camp where he was incarcerated: "Beyond this war, I do not think that we will be able again to direct and contain the world. I think it will contract upon itself, but at the same time open itself up, becoming porous at once. It is perhaps high time."[54] The world has contracted, but has it become porous? Harvey's hypothesis has been so successful because it buttresses the analysis of the acceleration of globalization with the critique of the processes of flexible accumulation.

Like temporal geography, this analysis of spatiotemporal compression could have an effect on literature, if it is based on the neo-Marxist, postmodern analysis of planetary fluxes. It could also be used to study what is called world literature. Spatiotemporal compression provides a framework for the narrative strategies of contemporary novelists, including Jean Echenoz and Michel Rio in France and Ray Loriga in Spain, among many others. In *Tokio ya no nos quiere* (or *Tokyo Doesn't Love Us Anymore*), Loriga creates a slightly futuristic context, but one that does not trouble the familiar geographical environment. The anonymous hero sells pills to facilitate forgetting. Potential consumers are numerous and closely monitor the market, but the protagonist himself develops a taste for the drugs. He loses all consciousness of time before being tossed to the four corners of the planet, from Arizona to Japan, from Thailand and Vietnam to Berlin and other places. The logical connections between these different geographical and psychological stops tend to blur. Temporal markers are erased; space seems totally open because distances almost vanish. The protagonist of *Tokio ya no nos quiere* is a more or less willing victim of spatiotemporal compression. The present is all that there is, and schizophrenia is lying in wait.

This brief overview was not intended to be exhaustive, of course. If we were to make such an attempt, it would need a much wider scope, because it appears that the study of space-time in literature, as in other fields of humanities and social sciences, is polycentric . . . or not. The second observation relates to the interdisciplinary character of theoretical exploration. The few examples listed here are drawn from fields as diverse as literature, history, and above all geography. Other related disciplines include architecture, urban studies, philosophy, anthropology, and more. It is inconceivable to consider systems of spatial or spatiotemporal representation in the field of literature alone, unless one wishes to isolate literature from the rest of the world. Questioning the place of literature in the world is the leitmotif of the following chapters. For now, in the section that follows, I will lay out several arguments and perspectives concerning the interdisciplinary dynamic of geocriticism, which should animate all approaches to space and time, regardless of the disciplinary background of their original proponents.

An Interdisciplinary Approach to Spatiotemporality

Geocriticism requires an interdisciplinary approach. Knowing the theory of relativity in detail is not necessary, any more than knowing real estate law is. However, I think that a more thorough knowledge of the spatial problems addressed in geography, urban studies, and architecture, along with anthropology and history, is desirable. The boundaries of literature are changing, and there is no clear roadmap to determine the route. The postmodern theorist knows that the ivory tower of Literature with a capital *L* is surrounded. Like many social sciences, geography has long since made way for relativity. More generally, is determinism, which constitutes the criterion for the split between the literary and the nonliterary, still legitimate in the early twenty-first century? I would argue that strict disciplinary boundaries have hindered research, and we must return to a model of interpenetration among the disciplines. As Soja has said in *Thirdspace*, "Space was too important to be left only to the specialized spatial disciplines (Geography, Architecture, Urban Studies) or merely added on as a gap-filler or factual background for historians, social scientists, or Marxist sociologists. The spatiality of human life, like its historicality or sociality, infused every discipline and discourse."[55] Jean Giono had expressed the same idea in *L'eau vive*: "One cannot know a country by the simple science of geography."[56] It seems clear that both are right. And to the extent that the discourse of spatiality is itself so interdisciplinary, interdisciplinarity becomes difficult to ignore. Without the big picture, the analysis becomes partial, incomplete, and somewhat frustrating for the informed reader. From all sides, critics call for interdisciplinarity. While Soja specifically connects geography, architecture, and urban studies, literature also becomes interlinked with other disciplinary fields as more scholars devote greater attention to the connections among them.

In cultural geography, the role of literature is far from negligible. Hervé Regnauld recognizes that "after all, as noted by some of its practitioners, geography is not just a social science, but also a science of nature, with which painters or writers deal as much as scientists do."[57] Brosseau points out that, "among the mass of written documents on which geography relies, literature has attained a place of honor as a field of investigation. If the real expansion of geographical research on literature seems to begin in the early 1970s, when there was no consensus about the legitimacy of using such sources, today it is generally assumed that literature is relevant to geography."[58] John K. Wright had called for the first hybridization of the two disciplines in the 1920s. In a 1926 article, Wright coined the term "geosophy" to indicate that geography was not the exclusive property of professional geographers, but that a "sphere of ideas" fed the history of geographical ideas, whether conventional (formal geographic science) or not (informal knowledge of place).[59] Geosophy had therefore to partake in fiction, sometimes in mythology. By the 1970s, the blending of geography and literature was being undertaken on a grand scale. As Brosseau recounts, the Institute of British Geographers in 1979 devoted its annual meeting to relations between the two. In the late 1980s and throughout the 1990s, such renowned geographers as Denis Cosgrove, Stephen Daniels, James S. Duncan, and David Ley consolidated the link. Derek Gregory's *Geographical Imaginations* surveyed this movement while also contributing to it. In France, it would take longer to achieve this result, despite the role of a geographer well known to literary critics: in Julien Gracq's *The Shape of a City*, literature and geography meet in Nantes, the birthplace of Jules Verne.

According to Brosseau, there are three main reasons why geographers have become interested in literature: literature provides a complement to the regional geography; it can translate the experience of places (via modes of perception, for instance); and it expresses a critique of reality or of the dominant ideology. The difficulty lies in the deterministic manner in which geographers treat a literary "document." The geographers' predilection for realism may limit their sources. From this perspective, Flaubert could be "exploited" as a surrealist novelist. As Brosseau puts it, "The overriding question often remains whether novelists are good geographers."[60] For this interaction to be effective, the two disciplines and their visions of space must share a common language: "If geography and the novel are wholly different, how can they communicate without establishing in advance—or en route—a metalanguage (or code) allowing transmissions from one to the other?"[61] Another good question is raised by Maria de Fanis in *Geografie letterarie*: "The artist appropriates a place, exploring it with active participation, moves off the beaten path, pulls it out of context, and in clarifying rules, invents others. In this view, the prerogative of the artifact no longer lies in the simple reproduction of reality. It is rather the product of a logical, conceptual construction . . . In meaningfully reordering what appears confused in the world, the text reveals . . . unlimited generative potential, which manifests itself in each new conceptual node of a new order proposed by the text."[62] The literary text therefore becomes a generator. I believe that this characteristic of the fictional Logos reveals the meaning of hidden realities, exploring the folds of reality, and may thus be worthy of attention from geographers as it is from literary critics.

To say that the study of literature and space is interdisciplinary amounts to a truism. Literature is already playing the game: texts have always looked at geography and at ways of representing human spaces. Trying to isolate the literary from other disciplinary points of view would only diminish literature and its role in the world. I cannot emphasize this enough: literature is a not a subordinate field, operating in the service of other humanities and social sciences, but literature can certainly help them in their projects. Unsurprisingly, writers are the first to become aware of this. For Stasiuk, "the domains of geography and of the imagination, so distant from each other, are more closely related to one another than is folly to wisdom. One reason for this is that to construct worlds, that noblest form of daydreaming, always supposes that one invest in space."[63] Furthermore, the alliance of literary studies and geography is itself a case of interdisciplinarity. It is not a question of theft, here. The interdisciplinary is not the kingdom of freeloaders, living off of the toil of others. Rather, it is like that land where people practice potlatch, which, at least on a symbolic and spiritual level, enriches the whole community and all communities. In England and America, literary studies moved toward geography earlier than in France and Continental Europe, as had also happened in the other direction, from geography toward literature. This "advance," at least chronologically, is explained by the fact that a proximity between literary and cultural studies is better established across the Channel and over the Atlantic. The simple relationship of proximity is sometimes supplanted by a synecdochical relationship, and the resulting literary phenomena encompass the broader expanse of the cultural sphere. In *Questions of Travel,* Caren Kaplan writes, "Topography and geography now intersect literary and cultural criticism in a growing interdisciplinary inquiry into emergent identity formations and social practices."[64] Occupying this intersection of disciplines is in no way degrading to literature, but this research will take us to the borders of what is traditionally the province of literary studies.

But even if we remain in the areas literature normally inhabits, we find other types of connections between literature and geography. In his *Atlas of the European Novel,* Moretti has proposed that we might move "towards a literary geography," and he then mentions two distinct levels of inquiry. In the microgeographic register, Moretti maps the spaces of the Paris of Rastignac and the London of Sherlock Holmes or Oliver Twist. On a macrogeographic level, he studies the movements of characters through different national territories or colonies. Moretti's literary geography is quite original, providing reflections on the perception and representations of metropolises in nineteenth-century novels. It also provides valuable lessons on the history of the novel, on the transhistorical modalities of the novel, and on the asynchrony of cultural spaces, among other things. Moretti's book is a good example of an interdisciplinary approach, since it assimilates literature and geography, the fictional and the real, in a broadly historiographic perspective.

It is doubtless unnecessary to point out the linkages between literature and geography or geography and literature. If it is in the nature of geography to probe the potential of human spaces, it is also in the nature of literature to touch on space, because all literature is in space, regardless of its thematic developments. But it is not only geography. Other spatial sciences, such as architecture and urban studies, intersect with literature, and these connections are becoming greater, denser. The methods of hybridization are analogous to those of literature and geography: reciprocal. The literary enters the domain of urban studies and architecture, which penetrate the literary. Calvi defined the architectural project as a "weak" project in the sense that Vattimo has given this epithet, a project inclined toward experimentalism, dialogism, and openness. Literature finds its place in this type of process because it becomes the cornerstone of the imaginary project, complementing the architectural one, but in a manner that is strong (not weak). Calvi's ideas were applied by Flavia Schiavo in *Parigi, Barcellona, Firenze: Forma e racconto.* To study the evolution of these three cities from the nineteenth century, Schiavo assembled a series of literary texts in which they served as geographic references. Schiavo argues that urban space is not simply an abstract framework that one identifies on a map but a mental and emotional framework that literature permits us to explore in time. As she puts it, "Hypothetically, could we assign literary representation its own creative role, but one that would be coplanar and integrated with conventional sources and orthodox documents?" Schiavo answers, a few pages later, "It is undeniable that literature tends to reveal a certain truth—but this truth is often subjective, animated by a rhetorical energy that, in general, does not achieve an ecumenical, normative, or total view. Contrary to the standards of urban studies, literary description is not valid *erga omnes*." And so we return to the gap between the objective and nonobjective. Schiavo nevertheless overcomes the obstacle by relativizing all forms of determination, in line with Vattimo and the postmodernists: "But is it really possible to affirm that there are descriptive systems capable of reproducing reality? And if they exist (which we doubt), why should it only be those that refer to technical language? Also, is it not true that each system of representation only expresses an intrinsic and relative truth, a truth proper to itself? . . . Is the distance between the *imaginary topography* that emerges from novels and the *real representation* conveyed by the map really insurmountable?"[65] These lines anticipate the much-debated question of referentiality, which I will address at length in Chapter 3. It raises another question incidentally, still implicit: that of the transversality of literary vision, of its possible extension to the whole ensemble of fields of spatiality studies.

Literary Order and Disorder

Why, suddenly, has literature drawn so much attention in a scientific universe where it had previously had so little influence? The phenomenon is too recent, critical distance too small, to propose a satisfactory response. There is impertinence—that of thinking in an ontological and epistemological context that tends toward the relative, in an environment deprived of a dominant order, deprived of *meaning*—and literature is presented in a different, if not unprecedented, light. (Let us not forget that for the ancient Greeks, literature was so ingrained in the concrete forms of understanding the world that it did not exist independent of the sciences.) The fragmentation of the coordinates of existence caused time and space to stray. If this world is a "possibility," and not an unqualified certainty, then this breakdown results in a loss of guiding signposts. But landmarks are not indispensible. At least, they do not always fit in a Euclidean or Cartesian perspective. The landmark is in the point, in innumerable points, silhouetted on the horizon of knowledge, one of untold horizons, which have multiplied after the single teleological line of "strong" knowledge, after uncertain progress, was shown to be unreliable. The effects of this (salutary?) implosion are not limited to the literary domain; they were felt by all engaged in reading the world.

Would it be untimely to say that determination has lived out its life? If this hypothesis is feasible, it has several consequences for literature. The first would be to reassure the practitioner or theorist of literature. Indeed, the risks that the literary critic takes every time he or she crosses boundaries into so-called deterministic areas would be partially if not totally removed. Anyway, one would develop in new and unknown directions, away from the hermetic old determinist models. Literature remains anchored in the familiar universe of the relative, while "hard," "strong," absolute," *deterministic* disciplines that tried to know everything would be sucked into the indistinctness that has gripped our society in the aftermath of the Second World War. The borders would become permeable, replaced by a threshold to cross. The second consequence would follow from the first: the literary topos would become a matrix. As an emblematic vehicle for a weak ontology, literature focuses itself and regains an honorable place in the epistemological universe. It appears clear that the position of literature in this arrangement is *absolutely* correlated with the degree of relativity that one assigns to the world.

What "lessons" would the other disciplines derive from the literary? From the preceding discussion, it appears to be pure discursivity that characterizes literature. Nothing very original, except that this discursivity—self-referential, often far from the "real world," with no direct effect on it, thoroughly fictional—has finally become instructive. The multiplication of visions of reality, once concentrated in an absolute determinism, and the infinite malleability of literary discourse seem consubstantial in the postmodern age. Literary discourse constitutes an entropic paradigm between points of inflection and lines that branch off, before turning into lifelines to carve a destiny in the palm of one's hand. In *The Mirror of Herodotus*, François Hartog says that a surveyor is "a rhapsode in the primary sense of the term. He is the one who *sews* the different spaces together; he is the linking agent whose task it is to connect one space to another, continuously, as far as the limits of the inhabited world."[66] Sewing has always been characteristic of the text, which is texture and fabric; but now the entire scientific class is involved in tailoring the jester's motley that has become the incommensurable reality of the contemporary world. All of them have recourse to the interdisciplinarity of which literature is the exemplum in this direction. Literature is a vector of assumed instability in a series of disciplinary landscapes traditionally characterized by stability and saturation. Determinism is the attempt to exhaust the world in the quest for absolute completeness: exactly what literature abhors. Inventing worlds and their perpetual reenchantment are the imperatives of literature. But literature does more than that. Complemented by theory, it is able to propose solutions, to project representational models applicable to shifting contexts. In *Time and Narrative*, Ricoeur has repeatedly invoked a mimetic dialectic whereby the arrangement of elements is prefigured in limbo, configured by the narrative, then refigured by the reader. This triple movement is spontaneous; like spirit, it blows where it wishes. Literary discursivity participates in this dialectic. It branches off at will, but it is always accessible to a theoretical metadiscourse, which nevertheless cannot monopolize it. As Ricoeur puts it beautifully, "Fiction alone, because it remains fiction even when it projects and depicts experience, can allow itself a little inebriation."[67] Intoxication facilitates transgression, and as long as it is powerful but still light enough not to be fatal, this form of drunkenness—"a little inebriation"—establishes discourse in the transgressive.

CHAPTER 2

Transgressivity

Wanderers with the Harlequin's Spirit

The first premise of geocritical theory states that time and space share a common plan, subject to an entirely oscillatory logic whereby the fragmentary ceases to be oriented to a coherent whole. Postmodern temporality is characterized by isotropy, which is the scientific name of this systemic indeterminacy, and this isotropy is then extended to the spatial representation. We must not confuse isotropy with isotopy. For some, like Henri Lefebvre, isotopy is characteristic of the old Euclidean geometric space, equal in all its parts, stable and fixed. *Isotropy* characterizes a space of movements and tensions with higher order and is not subject to a hierarchy. It marks the transition from a reading of the world still guided by residual grand narratives to an erratic reading arising from a full-fledged postmodernity. The second premise of geocriticism is that the relationship between the representation of space and real space is indeterminate. Rather than considering a spatial or spatiotemporal representation as not "real," we view every representation (whether literary, iconographic, etc.) as referring to a broadly imagined reality that, in and through its extreme extension, is subject to a weak ontology.

From these two premises, we understand that space cannot be understood except in its heterogeneity. Of course, this complicates its representation, but we agree that this is not the age of simplicity. The Euclidean homogeneity that had long been the guiding principle for understanding the world is now being undermined. We cannot, as they did in the nineteenth century, "inscribe within each part of the world an essence that one believes to be the fate of all humanity," as Pierre Auriol puts it.[1] Those who seek to prove that this theory of the world is valid, in spite of the evidence to the contrary, will tend to resort to bombs to do so and thus break it. In his own style, Braudel weighed in on the relative stability of the human landscape of the German prison camps: "Poor and fragile sketch that is the living world! Only when the paint is dry, the model ceases to look like his portrait. Discover, rediscover, describe, describe again, the task is endless."[2] It is like the labors of God in certain Talmudic texts; after failing 26 times in the creation of the world, he returned to the task. And, as Prigogine and Stengers note, after each attempt, "'Let's hope it works' (*Halway Sheyaamod*), exclaimed God as he created the World, and this hope, which has accompanied all the subsequent history of the world and mankind, has emphasized right from the outset that this history is branded with the mark of radical uncertainty."[3] It is not surprising that the poor creatures who later were expelled from the Garden of Eden had shown such audacity. Their souls could not be immaculate, but their motives were pure. Without thinking of our distant ancestors, Michel Serres has summed up their fate, and that of man and woman together in the postmodern condition: "Without fixed roots, we have all become wanderers with the harlequin's spirit, taking on and mixing with the spirits of the places we passed, for good or evil."[4]

This radical insecurity affects space as well as time. Henri Lefebvre analyzes this spatial heterogeneity throughout *The Production of Space*. Like others, he attempts to dismantle the myth of spatial uniformity, which for him lies under the "phallic" sign, which is to say that of the political powers, the chief of police, the army, and the bureaucracy. "Under the cobblestones, the beach," as the May 1968 militants chanted in the streets of Paris six years before the publication of Lefebvre's book. In the heat of action, it was found that the space was composite. "Just as white light, though uniform in appearance may be broken down into a spectrum," writes Lefebvre, "space likewise decomposes when subjected to analysis; in the case of space, however, the knowledge to be derived from analysis extends to the recognition of conflicts internal to what on the surface appears homogenous and coherent."[5] It would be easy to play with the word spectrum [*spectre*], and say that *The Production of Space* serves as the epitaph for the old empire of that totalizing space, of positivism, of colonialism, of the always absolute and inhuman constriction. In Lefebvre's book, the ghost of that space is made visible. Lefebvre, however, declined to isolate the *types* of space. He said there is indeed a single, abstract space, which has a "contradictory character within the framework of the dominant tendency toward homogeneity."[6] The contradictory nature of homogeneous space incorporates the elements of heterogeneity: "It is not, therefore, as though one had global (or conceived) space to one side and fragmented (or lived) space to the other—rather as one might have an intact glass here and a broken glass or mirror over there. For space 'is' whole and broken, global and fragmented, at one and the same time. Just as it is at once conceived, perceived, and directly lived."[7] The definition of a heterogeneous (and socially open) space, the part that consistently escapes political control, continued in other works of theory throughout the 1970s.

In their *Capitalism and Schizophrenia* volumes, Gilles Deleuze and Félix Guattari distinguish *smooth space* from *striated space*, a distinction that is analogous to that between heterogeneous and homogeneous space. Homogeneous space is subject to gravitational forces: "It is striated by the fall of bodies, the verticals of gravity, the distribution of matter into parallel layers, the lamellar and laminar movement of flows. These parallel verticals have formed an independent dimension capable of spreading everywhere, of formalizing all the other dimensions, of striating space in all of its directions, so as to render it homogeneous."[8] Striated space, then, is the space occupied by the state apparatus. This is the space of the polis, politics, the policed, and the police, as opposed to the space of the nomos, which is smooth space. This is the space of *hadara* or city life, as opposed to *badiya* or bedouinism, to use the terminology of fourteenth-century Arab historian Ibn Khaldun. Of course, it is smooth space, heterogeneous and nomadic space, that the two philosophers embrace, since "sedentary space is striated, by walls, enclosures, and roads between enclosures, while nomad space is smooth, marked only by 'traits' that are effaced and displaced with the trajectory."[9] The nomad aims to read these traits without becoming imprisoned by the subsequent definition: "Smooth space is precisely the space of the smallest deviation: therefore it has no homogeneity, except between infinitely proximate points, and the linking of proximities is effected independently of any determined path."[10] It goes back to punctual logic, which Deleuze and Guattari would say is part of the intermezzo. Here we return to isotropy, because "variability, the polyvocality of directions, is an essential feature of smooth spaces."[11]

Smooth space unfolds between points, between points that can connect as many lines as one chooses. Virtually open to infinity, it arranges all the minutes of each individual's life. Every minute of a story and every acre of it as well? This would imply a veritable conquest of the moon, because it would have to restock the innumerable books of life's library, as José Saramago humorously depicts in his *Terra do pecado*. Pushing to the extremes the consequences of postmodernism's totalizing ontological vision (the only conceivable totalization), considering that the storylines of a life are endless and beyond the scope of narrative, the Portuguese writer eventually eliminates all strong punctuation, all reductive textual guidance, from his novel. Like many of his contemporaries, Saramago uses schismatic strategies to register the failings of consciousness, resulting in a narrative of everyday life that flows through smooth space.

Deleuze and Guattari had begun an inventory of smooth spaces. Their census could support a thematological approach to the spaces in literature. There is the sea, of course, and ice and the desert: "The creaking of the ice and the singing of the sands."[12] But there is also the calculation of longitude, the cartographic survey of the desert, cryology. The sea is also a laboratory: "the sea, the archetype of smooth space, was also the archetype of all striations of smooth space . . . It was at sea that smooth space was first subjugated and a model found for the laying-out and imposition of striated space, a model later put to use elsewhere."[13] Smooth space is constantly threatened by the striating that civilized, settled society imposes. We must at all costs render smooth space metric, or measurable. The distinction between the smooth and the striated eventually become tenuous, no longer to be understood in terms of unsettled versus civilized spaces. Deleuze and Guattari assert that "a stroll taken by Henry Miller in Clichy or Brooklyn is a nomadic transit in smooth space; he makes the city disgorge a patchwork, differentials of speed, delays and accelerations, continuous variations."[14] The striated can become smooth, just as smooth space is exposed to striation. As with Lefebvre, here we come to the conclusion that space is essentially heterogeneous, but it is always subject to homogenizing forces. Anyway, it is chronically diverse. Striated space and smooth space, this mixed space slowly moves the white sands of Alamogordo, New Mexico—a gypsum desert where, as a result of endless evenings of striating breezes, some sands are whisked to the top of the dunes, while other sands are frozen in moisture between the dunes, constantly changing, over millions of years.

The definition of smooth space will not, in any event, be singular and is not limited to theory from the 1970s. Few people have continued to invoke homogeneous, striated space. Faced with Saddam Hussein, two generations of the Bush family and an inconclusive Operation Desert Storm ("We have to finish the job")[15] were involved in striating the smooth space of the Iraqi desert in an effort to create a simulated-American or simulated-democratic striated space. But according to other, more credible sources (although, unfortunately, they received less attention), space is now dedicated to heterogeneity. This is the opinion of nearly all postcolonial critics, for whom space is subject to conflicting tensions that arise from incompatible systems of representation. It is also the opinion of such postfeminist, multiethnic, "multi-inter-trans-ethnic"[16] critics as bell hooks and Gloria Anzaldúa, for whom the displacement between the sexes and among ethnic groups leads to a plurality of perceptions of space. It remains the opinion of those, such as David Harvey, who observe the time–space compression that has accompanied the processes of globalization.

"Being-there expands," notes Serres, and with it expand the tendencies to penetrate everywhere and to standardize what has been conquered, to "mesh" space "by the virtuoso techniques by which distance and time are partly abolished."[17] This is thus the era of *pantopia*, total space, which according to Serres is the place of "all places in every place and every place in all places, centers and circumference, global conversation."[18] A class of heralds embodies this type of contact with the environment: messengers of the gods and bringers of tidings have always interested Serres. There is Hermes, or Mercury, and there are the angels. As Serres explains, "If Angels become rowdy, move or swirl like flies and atoms, they weave together the universe of divine omnipresence. In what ways do they get their message across? By routes of chaos. Thus, via this mixing, they arrange all of the constituting atoms and places and the Universe: by capricious changes to the there, to being there, to out there, they fashion the global."[19] Globalization seems to share the paths of chaos; it seems to travel by angelic communication. But, pausing a moment to suspend disbelief, we will ask the fatal question: Do angels exist? And, hurrying to respond precisely in order to avoid a passing angel, we reply, "No, as everyone knows." Globalization is the word of angels against that of a flickering Reason, whose vestiges, despite everything, have retained their legitimacy. Globalization assumes the homogeneity of space, but space is inherently heterogeneous. Serres remembers Dante and the gateway to a place that one is usually reluctant to enter: "Abandon all hope, ye who failed to pass the threshold of this new world; but freely enter, those who have leapt across."[20] All limits call for a crossing. A wanderer with the harlequin's spirit, the postmodern individual cannot be thrust into any world other than this absolutely mixed-up one. Heterogeneity is his profession (a profession of faith). Transgression is his lot: *Lasciate ogni speranza, voi ch'entrate.* Dante's *Inferno* always attracted more readers than *Purgatorio* and *Paradiso* combined. Moreover, it combines all possible worlds, even Limbo, which forms the first circle of the abode of the former angel Lucifer and which is a place of great prestige, a place populated by the great transgressors of the spirit: "We were still at some distance from that place, / but close enough for me vaguely to see / that honorable souls possessed this spot."[21] Dante is about to meet the likes of Homer, Socrates, and Orpheus. We forget that Hell is hellish and, at this moment, we envy Dante.

From Transgressions to a State of Transgressivity

The word *transgress* derives from the Latin *transgredi*, whose meaning has a spatial origin. Among the Romans, one transgressed when passing to the other side of a boundary or river, or when moving from one argument to another. Something that exceeded its measure also transgressed. The verb *transgressio* was derived from the predicate nominative *transgredi*. The noun reflected the verb, but *transgressio* was also a figure of rhetoric (in Cicero), one that is now referred to as "hyperbaton." Hyperbaton was initially a figure of inversion or dissociation, distancing for rhetorical effect words normally kept in close syntactical proximity. For others, the specific effect of hyperbaton is rather "a spontaneity that requires the addition of some obvious or intimate truth in a syntactic construction that seemed closed."[22] Maybe this effect is the same in transgression, which would create an intimate space outside of the enclosure. The *transgressio* could also be an infraction: one does not cross a boundary without departing from the norm. But the Romans did not give priority to that sense of the word. For them, as for the Greeks earlier, one transgressed in space: "To transgress means, through *hubris*, to step outside one's own space and enter a foreign one."[23]

Over the centuries, the meaning of *transgressio* has become more precise. In modern French (and in other Romance languages), *transgression* has taken on a significance that emerged from the margins of its etymological precursor: transgression means violating a moral, rather than a physical, limit. One transgresses against the law. The spaces of our transgressions are not those of the Romans. For the latter, it would have been a matter of seeing what unfolds beyond the threshold, though the threshold itself was seen in two different ways: it was a *limes*, or boundary line, intended to make one stop, but it was also a limen, or porous border, intended to be crossed. The *limes* was a sort of border between two states of things, one accepted and thus existing, the other impermissible and thus (officially) nonexistent. Ovid faced this alternative space when he was exiled to Tomis, on the shore of the Euxeinos Pontos, what we call the Black Sea. Tomis was for him and the Romans the edge of the world, *ultima tellus*. When Ovid observed the world of the Dacians and Sauromatae, known as "barbarians" in his language, and when he perhaps also looked across to the opposite bank of the Hister (the Danube), he saw nothing Scythian. Porous, the limen was a border that opened onto an unknown novelty, but that *opened* toward the place rather than closing down upon it. Perhaps Ovid transformed the *limes* of the empire into a limen. I say "perhaps" because we know nothing. In this hypothesis, Ovid committed a crime more serious than the one (which one, by the way?) that caused his expulsion to the relatively frozen north of the Roman Empire.

Transgression is not just crossing porous boundary lines. It assumes a closed and striated space and a will to penetrate, which the state apparatus (following Deleuze and Guattari) establishes as a form of burglary. Striated space is sometimes the space of the gods high on Olympus or in heaven, making rules for places and lives. Transgressing their domain can be dangerous, as much so as subverting the political norms. When Xerxes, king of Persia, used his ships to build a bridge to cross the Hellespont (the Dardanelles) and invaded Greece by land, he committed an act of hubris, which Aeschylus denounced in *The Persians*. Hubris is a crime, because by it divine nature and human nature cease to be distinguished. In François Hartog's words, "This spatial transgression is also a transgression of divine space and aggression against the gods."[24] The gap is certainly narrow between action and transgression. This gap has a name, according to Deleuze and Guattari: it is the *epistrata*, the margin of tolerated deviance. The problem, as Mark Bonta and John Protevi summarize, is that each "social institution will have different thresholds of tolerance for deviation from a norm."[25] The angels have experimented with this restriction of variable geometry. One of them, Lucifer, eventually fell: he had transgressed without taking full "measure" of the epistrata. The measure, which is the opposite of the survey, is not itself a transgression. One does not survey the transgression. One takes in the brilliant view.

Evidently, the Romans were more interested in novelty than prohibition. Over time perhaps, we came to believe that novelty could not be situated in space without becoming a sort of violation. In this changing context, to speak of "spaces of transgression" is not a simple matter. We take part in this space of transgression, which is a sort of zone of intimacy beyond a closed construction. This space could be examined from a sociopoetic point of view. One would then determine the rules and identify the threshold, the space of movement beyond which would constitute transgression, and one would determine the manner in which these rules would be applied, disregarded, or violated. There are several codes governing the limits: the code of hospitality is one of them. The intersection, or contact zone between social actors, is regulated by explicit rules. These rules assume a shared rhythm, a spatiotemporal correlation. In the absence of a common rhythm, transgression is inevitable. In certain cases, transgression is massive, becoming a deliberate intrusion—hence war, a vast state transgression. Transgression is disparate, perhaps by definition. But it also meets a minimum set of defining criteria. Hence, there can be no transgression without the contravention of a code or rite. Transgression exists only in the presence of two figures: one who contravenes and one who attests to the contravention. Sometimes it seems that this is the same person. On his island, Robinson Crusoe traces lines of demarcation and delights in the dual status of judge and defendant. But Robinson himself quickly loses his isolation: the presence of a Friday is required, doubtless because transgression by nature lies in interaction. Do we let ourselves off too easily when we form our own tribunal? The code is in principle monological. Whether it is made explicit in speech or in writing, it is in every case articulated, entered into a concatenation of laws, leaving as little room as possible for interpretation. Of course, the monologic of the code extends to its environment: it assumes that every moment is part of a homogeneous time and that every place is a uniform space. Transgression occurs when there emerges an alternative to the straight line of time and to the rather geometrical figures of policed space. In the *sidestep*, one discovers the incalculable variations of space-time.

The code of space-time necessarily forms a unique bloc. But transgression imposes heterogeneity, along with polychrony (the combination of different temporalities) and polytopy (the composition of different spatialities). Polytopy is space understood in its plurality. But the polytopic view of space reserves for an individual a zone of intimacy, guarded against external intrusions. This is a secret space, a space of hyperbaton, one where the individual deploys a supplemental personal truth, protected from the eyes of the world and from the prescriptions of the code. This tension between the desire for a normatively sanctioned unity and the need for freedom emerging at the margins of the law inscribes the individual in a society where different, more or less compatible but asynchronous, rhythms coexist. Not everyone lives at the same speed. And speed is itself a relative concept. For a Hopi Indian, the construction of a highway does not necessarily justify slashing the desert landscape with lines of asphalt in northwestern New Mexico. What's so good about highways? The slow cycles that punctuate the life of the Hopi have nothing in common with the frenzy of white people. Polychrony and polytopy produce a polyrhythm best suited to anthropological study. In literary theory, the concept of polyrhythm is somewhat forgotten. This is unfortunate, because the plurality of inscriptions in space-time and the proliferation of rhythms that spring from them could form the basis of a sociopoetic approach. The written code is certainly monological, but it is completed and sometimes supplemented by a number of unwritten norms that regulate the margins to ensure peaceful transitions.

Transgression is not necessarily the result of a volitional act; it sometimes emerges from a poorly negotiated transition, an involuntary movement that causes turbulence. I anxiously wonder what would happen if a guest to my Limousin region refused to obey the injunction "Finish entering!" (or, in Occitan, "*Chabaz d'entrar*!").[26] Veritable rituals serve to make acceptable actions or behaviors that would otherwise be seen as a string of transgressions. One of the best examples of a similar system is provided in the region of Rrafsh, bordering Kosovo. There was the celebrated *kanun*, customs or laws of the clan of the Albanian hero Lekë Dukagjini, who organized (along with Gjergj Kastrioti) the resistance against the Ottomans at the end of the fifteenth century. Transcribed at the time of national independence in 1912, the *kanun* defined a code of conduct that was supposed to resolve all aspects of daily life. It was supposed to address almost everything. What would happen, for example, if a stranger wanted to enter one's home? The well-known rule would allow a stranger in, following the ancient Greek idea that the *xenos* could be a *theos*. Barring entry constituted a transgression perceived as aggression. Consequently, transgression was a form of poor management of the spatiotemporal interface (nonsynchronization) and interactivity (incongruence). In general, transgression involves several moving parts: sometimes malice, often fleeting and imperceptible or even infinitesimal, results from a simple misunderstanding of the code. Ismail Kadaré, the great Albanian novelist, has inspired many variants of this code in some of his most famous books (*The File on H*, *Broken April*, etc.). He actually explores "how people are tied together and yet isolated from each other by invisible threads of rhythm and hidden walls of time," in the words of Edward T. Hall.[27] The management of the spatiotemporal interface, which results in a rhythmic concord or discord—discord is both more likely and more formidable as we approach the threshold, the line dividing coherent social or cultural formations—lies at the heart of all legal measures to regulate movements, to defuse transgressions, to render familiar that which is exogenous. This is, of course, the role of the code of hospitality, which seeks to avoid confusing the statuses of the *hospes* (host) and the *hostis* (enemy).

The typology of interfaces is not limited to studying the code of hospitality. It encompasses all aspects of border crossings. Transgression is coextensive with mobility. Transgression is proper to Serres's wanderers with the harlequin's spirit, to Deleuze and Guattari's nomads, and to all who reject the static and the sedentary. Spatial transgressions cross over small unities and even over the sphere of intimacy. At the other end of the scale, they relate to large groups. At a macroscopic level, any movement can result in transgression. The traditional definition of a code, a compendium of norms and benchmarks one may not transgress, lays the groundwork for such an interpretation. Indeed, according to French law, the code governs a domain. Of course, the legislator means to identify the abstract areas in which the law is exercised, underlying the typology. But *domain* also has a strictly spatial sense. Domain is a vast unity of place, one whose coherence is ensured by a sense-making community, a consecrated synchrony. If this rule is general, so is its discussion. Indeed, it appears that transgression may become inseparable from space and apply to large groups. Space is generally seen as stable (except when it is ravaged by war, which aims to alter the established order). From a Heraclitean view, we may consider that space is essentially transgressive. It is not fixed, it fluctuates, and it is caught by forces (or generates dynamics) that cause (or are caused by) permanent flows. Perhaps this *perpetual motion* applies less to a transgression than to the inherent transgressivity of all spatiality and of every perception of place.

Philosophy has sought to address this perpetual mobility. *Panta rhei* (everything flows), as Heraclitus said. Some of this principle's literary applications may be seen in Yuri Lotman's reference to the "semiosphere" and also in Itamar Even-Zohar's theory of polysystems and Deleuze and Guattari's veritable territorial dialectic of deterritorialization and reterritorialization. The effects of this transgressivity also are reflected, at a more visceral level, in literature engaged in minority discourse (e.g., ethnic, sexual, religious, and so on) that struggles to be heard in the dominant discourse. Depending on the approach, the field changes its name. For a logician like Lotman, it is a "semiosphere"; for Deleuze and Guattari, it is more of a "territory"; for Anzaldúa, feminist and Chicana activist, is the borderlands, or *la frontera*, the barriers raised to hinder transgression and all other movement across them. But in all cases instability is the distinct feature of a unity formerly taken for granted. No representation can define space in a static condition. Entropy appears to be overtaking all levels of existence.

Transgression is a process that accompanies movement and motive. Contrary to what occurs in a closed sphere, fixed codes no longer provide benchmarks. Here, the transgression corresponds to a nascent overlapping of movement that disturbs the dominant equilibrium. Transgression is somehow the result of an oscillation, little attributable to a singular, individual responsibility but more like continental drift, the shock of geological plates. When it is deemed permanent, transgression is not the result of isolated and spontaneous action; it becomes a state. The state of transgressivity characterizes the forces continually acting upon heterogeneous spaces, forces that make them a multiple "territory of germination" (in the words of Paola Zaccaria).

The principle of transgressivity, which is inherent in any dynamic (as opposed to static) representation of space, is at the heart of most literary theories as well as semiotic and philosophical reflections on space, broadly speaking. Heterogeneity characterizes the natural habitat of *most* postmodern formulations of space. Rather than elaborate further on this hypothesis, I will just point out that, if the deconstruction of the timeline is one constitutive criterion of postmodern aesthetics, the view of space in its heterogeneous dimensions, in its transgressivity, is another. Therefore, I stand corrected: heterogeneity characterizes the natural habitat of *all* postmodern formulations of space. The language of multiplicity enters almost every study of spatiality and, more generally, of the different forms of spatialization of the Logos. We are long accustomed to "fields," "domains," and other "areas" that interconnect or form specializations in discourse. Now we integrate into this geography of categories a more elaborate semantics, involving mobility and interaction. In *Le nombre et le lieu*, François Dagognet, who is not exactly a postmodernist, invokes the logic of "multifitting" [*multi-emboîtement*] or even "pluri-envelopment" [*pluri-enveloppement*], verbal creations he used in describing certain Dutch paintings.[28] Others speak of "concrescence," which is when two or more distinct natural beings eventually grow together. Still others speak of "arrangements." Space, like any territory that aims at representational stability, is, in the apt phrase of Deleuze and Guattari, "a 'holding-together' of heterogeneous elements."[29] This "holding-together" [*tenir-ensemble*] is not a symptom of structural weakness, a vague makeshift support for a crumbling edifice; it just means that subtle mechanisms allow the contemporary space to take part simultaneously in all the dynamics that traverse it. Fluid and blended, space becomes "the locus of interaction of dynamic forces of material systems."[30] But there is another, perhaps more poetic, way to say this. In his fifteenth-century *Intercoenales*, Leon Battista Alberti—thinking of the multitude of small, diverse, warring states that made up his native Italy—coined the epithet *naviculae* (Latin for "little ships"). Despite the intervening centuries, the navicular state of postmodern spaces reminds one of Alberti's quattrocento Italian *naviculae*. Transgressivity remains because it presents itself as the only constant in an environment of transgression, digression, proliferation, dispersion, and heterogeneity.

Polysystem and Semiosphere

A geology of large ensembles requires a preliminary examination of at least two types of movements. One, which is digressive, would be intrinsic to each base, or to the constitutive elements of a single system, and it would in this case be the "territory" ineluctably leading to those earthquakes that annul any fanciful notion of stable and homogeneous representation. The other, which is transgressive, would result from crossing the spatial boundaries of several continents, of several competing systems. Even-Zohar speaks of intrarelations within a single system and interrelations among distinct systems as "the correlations a system maintains with systems controlled by other communities."[31] Whatever terminology we adopt, in the former (intrarelational) case, two or more types of dynamics may be struggling. These dynamics are flexible, but they are subsumed under Deleuze and Guattari's concept of deterritorialization or under the binary opposition between center and periphery—this latter concept has been deployed in semiotics by Even-Zohar, among others, and in literary studies by those who consider questions of liminality and of the boundary (with respect to space, identity, and culture). In the second (interrelational) case, we might briefly mention the effects of a clash of semiospheres in a thoroughly mobile environment, as described by Lotman. But it goes without saying that the distinguishing characteristics between intra- and inter- are not preestablished, because, as Even-Zohar usefully notes, "the very notions of 'within' and 'between' cannot be taken either statistically or for granted."[32]

Transgression corresponds to the crossing of a boundary beyond which stretches a marginal space of freedom. When it becomes a permanent principle, it turns into transgressivity. The transgressive gaze is constantly directed toward an emancipatory horizon in order to see beyond a code and territory that serves as its "domain." But transgression equally lies in the swerve, in the new trajectory, the unexpected, and the unpredictable. It is centrifugal, since it flees from the heart of the system, from the space of reference. As Michel Maffesoli puts it, "It is a place one creates in order to leave the place, breaking the links from which this one or that one takes its meaning; they must be, in reality or in fantasy, denied, overwhelmed, transgressed. This is a mark of the tragic sense of existence: nothing is resolved in a synthetic overcoming, but all must live with tension, with incompleteness."[33] Putting it another way, we might say that transgression is digressive because it takes alternative pathways, because it takes all the forking paths of Ts'ui Pen's garden toward elsewhere. Transgression is digression: whereas movement is in the Latin *gredi* (to walk, or to go), the modalities of *other* movement lie in the incompleteness of *trans-* and *dis-*, prefixes of instability. For the Romans, *dis* primarily designated a separation from a point of completion and plenitude, as if the disparate had been valued at the time. *Dis* was also an epithet that reflected the opulence and riches of the land. Finally, Dis was another name for Pluto, god of ascendance and *katabasis*, god of that hesitation between the top and the bottom of the earth. This Dis then lends his name to the capital city of Dantean devils, toured by Dante and Virgil in canto 10 of the *Inferno*. At the level of large ensembles, the principle of transgressivity is expressed in a singular way. It is no longer flight from the center, from the "canon," or from the state machinery but is an aggregate form that confronts rather than fleeing. For, as Jean Roudaut sharply observed, "The center has long seemed the only principle to coordinate spiritual forces (the one God), political tensions (the king by divine right), linguistic dispersions (the language of the court); yet it is only one vision of theological essence, among many others."[34] The center does not always drive the system. Wrapped up in its own status, the center has lost its centrality. The center is the crystallization of a moment that *was*; its status is affirmed at the precise moment when it imprints itself on a memory: memory only, a paradoxical recognition that inflects the present with the power of the simulacrum, a hollow presence, effectively a vacuum. In this regard, the periphery signals its simple *recognition* of debt, which confirms the presence of the past, the strength of that which is to be no more. The center is in fact the *stanza* as defined by Giorgio Agamben, namely a nothing, "but this nothing safeguards unappropriability as its most precious possession."[35] It is a phantom, a phantasm. Therefore, as in Julien Gracq's city, which is also a centralized system, the "lasting image of a city where one has lived for a while tends to grow—in a prolific, anarchical manner—from a single, germinal cell which does not necessarily coincide with a functional, or nerve, 'center.'"[36] This germinal cell is often—or always?—found in the margins. Peripheral entities take aim at the center, reducing the distance from it, cancelling it, and replacing it. Thereby, digression takes on a centripetal valence. Once again, the primum mobile can be found in a principle of the temporal order: synchrony is not homogeneous; it is crossed by a multitude of diachronic lines. Clearly, reality is a combination of more-or-less contradictory (or entropic) forces that disrupts the coherence of a homogeneous present. The present is already past.

This means that the spatial center and reality, as ontological markers, coincide, but this coincidence is impromptu, illusory, and, in any event, provisional. Just as synchrony is subject to disruptive diachronic forces, the center in the singular (of an apparently unique system) is coupled to a periphery that is always plural. "It is, therefore, very rarely a uni-system but is necessarily a polysystem—a multiple system, a system of various systems which intersect with each other and partly overlap,"[37] says Even-Zohar, who provides the following definition of *polysystem*: "The polysystem, i.e., the 'system of systems,' is viewed in polysystem theory as a multiply stratified whole where the relations between center and periphery are a *series* of oppositions."[38] It goes without saying that such an approach incorporates the notion of transgression, and, to a certain extent, removes its negative connotation. Transgression is part of the system. It is that which makes what had appeared to be a homogeneous system a heterogeneous polysystem. It opposes the static, which would forever fix the poles of reference (that is to say, the center and the periphery), the privileged center point and the infinite series of points that are situated in a more or less distant array. In overcoming this bipolarity, the state of transgressivity is the name we give to the perpetual oscillation between center and periphery, to the reconciliations of peripheral forces operating with respect to the center. It corresponds to the principle of mobility and animates the examined life. It will not weigh in on the scale of values sanctioned by a preconceived hierarchical legitimacy. The limit is integrated into a dynamic field where that which evolves in the periphery is destined to approach the center according to a law of interference. Consequently, transgression is neutralized: it is not necessarily affected by a negative nuance but corresponds to a simple act of border crossing inherent to the system or "system of systems."

The theory of polysystems is provocative, although its promoter has not yet pushed it to its ultimate consequences. Even-Zohar has mainly concentrated on two of its practical applications: the study of literary value and the question of translation. For him, the literary canon is an illusion because "no field of study, whether mildly or more rigorously 'scientific,' can select its objects according to the norms of taste."[39] Others, like Goethe, had remarked upon this before. But Even-Zohar goes further in the direction of semiotic generalization: "The tensions between canonized and non-canonized culture are universal. They are present in every human culture, because a non-stratified human society simply does not exist, not even in Utopia."[40] This reflection on the literary canon has a corollary: the position of translation in the polysystem (discussed through examples of translations from Russian into Hebrew) and in comparative studies, which is often accused of not placing enough emphasis on the theory of translation. (Although this criticism is not unfounded, many efforts have been undertaken in recent years to fill gaps.) The temptation is great, however, to extend polysystem theory to a broader plane, which would imply a meditation on human spaces subject to competing cultural systems. One might consider using polysystem theory and the diverse theories derived from Russian formalism in postcolonial studies, women's studies, or other forms of cultural studies. This usefulness is because, in what is only an apparent paradox, we might say that liminality is at the center of each of these approaches. "In fact, the Borderlands are physically present wherever two or more cultures edge each other, where people of different races occupy the same territory, where under, lower, middle and upper classes touch, where the space between two individuals shrinks with intimacy," says Anzaldúa, who describes a polysystem infused with quotidian forces.[41] At the macroscopic level, large ensembles would find a resolution, in the photographic sense of the term, in the experience of peripheral minorities fighting against the polysemic canon of the majorities, whose hegemony (or centrality) is always and only temporary.

An heir of Russian formalism and founder of the famous school of semiotics in Tartu (Estonia), Lotman, with his theory of the *semiosphere*, undertook a task comparable to Even-Zohar's project. For Lotman, the conflict between forces of uneven distribution is not really internal to the system but occurs at the intersections of systems. I will not dwell unduly on the idea because it is clear that the distinction between the intra- and the intersystemic is tenuous. Moreover, in some cases, what appears to be a dilemma for Even-Zohar's argument is settled in Lotman's theory: the system of semiospheres not only is cognitive but also incorporates affects. As Jacques Fontanille explains, "these perceptions [of cultural facts] trace two complementary directions: the first, rather cognitive one, is interested in the internal structure of cultures and discourses, notably the relations between their parts and their totality (*harmonious* in one case, *chaotic* in the other); and the second, more affective and emotional, is concerned with the effect produced by the presence of the *them* on an *us* (*security vs. menace*)."[42] This cognitive–affective valence allows a spatial understanding of the semiosphere, whereby we perceive it as a spatialized unit of meaning or, as Lotman says, "the semiotic space necessary for the existence and functioning of languages."[43] Like Bakhtin, Lotman imagines a dialogue, but a dialogue carried into the macroscopic sphere. Fontanille offers a useful view of this development: "The notion of dialogue is not yet entirely appropriate, since the participants are persons and nonpersons—*us* and *them*—so the concept of polyphony would be more appropriate. Anyway, the interaction between this *us* and this *them* leads to different layers of meaning."[44] Moreover, Lotman has partially modeled his idea of the semiosphere on Vladimir Ivanovich Vernadsky's concept of the biosphere: space is thus prominent in the matrix. For Lotman, the semiotic systems that animate the space sketched by the semiosphere "are in a state of constant flux."[45] Transgression again becomes the active principle embodied in the mythological or romantic heroes and embodied in "peripheral texts" where one "reconstructs a picture of the world in which chance and disorder predominate . . . So the world-picture is as a rule chaotic and tragic."[46] Mobilizing a range of literary examples, Lotman returns to the Ulysses of Dante's *Inferno*, who, according to Lotman, is the prototype of the voyager plunged into *real* geographical space. And, with respect to the relation between real and represented space, "real space is an iconic image of the semiosphere, a language in which various non-spatial meanings can be expressed, while the semiosphere in its turn transforms the real world of space in which we live into its image and likeness."[47] This is important because it postulates communication, and even an authentic interaction, between the real and the unreal. In this theoretical context, it is not surprising that Lotman reaches conclusions similar to Deleuze's, considering that the spatial image is a "heterogeneous mixture which functions as a whole."[48]

Deterritorialization and Reterritorialization

As for the mobility of spatial representations, I think that the most complete macroscopic theory is the one elaborated by Deleuze, often with the help of Guattari. Like Lotman and Even-Zohar, Deleuze and Guattari eventually neutralize the concept of transgression, because "it is not exactly a question of extracting constants from variables but of placing the variables themselves in a state of continuous variation."[49] When variation is continuous, the punctual transgressive act (the variable that will not remain a constant) is in a state of permanent transgressivity, which in turn affects *territory*, another name for a system of spatial reference that would like to be homogeneous and that is not homogeneous. Transgression belongs to homogeneous and unitary systems, those expressing explicit and stable limits, which one can then courageously cross. It changes character in heterogeneous and multiple systems that can create their own escape routes. Transgression is difficult to imagine in an order in which the way out of the code is always an option, in an ensemble perceived as a territory open to deterritorialization, to escapism. As Deleuze and Guattari say, a particular territory "borrows from all milieus; it bites into them, seizes them bodily (although it remains vulnerable to intrusions) . . . It has the interior zone of a residence or shelter, the exterior zone of its domain, more or less retractable limits or membranes, intermediary or even neutralized zones, and energy reserves or annexes."[50] Hyperbaton remains the dominant trope of this intimate space. A simple membrane suffices to protect it from the assaults of a code that seeks to infringe on its liberties: "The essential thing is the disjunction noticeable between the code and the territory."[51]

Nevertheless, a system that integrates and validates the possibility of a shift automatically deactivates transgression. It no longer maintains a center and a periphery; there is no hierarchy other than that emanating from the fundamental divide between two visions of space: the smooth and the striated. The internal qualities of each of these spaces tend to fade. Deleuzian territory is unpredictable in its appearance and its manifestations. It lacks roots. It does not appear even as a system of roots in which all *order* winds up, in the last resort (in extremis, at the extremities), diluted by *disorder*. It is a rhizome, like a bulb or a tuber, with no beginning or end: "any point of a rhizome can be connected to anything other, and must be. This is very different from the tree or root, which plots a point, fixes an order."[52] Rhizomatic territory is subject to the delinearization of time, to its fabric. This anomic space-time is appropriate for the fluid forms of the postmodern. In its rhizomatic character, territory lacks all stability in time; similarly, its spatiality is always changing, even fugitive. It is crisscrossed with lines of flight, causing an "asignifying rupture." The line of flight feeds a dynamic of the unexpected and the impermanent, a dynamic that acts throughout the territory. According to Deleuze and Guattari, this is "molecular" insofar as the line "no longer forms a contour, and instead passes *between* things, *between* points. It belongs to a smooth space." It is opposed to the "molar" line of striated space, where the "countable multiplicity . . . remains subordinated to the One in an always superior or supplementary dimension."[53] These discharges of chaotic energy function to evacuate all stable identity from the territory. Within a dialectic that escapes the grand narratives of legitimation (the ideologies identified by Lyotard in *The Postmodern Condition*), territory ceases to be univocal. The lines of flight begin a deterritorialization. And territory, driven by this deterritorializing force, is subject to a provisional reterritorialization that itself leads to a further deterritorialization, and so on. As permanent transgression eventually becomes transgressivity, a territory rendered incessantly mobile will eventually be governed (so to speak) by an almost impalpable deterritorializing and evolutionary dialectic. Therefore, territory is occluded in favor of evolving territoriality, as any attempt to demarcate territory would be ephemeral.

For its part, deterritorialization is absolute when it engenders the new; it is relative when it ends up reconnecting with tradition, although the territory, like the Heraclitean river, is never the same twice. This dialectic is not involved in any axiological system. That could only lead to an "abject reterritorialization." Thus in *What is Philosophy?* Deleuze and Guattari suggest that Martin Heidegger "lost his way along the paths of reterritorialization because they are paths without directive signs or barriers."[54] The tawdry tinsel shines above the parapets; Heidegger's Nazi uniform worn at the University of Freiburg is one of them. Above all, deterritorialization proves to be perilous. Indeed, the deterritorialized perception of identity is proper only to those for whom the lack of signposts does not lead to a quest for an alternate order, a "radical" order rebuilt around some notion of "roots." The abject is never anywhere but in the alternative roots, which claim progress in its regression. The road is narrow, however: reterritorializing the old is a dull operation; reterritorializing the new is necessarily an ambitious enterprise but an adventurous one. Deleuze and Guattari have attempted to clarify the concept of Deterritorialization (here using the abbreviation "D"):

> Is there *absolute* D, and what does "absolute" mean? We must first have a better understanding of the relations between D, the territory, reterritorialization, and the earth. To begin with, the territory itself is inseparable from vectors of deterritorialization working it from within . . . Second, D is in turn inseparable from correlative reterritorializations. D is never simple, but always multiple and composite . . . Now, reterritorialization as an original operation does not express a return to the territory, but rather these differential relations internal to D itself, this multiplicity internal to the line of flight . . . Finally, the earth is not at all the opposite of D: This can already be seen in the mystery of the "natal," in which the

> earth as ardent, eccentric, or intense focal point is outside the territory and exists only in the movement of D . . . We could say that the earth, as deterritorialized, is itself the strict correlate of D. To the point that D can be called the creator of the earth—of new land, a universe, not just a reterritorialization.[55]

The cardinal principle that Deleuze and Guattari define here suits an essentially mobile representation of spaces. Human spaces, which are caught up in discourses (political, philosophical, geographical, literary, or otherwise), are spaces driven by a dialectic that expresses the ability for movement. What remains to be known is which "new" direction deterritorialization will take in a "modernity" that makes "territoriality" fugitive.

The impact of Deleuzian *geophilosophy* on the recent history of spatial ideas has been considerable. Admittedly, this geophilosophy could be attacked. Caren Kaplan has criticized Deleuze (forgetting Guattari) for having developed an approach that contributed to imperialism, or rather, an approach that could *only* support imperialism: "Can colonial spaces be recoded or deterritorialized without producing neocolonialism?"[56] The question is surprising because it takes no account of the ontological and epistemological environment from which Deleuze and Guattari's ideas emerge. If deterritorialization is a necessary process in evolution, in a context where the notion of linear progress is rendered dubious, it does not inevitably lead to a "bad" reterritorialization, as Kaplan seems to believe, let alone a reterritorialization made (deliberately) imperialist. Deleuze and Guattari are well-known champions of nomadism (personal, intellectual, and cultural); nomads subtend all minorities. In his study of Scythian nomads, Hartog is much more circumspect than Deleuze and Guattari on the relationship of nomads to the state apparatus, to its homogenizing centrality.[57] He highlights a bizarre aspect: Hermes, master of the *agros*, the land reserved for pasturage, had no equivalent among the nomads living north of the Hister. But Hermes is a nomad god . . . just as Venice is a nomad city. With one winged foot, he sweeps the world; with the other, he floats over the surface of appearances. In the words of Maffesoli, "A foot to touch the earth, and wings to fly, when the instinct of adventure was too strong to be satisfied by the day-to-day routine. The figure of Hermes combines well with the Venetian mask, with a face sufficient in itself, but of ruse and duplicity. The mask is disquieting, but at the same time it encourages the rendezvous. It is an enticement and measure of flight. Hermes returns to an errand that touches the ground without becoming attached to it."[58] Maffesoli's impromptu connection between Hermes and Venice notwithstanding, let us for a brief moment leave Venice and return to Hermes—or the lack of a Hermes—among the Scythians. The main deity for the Scythian nomads was in fact Hestia, goddess of the hearth or home, the center of domestic space, a symbol of fixity, immutability, and permanence.

Why Hestia, and why not Hermes? According to Hartog, whose hypothesis seems justified, Hestia embodied royal power. In other words, in the system of the Scythians, the king occupied the center of power and with it the center of the world. Reterritorialization therefore operates on a center that is displaced in the relative space of the nomad, but one that retains its position in the absolute space represented by their code.

Pier Paolo Pasolini brilliantly exposed this (apparent) paradox in his film *Medea*. Medea, the princess of Colchis who was carried away by Jason on his ship, the Argo, preserves a nomadic identity as long as she can situate herself at the center of his world. However, upon debarking in Greece, on a virgin land, treeless, and lacking signs, she loses the measure of the axis mundi. That is when the first cracks appear in her passion for Jason. Meanwhile, Jason believes he has the power to designate a center while his companion is in mourning. The Argonaut pretends to replace the Golden Fleece and the tree that held it with a new omphalos, the navel of the world. But this attempt is in vain, disproportionate—in a word, hybrid. Medea's gaze turns dark, while Jason, for once, perhaps for the first time, is confused. One time, the experience of carnal love restores balance, but one time only: the rest is history.

This insight calls for two observations. On the one hand, deterritorialization is not necessarily transgressive because, just as the wolf may be in many folds [*bergeries*], power is in many folds [*plis*]. On the other hand, Deleuze and Guattari's theory is only marginally Manichean, as the smooth and striated are not totally opposed: sometimes the smooth conceals the striations relevant to customs. The nomads of postmodernity move well beyond the traditional category of nomadism, which is defined in the opposition of the mobile and immobile. Nomads represent the ensemble of minorities. Their space is smooth, or it arises from the smoothing of a striated space; their history is, as Derrida would put it, "alter-native." From this point of view, postcolonial space is certainly nomadic; postcolonial history is, too. One and the other are constantly deterritorialized and reterritorialized according to a logic that is not neocolonial, or at least that should not be—otherwise, the world itself is without hope, rather than just Deleuze and Guattari.

Does territory exist only in a state of spatiotemporal stasis? Wouldn't it be better to invoke a "territorial dialectic" that is inconceivable except in a dynamic system, in perpetual motion, and in the responsibility that accompanies any movement? Geophilosophy has formulated this question and attempted to provide answers. Perhaps it is through this attempt that it marked a decisive shift from a historicized philosophy to a spatialized philosophy in which the concept of temporal progress yields to the concept of spatial deterritorialization. From near or far, geophilosophy has inspired a great deal of speculation in multiple disciplines, beginning with philosophy. In 1994, Massimo Cacciari, who had been the mayor of Venice, that paragon of deterritorialized cities, published *Geo-filosofia dell'Europa*,[59] which then appeared in French under the title *Déclinaisons de l'Europe* (thus obliterating the reference to geophilosophy). No doubt the French publisher thought, while a bloody conflict raged in Bosnia, that Europe was better suited to declension in the accusative case than as the object of geophilosophy. Cacciari has made some interesting additions to the Deleuzian theory. He begins by applying geophilosophical principles to the Greek prolegomena to the entity that is Europe, and then he allows his thoughts to run toward the contemporary scene. Along the way, Cacciari takes advantage of the subtle nuances that the Italian language offers—for instance, when the words *essere* and *stare* flow together in the common participle *stato*—to distinguish two qualities of being, one dynamic and the other static. In Europe, as in any space, *essere* must fight against *stare*; it must move. And according to Cacciari, it does, but only in one direction—toward the west, conforming to the ancient impulse that the Greeks called *exokeanismos*. This "ex-oceanization" reflects that the search for identity leads beyond cultural boundaries (beyond the realm of the living) and beyond geographical boundaries (the columns of Hercules) for the *neoteropoioí*, the "innovators," of whom Dante's Ulysses serves as the exemplar for Cacciari, just as he had for Lotman before him. Europe, with its considerable space, has never been stabilized; it has *been*, without ever *being*, as in *stare*; it is, as Cacciari would say, a *tópos átopos*, elusive homeland of the Athenian *áoikos* (without fixed home), spiritual heirs of the man from Ithaca, subject to the whims of winds and gods. This explains the many vicissitudes, too often tragic, of history. As Cacciari points out, the West is also the land of twilight. Of all the slow deterritorializations, maybe this one has consumed the most creative energy. Old Europe? The West, land of the evening, is also the place where we find rest from the efforts of a long day, where we pause to recover our spirits. And the lovely shade of Scarlett O'Hara offers again in a plaintive voice, "Tomorrow is another day."

Cacciari did not just lay out a geophilosophy of Europe; he has also established an inventory of terms for the study of spatial mobility in the recent history of ideas, and sometimes of bad ideas. Drawing on the philosophy of Giambattista Vico, he recalled for his readers the Hegelian notion of *Flüssigkeit*, Nietzsche's *Bewegtheit*, Carl Schmitt's *Entortung*, and even Ernst Jünger's *totale Mobilmachung*. Seductive formulations, *Entortung* (or delocalization, similar to deterritorialization) and *totale Mobilmachung* (preparing for full mobilization) would seem to be appropriate for the foundations of a Deleuzian geophilosophy. But they are not. For Jünger, and even more for Schmitt, the dynamic nature of these centrifugal forces leads to a crisis inspired by the impossibility of reforming the large-scale construction of the state (*lo Stato*, in Italian) and of stabilizing the *nomos*. For Schmitt, as with the Greeks, the *nomos* is the conquered pastoral area that is divided, inhabited, and made knowable (notably, the term for "divide" is also a term for "taking"; *némein* in Greek and *nehmen* in German, each related to *nomos*, are words meaning "to seize," among other things).[60] This place of knowing and dwelling [*savoir habiter*] here establishes a strict equivalence between *Ordnung* (order) and *Ortung* (localization). However, for Deleuze and Guattari, the *nomos* is the disparate rather than the encompassed; it is nomadic rather than conquered space, traversed rather than settled. The nomadic trajectory off the beaten path (in the overused phrase) "distributes people (or animals) in an open space." In contrast, the sedentary practice—one circumscribed by paths—is to "parcel out a closed space to people."[61] The *nomos* of Deleuze and Guattari is a euphoric nomadism; the *nomos* of Schmitt is a dysphoric sedentarity. Ultimately, *Entortung* and deterritorialization have no relationship to one another.

Geophilosophy has inspired similar studies in aesthetics and literature. It is true that Cacciari has continually used literary sources, as has Deleuze. Luisa Bonesio has employed what she calls "geophilosophy" to establish an ecological critique of today's urban landscape, but she based it on the writings of Jünger and Jean Baudrillard. Borrowing the latter's concept of the simulacrum, Bonesio has described the postmodern landscape as "a philological and simulacral restoration of something that no longer exists."[62] Bonesio would seem to have more affinity with Kenneth White's *geopoetics* than with Deleuze and Guattari's geophilosophy. It could be that the use of the term "geophilosophy" has come to be dictated by fashion. It is also possible that, in an extreme case of deterritorialization, geophilosophy has been condemned to be deterritorialized in a direction that it never meant to go. Would it be creative chaos? Prigogine and Stengers have studied the competition between center and periphery, between mechanisms that amplify fluctuation (provocative innovation) and the system's power of integration (its "response"). Bonta and Protevi have adapted this type of vocabulary to Deleuzian theory in distinguishing attractors ("patterns of behavior"), bifurcations ("thresholds where a system changes patterns"), and "symmetry-breaking events" in "zones of sensitivity."[63] These distinctions are interesting, amounting to a complementary terminology. Here is how Prigogine and Stengers put it: "In the indifferent chaos of equilibrium has been established a creative chaos, similar to that ancient, fertile chaos that can produce different structures."[64] This connection between the postmoderns and the ancient Greeks is only the first of a series. For, on the spatial plane, postmodern transgressivity corresponds to the creative chaos of the Greeks. Moreover, Chaos was also the name of the incarnation of chaos. The genderless deity autogenerated two children: Erebus, or absolute darkness, and Nox, or night. They then gave birth to two children: Aether, the "ether" or luminosity, and Hemera, or day. It is creative chaos that gives birth to the light and the day. Surreptitiously, the memory of this astonishing genealogy feeds that labile, postmodern faith in tomorrow: "Tomorrow is . . ."

The Torments of the Postmodern Cartographer

The logical consequence of this transgressive vision of macroscopic space was to cast doubt on any stable representation, any sclerotic representation of space in a codified system and in an indefinitely extended moment. Two targets were designated in advance: the survey and the map, which are regarded as the results of a static iconography. From its beginnings with Anaximander of Miletus, a pupil of Thales in the sixth century BC, the map was "speculation about the order and harmony of the world."[65] But this speculation was not disinterested. To be sure, it was better to understand the world and to organize knowledge in a comprehensible system of representation, but knowledge was not an end in itself. According to Christian Jacob, the history of the map has followed three stages of occupation of global (or Western) space: the founding of cities and settlements in the Mediterranean region (between the sixth and fifth centuries BC); Alexander's expeditions into Persia and India (in the fourth century BC); and the Roman expansion, which resulted in the official surveying of familiar spaces and the universality of the descriptive and cartographic projects (favored by such Hellenistic geographers as Strabo or Ptolemy, the latter being the author of a famous map whose objective was the *imitatio picturae totius partis terrae cognitae* [mimetic picture of all parts of the known world]). If we examine these stages in order, we see that the map has had three key functions: a political and commercial function, a military one (already sketched in the catalog of forces in the *Iliad*), and a fiscal one (after the invention of the survey). Deleuze and Guattari could have easily related this cartography to the restrictive development of striated space, a closed model of the world. But in these heroic epochs, heroes dictated the law. The geography of the world was still uncertain. The link between the *real*, which the map was supposed to reduce to a synoptic glance, and the *imaginary* was fluctuating; geographic space was predominantly an anthropological space in which heroes (Odysseus and Jason, or such legendary explorers as Hanno, among others) had to prove themselves with bravery, *metis*, and cunning, sometimes at their own expense. When the map was to support a specific decision, it became ambivalent. In *Géographie et ethnographie en Grèce ancienne*, Jacob relates a significant anecdote: in 499, the Ionian Aristagoras had visited Cleomenes of Sparta to convince him to organize a campaign against the Persians; in doing this, he unfolded a map, to be used to support his speech. But Aristagoras failed: seeing the space laid out visually, Cleomenes realized that it would take three months to reach Persia by sea, so it seemed out of reach.[66]

The Middle Ages maintained some of the spirit of the ancient Greeks, but by placing all representation of the world under the patronage of God. One example is sufficient to explain this perspective: the voyage of the legendary monk Saint Brendan through the ocean unfolding beyond his native Ireland. In the *Navigatio Sancti Brendani*, no attempt was made to account for the physical, *objective* world, but only for a world designed by God and recognized by men. Thus Brendan sailed amid the waves of an unknown sea as a space governed by the liturgical calendar. As Giuseppe Tardiola points out in his atlas of fantastical places of the Middle Ages, "the image of the world is above all a divine image, a code laden with messages, quotations, and *senhals*, a paradigm that God himself created that reveals and leads to Him. Geographical space is a framework for interpreting signs; the image of the world is a semiotic encyclopedia open to meditation."[67] Medieval cartography was oriented toward the future. The world was articulated around an axis passing through Jerusalem originally, as figured in the "O-and-T map," *orbis terrarum*, where *O* referred to the orbit of the Earth and *T* to the limits of the three continents surrounded in the circle (Asia *oriented* the gaze by being located above the horizontal bar of the *T*, with Europe and Africa below, to the left and right of the vertical line). As the results of further discoveries, maps and mapmaking improved, but God was always present, as were the imaginary or fantastic elements that one also finds in the *Odyssey*. The seas and oceans that determined the labile lands were populated by monsters. In his map from the *Cosmographia*, published in 1500, Sebastian Münster reserved a place for sea monsters; another, drawn from the *Nuremberg Chronicle* of Hartmann Schedel, which dates from 1493, featured a human teratology. Umberto Eco has made brilliant use of this catalog of monsters in *Baudolino*, a novelistic recasting of the legend of Prester John, a Nestorian monarch who reigned somewhere between India and the Muslim world at the time of the Crusades.

Cartography has evolved considerably since the sixteenth century. It is not my intention to continue this history in detail. Suffice it to say that, during the Renaissance and the centuries that followed, the perception of the world changed. Whereas previously one privileged the sensuous qualities of the human (and divine) environment, now one attempted to anchor it in the rational. Medieval monsters tended to disappear from the planet, just as the brontosaurus had before them, but at least the dinosaurs left fossils. Symbolism became increasingly abstract, as did the scale needed for the vertical point of view. With the somewhat belated resolution in the seventeenth century of the problem of calculating longitude, one could finally fix the coordinates of the newly discovered lands; the world would be stabilized at the same time that maps could be refined and that colonization was expanding. Deviations from this rigorous, rational code were rare, but they existed: in the second half of the eighteenth century, for instance, the Spanish crown organized a serious expedition to discover the floating island of San Borondón, the Isle of Saint Brendan, thought to be located off the Canary Islands. It did not produce any tangible result. San Borondón was elusive then, and it remains so. A little later, Joseph

Conrad had the privilege to witness the last coloring-in of the blank spaces of the map, recounting the experience through the fictional Marlow in *Heart of Darkness*. Remembering the large white areas that still filled the "Africa" pages of the atlas of his youth, Marlow notes, "True, by this time it was not a blank space anymore. It had got filled in since my boyhood with rivers and lakes and names. It had ceased to be a blank space of delightful mystery—a white patch for a boy to dream gloriously over. It had become a place of darkness."[68] There was, however, a last square of virgin land: the one that Kurtz designated at the heart of the jungle. A dramatic acceleration occurred in the last years of the century, because even in 1886, in Jules Verne's *Robur the Conqueror*, the narrator regretted that all geographers did not make use of a balloon such as his *Albatross*, for "There would then be no huge blanks on the maps of Africa, no dotted lines, no vague designations which are the despair of cartographers."[69] In the late nineteenth century, a form of despair fell upon those who desired to push the limits always a little further, where they would be subject to transgression, elusive, and inaccessible. As Auriol writes, "The map of the earth will soon be superimposed on the earth itself, printed on its surface, and the world, previously conceived according to boundaries between the known and the unknown, understood by the thin and moving line of a horizon constantly pushed back and opening onto an ever-renewed frontier, will become representable in its entirety, finally apprehended as a totality, something closed in upon itself."[70] The horror! The horror!

When everything is filled, we must remake the place, for if nature abhors a vacuum, man often finds horror in a plenum. Postmodernity is always confronted with the sense of a universal filling-in. Literature, like all forms of mimetic art, becomes in this context the experimental field of alternative realities, aiming to restore the imaginary margins and that which art feeds: its referent. Cartography is not immune to this tendency, as it has continued to grow in synergy with the science of geography. We may very tentatively conclude this overview of cartographic history with what British geographer Paul Rodaway calls "the ultra-map, even a kind of post-map," as figured in the satellite photo, for example.[71] The cartographic experience of the contemporary era tends toward the visual: the map is often substituted for the "reality" of space, while imposing a macroscopic view of it. Generally, one uses the map to move in a space that is not readily intelligible, that is not comprehensible in its totality: a university campus, an exhibition, a city, a region, or one or more countries at a time. The map is an icon of the macroscopic representation of space. And it is doubtless for this reason that the postmodern cartographer suffers torments that his predecessors, experiencing the euphoria of filling in the blanks, did not know. What are these torments? Those associated with excessive stabilization, the denial of transgressivity, and the consecration of the static.

The map privileges the name to the detriment of the sentence and of variation. This leads to a reduction of the world. Astonishingly, but elegantly, Franco Farinelli establishes a link between the beheading of John the Baptist and cartography. The plate (or *plateau*) on which the head (now separated from the body) of the Jordan River hermit was presented to Herod constituted the first map: "That the table of Salome was a map—and even that the episode of John the Baptist's beheading is nothing other than the first complete illustration of the terrible consequences of what we casually define today as the process of cartographic reduction—is certainly suggested by the term used to describe it, but also by the mechanism of language for which the daughter of Herodias (who neither desires nor thinks) is a mere mouthpiece: a language that proceeds exclusively by proper names, which happens only on maps."[72] The Baptist is reduced to a proper name, his own. The table on which his head is exposed is the first illustration of a world reduced to a denomination that leaves no place for transgression. This same logic, in a context that only appears to be distant, has animated the entire history of colonization, which cartography accompanies and sanctions as it surveys the territorial advances. For José Rabasa, territories acquire an unambiguous "semanticity" as they are included in a map. Mercator, in preparing the first atlas (in the modern sense of the word), immediately helped to impose a Eurocentric perspective in his great cartographic work. Spatial representation functions as a palimpsest, with successive "erasures and overwritings."[73] The original names ascribed by the aboriginal population are effaced and replaced. In *Tiepolo's Hound*, Derek Walcott refers to this phenomenon in Saint Thomas, the Caribbean island birthplace of painter Camille Pissarro: "The empire of naming colonized even the trees, / referred our leaves to their originals; this was the blight on our minds, a speckled disease." Some lines later, he adds, "Reality was riven / by these reproductions, and that blight spread / through every noun, even the names we were given, / the paintings we studied, the books we loved to read."[74]

Sometimes, the old name is preserved as a watermark. The English name of Tucson in southern Arizona, for example, owes nothing to any British founder. Tucson was established on the traditional territory of the Tohono O'odham, who lend their name, anglicized, to the place. But the retraction does not always work over time; as Rabasa points out, "The imperfect erasures are, in turn, a source of hope for the reconstitution or reinvention of the world from the native and non-Eurocentric points of view."[75] Sometimes the return to source materials is deceiving. Since its beginning, Limoges has taken its name from the ancient Lemovices, but what good does that do them? The toponym may retain traces of a vanished people, like fossilized creatures in amber. Rabasa's hope relates to recent decolonization, to the return of a people to an identity that is still alive, to the flame still smoldering under the ashes.

The stratification rendered visible through the history of mapmaking also finds several illustrations in literature. Australia and Canada, in anglophone literature, offer fertile fields of study. Africa is another. In a study devoted to the use of place-names in the novels of Ahmadou Kourouma, the Ivorian scholar Bi Kacou Parfait Diandué examines the relations between the old toponyms and those new ones bestowed by the colonizers in the works of his compatriot. Unable to reinstate the original "topolects," Kourouma has reinvented an onomastics. Thus Horodougou, which is described in *Allah Is Not Obliged*, becomes a "macrospace for moving borders," as well as a "space of sovereignty, an example of the inviolability of African ancestry."[76] Also in *Allah Is Not Obliged*, Worosso represents a supranational space of the Malinke, situated on the border between Côte d'Ivoire and Liberia, but it actually refers to the ancient empire of Sundiata Keita, Mali's great thirteenth-century monarch. The problem here lies not so much in the relations between the referent and its imaginary representation, but in superimposing two distinctly diachronic spaces: the colonial and the postcolonial. The cartography between these, in a generally stratigraphic logic, will be one of the components of geocritical study. Rabasa posits that the atlas, a pure product of the *art* of cartography, is not a generic object of study, and since it is subjective (the atlas being nothing other than a representation), it appears eminently open to combinations of texts and conducive to intertextual analysis.[77]

At the same time as that colonization played itself out, losing its pretenses and revealing its ulterior motives, cartography became suspect. Its ideological undercurrents would eventually be made manifest. It was trying to pass off symbols as reality, disingenuously feigning ignorance that this was the practice. In so doing, the map cut itself off from the world: it was no longer in the real world; it was deprived of any ontological extension; it was part of the project of homogenization embodied by Deleuze and Guattari's striated space. And Tanzania became orange, as on the map. In any case, that's what happens in *Alphabetical Africa* by Walter Abish, where the *National Geographic* map of Africa winds up influencing the physical geography of the continent itself. It could be blue like André Breton's surrealist oranges, or green, or pink. In the 1960s, with the aid of maps, Jean Gottmann conceived of the entire northeastern United States as a vast megalopolis that included New York, Boston, Philadelphia, Washington, and Baltimore; yet moving between these cities is enough to realize that their linkages are far too loose to be understood as a single space or even a multipolar space. And Farinelli comments, "In other words, one suffers without knowing the ontological power of a representation that, while presenting itself as a mere instrument, is actually posited beforehand, where it influences each of our worldviews."[78] It goes back to Heidegger's idea of the *Weltbild*. The *Weltbild*, as Farinelli points out, is not a "representation of the world," but a "world as picture." Cartography is situated somewhere in between.

In literature, the example taken from Abish's novel is far from isolated. Mapping, the mapmaker, and maps, respectively, become important themes and characters in contemporary literature and film, as does the surveyor, like K. in Kafka's *The Castle*. One might mention Robert Louis Stevenson's *Treasure Island* and all the pirate maps that have engendered deadly rivalries in the mimetic arts of the twentieth century. But there are other alternatives, more recent and overtly postmodern. Take two films, *The Element of Crime* by Danish director Lars von Trier and *The Pillow Book*, directed by Peter Greenaway. Von Trier establishes a German landscape and a rainy night, recalling the darkly futuristic Los Angeles that Ridley Scott created in *Blade Runner*. This place is the scene of serial crimes. Placed in charge of the investigation, Detective Fisher acts according to a consistent method of identifying with the murderer, one Harry Grey. The location of each crime appears to refer to a logical geometry. The first map seems to show a square, but Fisher finally grasps that it is the letter *H*, which the serial killer has traced, murder after murder. Moreover, to achieve its ends, he selects only cities or towns whose names begin with that letter. Fisher rushes to Halle, where the investigation arrives at its disturbing conclusion. Would Fisher—fisherman and sinner[79] in the aquatic environment—eventually adopt the identity of Grey? In this first feature film by von Trier, the map expresses the only anchor in a world deprived of benchmarks, where identities fluctuate at will in a mutable space characterized by a swampy, uncertain existence. The investigator becomes confused with the murderer; their profiles coincide. As for Harry Grey, he seems to kill with the goal of having his initial inscribed on a piece of paper. The map is part of an aesthetic of crisis. The same hypothesis applies in *The Pillow Book*, this time set in Kyoto. Nagiko's father, a famous calligrapher, had previously drawn ominous ideograms on his daughter's forehead. Now an adult, Nagiko goes in search of a man who would be willing to transform his own body into a map or paper. After some setbacks, she meets Jerome, a young Briton, whom she quickly discovers is the lover of the publisher who was responsible for the death of her father, the calligrapher. She then uses Jerome's body, and those of other men, to send messages to the publisher. In the process, she composes a work of 13 books and of 13 painted bodies. The story ends badly. Jerome dies and Nagiko paints an erotic poem on his dead body before burial. The publisher exhumes the body to extract the poem, which he turns into a book for his pillow: *The Pillow Book*. With Greenaway's use of the *makura no sōshi* (pillow book) of the courtesan Sei Shonagon, written at the turn of the millennium, the film-viewer witnesses once again the postmodern (and critical) reification of the body, its transformation into "semaphore," a pure space for investment—by violence in von Trier, by art (and force) in Greenaway.

In literature, the map of Tendre, conceived in its time by Madeleine de Scudéry, has seen a number of postmodern avatars, often under the sign of a woman. In *The Scale of Maps*, the Spanish novelist Belén Gopegui imagines a geographer specializing in topography, Sergio Prim, whose ambition is to map the hollows or empty places, the metaphorical adjunct to his own existence, which are partially filled with the arrival of the beautiful Bruyère. Based on the physical principle that "matter is discontinuous, such as energy" and that "under certain theories, space and time are too," Prim conjectures that there exist, between "blocks" of time and space, what he calls "topons and chronons," in the "cracks, the interstices, the line that we never want to cross and by which I desire to make my way." In sum, Prim plans to map the emptiness, which would allow him to leave space . . . in the company of Bruyère: "Stop space and invite you to a hollow, a place for rest, and spend time with you without committing errors."[80] The map no longer serves to cover the entire world in its fullness, but to discover the empty areas, the hollows, where one may produce a space of freedom. It is in any case a paradoxical cartography. In *Atlas de geografía humana*, Almudena Grandes also employs a cartographic theme, but on a more rigorously metaphorical level than Gopegui's. Here, human geography is recorded by four women in an atlas designed to be sold on newsstands in the form of booklets. But this geography reproduces the trajectory of their lives in a midlife crisis traced to the heart of Madrid's Movida. Evidently, the uses of the map are multiple, but all seem oriented toward the reduction of that anxiety that has gripped the postmodern society. Are we faced with a new avatar of cartographic "reduction"?

Bodies and Movement

The study of cartography, and of its literary and cinematic applications, offers a number of lessons about relations between spaces and their representations, between reality and fiction, between the present and the past, and so on. It also posits "a rapport between intimacy and immensity"[81] at the intersection between macroscopic space and intimate space, between the space Deleuze and Guattari have attributed to the state apparatus and the mobile space that the body occupies in a free zone, space that Michel Foucault has characterized as *heterotopic*. Heterotopias are "countersites" where "real" sites are represented, contested, and reversed. The Foucauldian heterotopia is the space imbued by literature in its capacity as a "laboratory of the possible," the investigator of the integral space that sometimes occurs in the field of reality and sometimes outside of it. Heterotopia enables individuals to juxtapose in the same site several spaces that had previously been incompatible. For heterotopia operates on a dual principle of opening and closing that makes these spaces, at various times, isolated or accessible. So it assures itself a practical function in, and in relation to, the dominant space. It acts both as a space of illusion and as a "heterotopia of compensation," to use Foucault's term, in order to form a space better organized than the dominant space: for example, the Utah of the Mormon settlers, the communities of the Amish, or the Paraguay of the Jesuits in Voltaire's *Candide* or in Roland Joffé's 1986 film *The Mission*. This heterotopic view of space is inherent in *third space*, which I address later. But it also encourages the return of a figure that the grand macroscopic theories like to ignore: the *body*.

What happens to the body when the flux is global, supraindividual, often abstract? In Cacciari's view, "The philosophy of postmetropolitan territory seems to require us to transform ourselves into pure souls or pure *dy-namis*, intellectual energy. And who knows, maybe our soul really is *a-oikos*, unhoused, like the Platonic Eros, but . . . what about our body?"[82] Are we doomed to whirl around like those souls in Dante's *Inferno*? For Cacciari, we are reduced to hoping "to touch the ground," to find a sense of *place* in the beautiful and immaterial ordering of a society tending toward the posthuman. Twenty years earlier, Foucault believed that heterotopic places were still the result of a choice. Heterotopia constituted the area from which the body (actively) withdrew from public space, space that is subject to the law. Here again, that hyperbaton of the rhetoricians returns. Heterotopia is another name for the sphere of intimacy that resists codification and that each individual tries to expand at leisure. It is the "hollow" that Gopegui's geographer is trying to study. The space where the body holds its intimacy is retrained, but the space where it dissimulates is all the more vast. Serres refers to this—to this place—as the minimal habitat of the impoverished Assisi: the *portiuncula*, the smallest portion, an "ineliminable, residual, and solely proprietary niche."[83] Paola Zaccaria envisions a geographic, or rather chorographic, approach: "Every man, every woman is a place, a land that one fails to discover or that fails to be fully discovered; its borders are based on the chorography that it describes or that describes it (chorography is what describes a particularized geographic zone). This is why, when entering space in its infinite forms, one seeks to multiply the points of view, and finally has a glimpse into one's own unknown territory."[84]

The definition that Zaccaria gives for *chorography* is accurate. This discipline, although it has partly disappeared from the lexicon, is not minor. If the geographer looks at the world at the small scale of the planisphere, the chorographer focuses on the perception of the regional space by using a much larger scale. Without heterotopia, without corporal *portiuncula*, no spatial interpretation would be conceivable. Space revolves around the body, just as the body is located in space. The body gives the environment a spatiotemporal consistency; above all, it confers a measure to the world and tries to give it a rhythm of its own, which can then be scanned in the work of representation. In Hall's work, he draws a parallel between the various rhythms that regulate great cultures. He describes the human quest for a sort of "rhythmic consensus," the individual's need to synchronize one's rhythm to the rhythms of those with whom he or she interacts (the "proxemic" relation).[85] But in both Hägerstrand's *tidsgeografi* and Hall's examination of proxemics, the result is a generalization that does not reflect the extreme diversity of postures that the body adopts in space or with respect to the space. One returns to Saramago and to the dreams of piling up books on the moon, evidencing the infinite variations of human life.

Drawing on the abstractions of large movements, macroscopic approaches to space often preclude studying the body, which can be understood as more physical and more intimate but also as social. Minoritarian discourse, however, is articulated around corporeality, which is sometimes a sphere of individuality and sometimes a space of community. Gender studies often involve spatial analysis, from the double point of view, cognitive and social. The cognitive perspective is not the most remarkable, as studies on the divide between male social point of view prevails, as may be seen in recent studies by Gillian Rose, Elizabeth Grosz, and others. The point of departure for this analysis is generally common: all homogenizing understandings of space exclude the particularity of minority perceptions, which are inscribed within a discourse of power. Rose has called for feminist geographers to explain that discrimination does not stem from the fact that urban space (often privileged in the analysis) is an ensemble subject to a process of uninterrupted fragmentation. Instead, it is the nostalgia for a hegemonic vision of a whole that favors exclusion.[86] Discrimination operates in reference to an imaginary—or conventional—totality to which all singularity must be reduced. Soon, a figure from Greek mythology appears. Along a road to Athens, Procrustes offered shelter to overnight guests, but in this manner: he gave his short guests a bed too large and tall persons a bed too small; then he stretched the limbs of the first to fit the dimensions of the bed and sawed off the legs of the latter to prevent them from exceeding the length of the bed. Procrustes was killed by Theseus, who did not share his sense of uniformity. When space is perceived in its mobility, it enables one to reflect on the crisis of the center–periphery model and stimulates the emergence of a minority perspective. According to Grosz, alienation begins with the metaphorical reification of the body in urban space. The city is transformed into a simulacrum of the body, while the body is absorbed in it.[87] It is not necessarily only a question of the female body, but it does apply well to it. This transformation reminds me of one version of the abduction of Helen, one recorded by Herodotus; it suggests that the woman whom the Greeks saw walking on the walls of Troy was not the wife of Menelaus, but merely a simulacrum, a pile of sails, made by Paris, who had accompanied Helen from Sidon to Egypt. The real Helen, beautiful Helen, found herself in Egypt, retained by Proteus, king of Memphis. According to Herodotus, Homer knew this version of history; Roberto Calasso notes that Homer alluded to it in book 6 of the *Iliad* and cites "fine embroidered work of the Sidonians," from which Hecuba chooses a fine specimen as an offering for Athena.[88] The Greeks lost ten years, perhaps, all for a piece of cloth. It is as if the female body, that of Helen, was destined to become a simulacrum, only an artificial thing holding the gaze of the men laying siege to the city and trying to force open its doors. Of course, the siege of an enclosed place has always been a metaphor for rape. Men force the gates of the citadel as if forcing the sex of a woman. But, at Troy, a circumstance confused the situation, made it paradoxical: how to penetrate Troy, how to violate a city that held (or hosted) Helen, the inviolable wife, under penalty of incest? Perhaps one had to defeminize Helen, turn her into luxury cloth, to preserve the erotic portal of the other, of Troy. From this perspective, Odysseus's crafty solution deserves some comment, because after all Troy was "taken" by a horse that the inhabitants themselves "introduced" to their city (at the same time that the seven men were hidden in its belly). Woman versus man, human versus animal: these are complex polarities Odysseus would be called to explore further during his odyssey. Another ten years!

The female body motivates another discourse, that of women of color, who have sometimes been ignored in minoritarian discourse, therefore making women of color a double minority. In Western society, racial discrimination has been strong for a long time and continues to be. The black feminist writer bell hooks remembers how, during her childhood, she moved from one home to another (from her parents' house to that of her grandmother, Baba), that is to say, from one "site of resistance" to another: "It was a movement away from the segregated blackness of our community into a poor white neighborhood."[89] By this movement, she perceived her body as an object subjected to the gaze. Arriving at her destination, she became again, in the intimate space, the subject of her own body. The same type of problematic that characterizes "white supremacist societies" governed by "racist domination," in the militant vocabulary of bell hooks, is confronted by several African-American writers, of whom Toni Morrison is probably the best known worldwide. In a novel like *Sula*, the conquest of territory remains a key challenge, but it has no ambition other than to establish the irenic presence of the body in space, to include some privacy in an acceptable relationship with the public sphere. This modest claim is defended with equal force by Anzaldúa in *Borderlands/La Frontera*, but with a Chicana twist, in a speech in which the border is by turns geographical, cultural, sexual, and related to one's identity: "1,950 mile-long open wound / dividing a *pueblo*, a culture / running down the length of my body / staking fence rods in my flesh / splits me splits me / *me raja me raja*."[90] In France, the conditions of and the approach to discrimination are quite different. If one speaks of immigrant literature, whose definition is controversial and risks creating a schism, one risks enclosing authors in a ghetto. Since the late eighties, the emergence of a Beur literature has raised the same categorical problems. In the United States, the land of the ethnic melting pot, the distinctions are clearly more numerous, more subtle. Without even mentioning Native Americans, one notes that Anzaldúa's ancestors have lived in Tejas, even in Aztlán (which to the Aztecs corresponded to the entire southwestern United States), well before the conquest of the land in 1836 transformed it into the future state of Texas. Ethnic categorization across the Atlantic due to intercultural communication has no exact equivalent in France, where assimilation (sometimes forced) was the common practice. In the United States, bell hooks is considered an African American; in France, thanks to obligatory assimilation, it would be difficult to maintain that status. All of this, which is barely sketched here, implies that at present the status of a "niche" minority (the *portiuncula*) is solicited with less force by a Beur writer than by a Chicana. But treating the body in space is comparable, regardless of definable identity politics. The body, in that it is heterotopic, is the germ cell from which the individuality shines through in the best case—or simply survives, in some less favorable cases.

From the feminine point of view, the perceived link between space and body is not limited to writing. In one of the essays collected by Alison Blunt and Gillian Rose in *Writing Women and Space: Colonial and Postcolonial Geographies*, Catherine Nash studies in depth the interactions between the female body and cartography, using the example of some of the works of Irish painter Kathy Prendergast, who in 1983 designed the *Body Map Series*. Prendergast joins female body and mapping in several paintings in the series. In *Enclosed Worlds in Open Spaces*, she represents a truncated woman's body serving as a map. In this new variation of *La Carte de Tendre*, the breasts become volcanoes, the belly a desert, and the navel a crater. Cartography is not the only model employed by Prendergast. Nash connects the cartographic body with nineteenth-century anatomical and gynecological plates. The originality of the Prendergast's project could be challenged, because after all the baroque era was already rich in amalgams of this kind. We remember the poems of John Donne, in which the lover is portrayed as an explorer navigating the female body. And what about the *Song of Songs*? In it, the bride is plunged into a living landscape in a garden of lilies, in fact turned into the geography of Palestine and Lebanon. The metaphor echoes throughout the entire world. In *Petals of Blood*, the great Kenyan writer Ngugi wa Thiong'o has his narrator compare a woman to a new world: "a woman was truly the other world: with its own contours, valleys, rivers, streams, hills, ridges, mountains, sharp turns, steep and slow climbs and descents, and above all, movement of secret springs of life. Which explorer, despite the boasts of men, could claim to have touched every corner of that world and drunk of every stream in her?"[91] The examples are many and varied. Often it is the image that serves as a vector. In *Domes of Fortune*, the dome maintains a metonymic relation with the lady Fortune: Alan Brien photographed breasts passing for geodesic domes, which then contain brief poems. The transformation of the body into a landscape is often achieved by a change in scale between man and woman. The hero of a short story by Charles Bukowski, a victim of a shrinking that reduces him to a height of six inches, becomes the sexual plaything of his wife, Sarah.[92] First introduced while in the young woman's vagina, he then promenades over her breasts. In fear of falling from the top of this promontory more dizzying than erotic, the little man decides to kill Sarah with a hatpin. The same process applies in Pedro Almodóvar's film *Talk to Her*. The nurse Benigno dreams of having sex with Alicia, a comatose patient in his care. This drive takes hold of him after he sees a particularly daring dream scene in a silent movie. It is now Benigno climbing the Mount of Venus, the center of all of this geography of desire. These examples belong to what Steven Marcus called "pornotopia."[93] Pornotopia consists of the integral eroticization of space, envisaged as the female body. For, in all these fantasies, the body to be conquered or penetrated is always that of the woman. We enter into what John Douglas Porteous has called the *bodyscape*, which in this case is more geomorphic (body as landscape) than anthropomorphic (landscape as body). In the grand scheme of things, this *bodyscape* is feminine.

This brings us back to the (geomorphic) cartography of Kathy Prendergast. Contrary to the authors I just mentioned, the Dublin artist has not confined herself to an erotic reading of the corporeal cartography. She associates the image of a cartography designed to take the measure of the female body itself with a more traditional form of mapping, which serves as a prelude to territorial conquest. She presents her native Ireland as a postcolonial world and refrains from giving any explanation, any access code for her tableaux: she invites the viewer to interpret the scope of the iconic "message." According to Nash, "the ambiguity of the series, the answers it does not supply, also has a subversive effect."[94] Prendergast has continued her cartographic efforts since the 1980s. In 1999, she presented a map of the United States and Canada, on which were included only those (real) places whose names contained the word "lost," which was also the name of the work itself. Lost Creek, Lost Canyon, Lost Spring, Lost Lake, and so on, are all natural referents whose *lostness* is punctuated relentlessly by authentic toponyms of disappearance, of eclipse. In her commentary on the earlier paintings, Nash had somehow anticipated the interpretation of *Lost* in reference to Ireland: "Places are named. This naming is linked to ideas of language loss. This decline of language is linked, in turn, to the idea of loss of a distinctive life-style and of a relationship to place considered to be more intimate and authentic than that of the present."[95] It comes back to the interaction between cartography and postcolonialism. Ultimately, the map and the territory, the body and minority discourse, constitute an inseparable ensemble that defines the crossroads at which macroscopic and heterotopic representations of space come together.

Third Space

At the intersection of these two models of representation, where their coming together leads to the emergence of a new type of spatiality, the turbulence is most noticeable. This tumult is positive because it returns again and again to the idea of creative chaos. What exists is turbulent; that which is productive moves. The territorial dialectic manifests itself here and operates at a rhythm chosen by the individual partially freed of the constraints imposed by its environment. Deterritorialization is accelerated and reterritorialization is more fruitful, as are the phases and the names that define the traffic moving at the crossroads between macroscopic and heterotopic. At the crossroads, an area of paradoxical liminality expands, an area that at the same time is open to the world and masterable by the individual. This area concentrates the largest variety of discourse. It allows the minority speech to express itself alongside the dominant discourse, which has lost its privileges. Those who are not aligned with the dominant type—be it ethnic, sexual, class, or gender—find a space of formation. It is sort of the center of the periphery, or more precisely, a contact zone between a center that dissipates and a periphery that affirms.

This space is anything but homogeneous; it allows for the synthesis of all differences, the reduction of certain fractures. Its name has constantly been changing over the last 15 or 20 years, perhaps because it is not in its nature to remain stable. The changing terminology reflects the dynamism that characterizes it. In France, we sometimes speak of the *entre-deux* (in-between), although for many this term refers to the interwar period [*l'entre-deux-guerres*] and, for the readers of Jacques Lacan, to the space "between two deaths" [*l'entre-deux-morts*]. For others, the in-between is the wasteland that English speakers call the no man's land. But the in-between is not just that. Instead of representing erasure or exhaustion, the in-between activates a hidden potential that reveals a point of equilibrium between one and another, between the One and the Other, as Serres would have it: "There is still neither one nor the other, and also perhaps already, both one and the other at the same time. Alarmed, suspended, and balanced in its movement, it recognizes an unexplored space, absent all maps, lacking an atlas, with no voyager to describe it."[96] The in-between is a deterritorialization in action, but one that loiters, awaiting the moment of its reterritorialization. It is the equivalent of suspending all determination, all identity; it imbues the intense and productive tempuscule that precedes the hour at which heterotopia will again struggle with the macroscopic dimension of existence. The in-between shelters the possible, "the ghost of a third man," as Serres puts it. The third man lives at the intersection of points of view, in a "median space"; it is pure fusion and transforms the in-between into a "third place of utopia," which can be extended to the world.[97]

Serres has expressed what could be the essence of this in-between, but some American critics have given it a content. In *Borderlands/La Frontera*, Anzaldúa described the tenuous existence of Chicanos and especially Chicanas in the southwestern United States along the border with Mexico. Anzaldúa begins by recalling what the border is, namely a line between what is safe and what is not, between us and them: "A borderland is a vague and undetermined place created by the emotional residue of an unnatural boundary."[98] This zone appears to be bipolar. But this is an illusion: in depth the border moves. According to Anzaldúa, *la frontera* is not a place of opposition between the one and the other; it is not even the place of their addition. It is rather the product of their multiplication. Anzaldúa creates a synthesis from what had been two worlds deployed on either side of the border. This synthesis represents "a third element which is greater than the sum of its parts. That third element is a new consciousness—a *mestiza* consciousness—and though it is a source of intense pain, its energy comes from continual creative motion that keeps breaking down the unitary aspect of each new paradigm."[99] The third element, which corresponds to the multiplication of the first two binary ones, enables one to outline a "third country," nourished by the "the lifeblood of two worlds."[100] The third space that Anzaldúa begins to delineate is a kind of space to be squared . . . whereby the square multiplies itself by itself, which is by no means the case here. The median space of which Anzaldúa speaks cannot be enclosed in a discourse of the border in a geographical sense; it extends to all sorts of margins, which are sometimes in the interior of a land. Third space opens whenever a space is given by the mestiza. As for the mestiza (or "mixing"), whose meaning is only partly ethnic, it constitutes the cultural identity of third space. The concepts of *third space* and *mestiza* go beyond mere terminology. In *Yearning*, bell hooks is interested in creating a third space, which she calls the "margin," a "space of radical openness."[101] As with Anzaldúa, the margin is not a rundown space of depletion, relegated to the wrong side of the tracks: "these statements identify marginality as much more than a site of deprivation; in fact, I was saying just the opposite, that it is also the site of radical possibility, a space of resistance. It was this marginality that I was naming as a central location for the production of a counter-hegemonic discourse."[102] Again, third space is defined as a margin animated by a discourse of another world, which hooks states is not mythical but is born of lived experience.

More theoretical than Anzaldúa and hooks, Homi Bhabha has devoted several pages of *The Location of Culture* to third space (indeed, he coined the term). *The Location of Culture* explores the problematic confluence of the old British colonial discourse and its postcolonial criticism, and Bhabha proposes to go beyond the binary structure of the limit and the speculation that it inspires. To do this, he begins by questioning the notion of "international culture." Instead of invoking the unquestionable diversity of cultures or marveling at the exotic tonalities of multiculturalism, one should rather see the "hybridity of culture," which dynamically incorporates the contingent nature of difference, the relativity of divisions. This approach seeks to avoid the "politics of polarity" denounced by Anzaldúa and hooks and, therefore, designates an in-between space, which is "third space." The connection takes an essentially spatial turn, but Bhabha does not forget to include it in a temporal logic. The individual, who is a "decentered subject," occupies a third space, thus gaining a kind of identity in "the nervous temporality of the transitional, or the emergent provisionality of the 'present.'"[103] The cultural environment is labile; it coincides with a perpetually mobile space, which is subject to a fluid temporality, a "borderline culture of hybridity."[104] Bhabha conceives of a cartography not unlike that envisioned by Sergio Prim, the geographer of Gopegui's novel, in that the hollows and the modalities should attract our attention. As Bhabha argues, "What must be mapped as a new international space of discontinuous historical realities is, in fact, the problem of signifying the interstitial passages and processes of cultural difference that are inscribed in the 'in-between,' in the temporal break-up that weaves the 'global' text."[105]

Bhabha adopts a position close to those of Anzaldúa and hooks, but his third space seems more rooted in the cultural landscape. Two years after Bhabha's book, Edward Soja offered his contribution to the theory of third space. With Soja, the third space is transformed into *thirdspace* to become a fully integrated place: "*Everything* comes together in Thirdspace: subjectivity and objectivity, the abstract and the concrete, the real and the imagined, the knowable and the unimaginable, the repetitive and the differential, structure and agency, mind and body, consciousness and the unconscious, the disciplined and the transdisciplinary, everyday life and unending history."[106] Soja also proposes an explicit breaking up of binary systems. His effort does not follow so much from those of Anzaldúa, hooks, and Bhabha, but rather from that of Lefebvre. For Soja, as for Lefebvre, productive space emerges from *thirding* (or adding a third element to break up binary oppositions), which triggers a *trialectics* "radically open to additional othernesses, to a continuing expansion of spatial knowledge."[107] Soja conceives of trialectics as an antidote against any efforts to build up grand narratives, permanent constructions, or totalizations. It develops from approximations that build upon successive forms of acceptable knowledge without falling into the hyperrelativism, the "anything goes" attitude, associated with radical epistemological openness. Trialectics has the triple motivations of spatiality, historicity, and sociality, and its final stage consists of an accomplished hybridization. It does not pretend to that degree of certainty claimed by dialectical thought. On the contrary, "Trialectical thinking is difficult, for it challenges all conventional modes of thought and taken-for-granted epistemologies. It is disorderly, unruly, constantly evolving, unfixed, never presentable in permanent constructions."[108] The third space, which constitutes the core space of Soja's trialectics, presents a strong analogy with the territory in emergence as described by Deleuze and Guattari. Third space is the spatial formulation of transgressivity, which is itself a movement, transition, or crossing in defiance of established norms.

Third space appears as a floating concept, but undecidability is part of its substance. In *Postethnic Narrative Criticism*, Frederick Luis Aldama returns to this idea, refining and expanding it. Looking at Salman Rushdie's narratives of "re-conquest," Aldama marks the distinctions between first and third space. Unsurprisingly, the *first space* is that which the Europeans inhabit, as in Rudyard Kipling's *Kim*, while the *third space* falls to the colonized, those who were not blessed to be Western. In the implicit hierarchy Aldama attributes to Kipling, the third space of non-Western characters is coded as "primitive and racially impure."[109] The distinction between first and third here rests on a peculiar conception of space, an "ethnoracialized spatiality," in force during the colonial era. Aldama then shows how, after a reconquest of postcolonial third space, Rushdie overcomes the binary logic of colonialism. The favorable outcome of this enterprise results in a new term, as third space is transformed into *fourth space*. According to Aldama, Rushdie's fourth space is characterized by the cohabitation among "cultural and racial hybrid protagonists and characters . . . in an enlarged contact zone where firstspaces (Spain and Britain) and thirdspaces (Latin America and India) coexist."[110] However, Aldama and Rushdie somehow attribute to fourth space those qualities that are found in the third space described earlier by Bhabha and others. I am not sure that this new partition of space is useful. The fact remains that the use of "fourth" rather than "third" responds to a distant echo. In 1507, cartographer Martin Waldseemüller in his *Cosmographiae Introductio* had lifted the continent newly discovered by Europeans to the rank of "fourth part" of the world, which he was the first to baptize America, after Amerigo Vespucci, to whom he gave more credit than to Columbus. Five centuries later, one returns to the "decolonized," to the "Other" of yore in order to rename a world, to find a new and unusually rich "fourth part," to find the intersection of the three others. It matters little, moreover, whether that part is third or fourth; what matters is that it authorizes renewal and freedom.

Deleuze and Guattari provide an apt analogy: "There is, at some moment, a calm and restful world. Suddenly a frightened face looms up that looks at something out of the field. The other person appears here as neither subject nor object but as something that is very different: a possible world, the possibility of a frightening world. This possible world is not real, or not yet, but it exists nonetheless: it is an expressed that exists only in its expression—the face, or the equivalent of the face."[111] Deleuze and Guattari here formulate the way that third space, in expressing a possible world, is inscribed. Terror is certainly written into the etymology of *territory*. Because *terrere* or *territare* was frightening, when Jupiter became more "terrible" than reasonable, he acquired the epithet *territor*. But the terror that comes from the territory is bound to fade when it is "mobilized" and deterritorialized. Deterritorialization leads to a possible world, which corresponds to third space or to fourth space, but in any case to a transgressive space. In the lines quoted at the start of this paragraph, Deleuze and Guattari were referring to Michel Tournier's novel *Friday; or, The Other Island*, in which the One becomes the Other, alternating and hybridized, "as expression of a world possible in a perceptual field."[112] If the constitution of space in third space engages the writer or artist, it also requires an analytical approach. Third space, which asserts itself in the abandoned territory, potentially frightening and with stupefying force, embodies transgressivity in action. It is the common denominator of space and time, of Utopia realized in the point and in the moment. This intersection is a priori in flux because it is outside the capabilities of perception and reaction of the individual, and yet it extends to the world. In theory, every space is situated at the crossroads of creative potential. We always return to literature and the mimetic arts in our explorations because, somewhere between reality and fiction, the one and the others know how to bring out the hidden potentialities of space-time without reducing them to stasis. The space-time revealed at the intersection of various mimetic representations is this third space that geocriticism proposes to explore.

Geocriticism will work to map possible worlds, to create plural and paradoxical maps, because it embraces space in its mobile heterogeneity. As Serres notes, "we are no longer moving toward a universe, but toward the multiplicity of possible worlds. So let them be charted."[113] But before tackling this delicate task, before drawing the map in the hollows of spatialized literary worlds, there remains a major challenge to confront. Is the representation of space in literature and in the mimetic arts confined to the fictional world? Could it be that it has overflowed into the "real" world? In his essay on magic realism, Aldama asks the same questions. But for him, confusion between what he calls the aesthetic (relating to the text) and the ontological (relating to daily life) leads to the relativization of *real* oppression and exploitation suffered in parts of the world: "We need to keep in mind that it is the role of the university to collect and disseminate knowledge, and that the role of mobilizing the millions of people needed for the abolition of racism, sexism, homophobia, oppression and exploitation present in every country and worldwide does not pertain to the university but to the organization built by the workers."[114] And he finds Jameson, Barthes, Kristeva, Derrida, and Lyotard guilty of not having made the necessary distinctions between the two projects.

The coupling of the real and the text concerns more than just those who would have more-or-less direct control over events. The most stimulating aspect of this reflection lies elsewhere. Is the split between text and reality truly absolute? Earlier I cited Ricoeur's praise for salutary inebriation in narrative fiction. But what Ricoeur did not see (or would not see) is that most discourses—not only that fictional discourse of which literature is certainly the chief incarnation—take part in the quest to get a little drunk: geography, architecture, urban studies, and many others. "*Trinch*," says the Oracle of the Divine Bottle to Panurge in *Gargantua and Pantagruel*. All these considerations are reversible. Insofar as these disciplines address the real inspiration of literature to better understand reality, is it conceivable that literature contributes to the formation of the "real" or to the formations of different realities that have been subsumed under the concept of real? Is literature doomed, by its nature, to remain a stranger to the real world? Is it at least entitled to propose a "reading"? All of these impromptu questions invite us first to reflect on the status of fictional text with respect to the referent, to the real. By that force that feeds the cult of the spectacle (as analyzed by Guy Debord and Jean Baudrillard, among others), the real and reality-based society have perhaps become fictional. If this were the case, the danger would be palpable, as the fictionalization of reality is susceptible to an uncontrolled derealization of the world, the effects of which are potentially harmful. The sorrows of our planet *are* real, and evidence of them, at least, is not illusory. Conversely, the potential derealization may open new horizons for literature and other forms of fictional representation. In partially filling the gap separating the literary from the real, a person takes responsibility for having an "impact" on the real world. And so we return once more to Serres: "How does one construct, place by place, a map of worlds yet unknown? One must take flight like a fly, or better, like the Angels, whose passages and messages constantly weave divine ubiquity, and move toward the universal through virtual sites?"[115] In the following chapter, I will examine the peregrinations of these angels around the world, on the paths of reality and fiction, between referent and representation. The angels were messengers, after all. They too had their referent, a divine one. One of them fell, but the fall did not result in the annihilation of the angelic tribe. It had the effect of introducing the concept of responsibility into the ethereal spheres and, on Earth, it inspired the point of departure for Dante's *Commedia*.

CHAPTER 3

Referentiality

Space and Its Representation: A Prolegomena

From Plato and Aristotle to the postmoderns, we have always maintained that fiction has a mimetic relationship to the world. It would be vain and presumptuous to try to establish a list of variations on the theme of representation here. I content myself with a minimal definition, that of Mark Bonta and John Protevi, for whom representation is "the duplication or tracing in mental images of things composing the world . . . Representation operates on the level of actual products, duplicating their extensive properties in words and arranging these properties according to the principles of identity, analogy, opposition and resemblance."[1] Representation involves the translation of a source into a derivative—the source is sometimes the "real" (the world), and the derivative is "fictional" (the mental image, the simulacrum). Because it connects at least two instances, this extension sustains comparisons: same, other, and analogue (à la Paul Ricoeur). Finally, representation is conveyed by the word, the image, sound, and so on. Under this simplified scheme, representation is based on a movement (a transmission), a relationship (of comparison), and a system of signs. Depending on the approach, one or another of these aspects will be emphasized. A real turning point came when phenomenology put forward a new model of representation that has profoundly influenced the reading of the contemporary world. The first innovation involved the overthrow of the hierarchy. Phenomenologists paid greater attention to the spatiotemporal characteristics of transmission and moreover to the defamiliarizing or derealizing nature of the links connecting the source and derivatives thereof. Through the work of representation, the model enters an unstable, at times aleatory, environment. It is resimulated in a discourse that tends to adopt the contours of the imagination. This is explained by Eugen Fink, one of the leading figures in the phenomenology of unreality: "Every re-simulated world is an imagined world through and through, when the imagination would not be fully productive and would assume the existing world. This assumption changes the whole tenor of the world, which then departs from the original temporality to enter a time of the world of imagination."[2] In sum, the representation fictionalizes the source from which it emanates. Representation, which is re-presentation, amounts to a staggered updating of this source in a new context. But it does not modify only the temporality of the world; it also affects spatiality.

A systematic spatialization of representation occurs in the twentieth century, but the most important figure in this may be Henri Lefebvre, who inspired parts of the postmodernist critique. Published in 1974, Lefebvre's magnum opus *The Production of Space* has proved to be particularly influential. As Edward Soja has said, *The Production of Space* is "arguably the most important book ever written about the social and historical significance of human spatiality and the particular powers of the spatial imagination."[3] Lefebvre's great idea consisted in distinguishing three categories of spaces, three modalities of spatial representation: *perceived space, conceived space,* and *lived space.* In making this taxonomic choice, Lefebvre sought to demonstrate that "space is never produced in the sense that a kilogram of sugar or a yard of cloth is produced,"[4] but that *representation,* and therefore the result of a correlation, itself initiates a comparison. Perceived space corresponds to a concrete practice of space. More interesting for us, conceived space is itself a representation of space: it is the space of urban planners, mapmakers, and others. As for lived space, it is constituted by the spaces of representation, which is to say, lived spaces are experienced through images and symbols. Consequently, it is lived space that we are mainly interested in here. If Lefebvre's first category of space is obvious, in that people manage to walk down the street without bumping into walls, the other two are more complex. Are they just articulations of the same thing? Here is Lefebvre's response: "The question is what intervenes, what occupies the interstices of representations of space and representational spaces. A culture, perhaps? Certainly—but the word has less content than it seems to have. The work of artistic creation? No doubt—but that leaves unanswered the queries 'By whom?' and 'How?' Imagination? Perhaps—but why? and for whom?"[5] This does not really answer the question. The Marxist Lefebvre adopts a rather postmodern stance, in his way; in any case, his work has fascinated many postmodern critics.

The contributions of Lefebvre and his heirs, who were often postmodern (and post-Marxist) geographers like Soja, open up spatial representation to a theory quite distinct from those earlier debates over the relationship between reality and fiction, between the referent and fictional representation. Before continuing, we should reaffirm the principle that strengthens the relationship between the source and the derivative: all representation becomes discursive or iconic (or acoustic or plastic) after being mental. The representation requires a discursive coherence, a coherence like a language's in its ability to expresses a more basic coherence with the world (that is, the derivative could meaningfully differentiate itself from the source or referent). The arrangement of words or images can be quite consistent without corresponding directly to the world. It is this arrangement that makes possible the construction of the space of representation, which is sometimes a fictional space. In an elegant passage, Lefebvre hazards a definition of this "space of speech," where speech [*parole*] produces space:

> Is this perhaps the space of speech? Both imaginary and real, it is forever insinuating itself "in between"—and specifically into the unassignable interstice between bodily space and bodies-in-space (the forbidden). Who speaks? And where from? As it becomes more and more familiar, this question serves increasingly to conceal the paradox of absolute space—a mental space into which the lethal abstraction of signs inserts itself, there to pursue self-transcendence (by means of gesture, voice, dance, music, etc.). Words are in space, yet not in space. They speak of space, and enclose it. A discourse on space implies a truth of space, and this must derive not from a location within space, but rather from a place imaginary and real—and hence "surreal," yet concrete. And yes—conceptual also.[6]

The interface between reality and fiction lies in words, in a certain way of positioning them along the axis of truth, verisimilitude, and falsity, away from any old mimetic fancy or all axiology. Words, along with gestures, sounds, and images, are also caught up in the movements that support the representation of space. Speech can be that of conceived space, as with the speech of the urban planner who projects a map of a place, but it may well also be integrated into the lived space, which (according to Lefebvre) is the space of representation. It is then that literature finds something to say, *to say*—yes, not only to transcribe—into the text. This is "poetic work," which Jean Roudaut says facilitates the passage from the real city to the imaginary city, but it could be extended to any correlation between reality and fiction. Poetic work gives *being* by naming; it gives birth. It makes possible "the real city, which is a crossroads of discourse. Thus, it is a theater of memory. It is through language that we must restore it, reinvent it."[7] This poetic work evoked by Roudaut has existed since the dawn spread her rosy red fingers. In Greece, the bard was the storyteller of the world, the midwife of worlds, so poetic work functioned to represent both the *oikoumene* and that which exceeded the *oikoumene*, which only the flight of the imagination could achieve.

Is Tomorrow the Day before Yesterday?: Representations of Excess

In *Atlas*, Michel Serres questions our present condition in its relation to space. Concerning extensions, ask Where to be? For propagation, ask What to do? and Who to be? For proximity, ask How to go? and From where to go to where? This renders whole a world affected by a sense of saturation. It also reflects an expanded world with new extensions giving birth to virtual propagations: "The rediscovery, exploration, and exploitation of virtual spaces opened by such distances, vast but quickly cancelled, outside of me and exterior to place, so that the ways to live, to learn, and to work, are prolonged in recent decades, the final conquest of the ancient borders of the world; when the real space no longer presented more lacunae in our travels, our scientific adventures, and our technological inventions, we began to occupy our virtual spaces."[8] If this is the hour of saturation, of escape from a world where reality and fiction can be found somewhere between virtual and actual, it has not always been so. The question of the referent for some time has elicited a series of often-contradictory responses. Before I turn to consider structuralist tendencies, the sphere of postmodernity, and the theories of possible worlds proposed by the logicians and their literary heirs, it seems salutary here to return to the beginnings of the Western world, to an age when the link between reality and fiction was firmly held and not subject to debate, because the referent and its literary representation were one. There was a time when one was less preoccupied with seeing the world as too full, thus channeling it in the direction of the virtual, than with seeing the world as still empty, a world devoid of narrative. What was it like at the time when the world was not yet the closed space we streak across today, with hardly any particular emotional investment, with no concerns other than having to get used to jet lag, an unusual temperature, or slightly different levels of hygiene—a roundness that is our planet? The poet Riccardo Bacchelli perhaps was not wrong: "We Europeans know the world too well. Columbus / did not realize the harm he was doing. History / which moves to the West will end up just where it had departed. / Is the earth so round for the sake of irony?"[9]

This irony, Odysseus, Jason, and the Argonauts had not yet experienced. Did they have only a referent? Yes, if they were coasting along the Aegean. But when they moved away from the *oikoumene*, it was different; the flux began to reign. For Dicaearchus of Messina, a disciple of Aristotle, the distance from the Peloponnese to the northern Adriatic was equivalent to that of the Peloponnese to the columns of Hercules. A glance at a map of the Mediterranean—go ahead, take a look today!—suffices to show just how obvious the error was. This Adriatic, the same Adriatic of Rimini's discotheques and Venetian gondolas, was then an unknown and terrifying sea. At bottom of this gulf is where Cronus had castrated Uranus, in the very beginning. At Kerkyra, or Corfu, rests the mythic scythe that forever separated Uranus from Gaia, the earth mother. Kerkyra is also the island of the Phaeacians, who were born of the blood of Uranus. It is also in the Adriatic that the ancient Greeks situated one version of their afterlife: the Isles of the Blessed. Bathing the northwestern coasts of Hellas, the Adriatic—the sea of Cronus—was enigmatic, *unheimlich*. Therefore, one can hardly imagine more distant spaces that could be represented. In *Iphigenia in Tauris*, Euripides is unable to distinguish the Bosphorus of Thrace and the Cimmerian Bosphorus: the first is what we know as the Bosphorus; the second marks the entrance of the Sea of Azov, near the Crimea. It seems difficult to confuse them. One reduces the extreme density of Europe, because it corresponds to the great arctic north. Ovid, in his "Letters from the Black Sea," evokes a chill when the shores of Tomis, his place of exile, are covered with ice for two years. One has trouble imagining the beaches of Romania studded with icebergs. Medea, at the eastern extremity of the Euxeinos Pontos in Colchis, is the niece of Circe, who (according to Hesiod) lives on the island of Aeaea at the western extreme of the world, Tyrrhenia, before the westernmost point was transferred to the Pillars of Hercules. The journey from one to the other can be done with the chariot of Helios (the sun), who was the father of Aeëtes, himself the father of Medea. And the sun makes its journey in less than one day. The Danube is the river that the Argonauts traveled upon so swiftly . . . to empty into the northern Adriatic. The Rhone flows into the ocean and is hardly distinguishable from the Eridanus, which should be the Po. In short, one floats on the waters as on the maps. And one could multiply examples of this type, each more fascinating than others. We realize that the unknown did not begin at the Pillars of Hercules, but in the Adriatic, in the Tyrrhenian, and in what for us is the Black Sea. In other words, the center of the world was organized using a much smaller scale than we are used to applying to modern spaces. A distance of a few nautical miles, or a few periods of time, was enough to travel beyond the known world. All travel took place along a line that crisscrossed the familiar and the fabulous, the one and the other, sometimes together at once.

The relationship between familiar and fabulous has evolved throughout the history of science. Today, the familiar has prevailed over the fabulous. Originally, the relationship was reversed. All was fabulous, an enormous void, blank spots on the virtual map. Odysseus is horrified by the spectacle that unfolds before his eyes almost everywhere in his journey. Massimo Cacciari, looking at the Odysseus of Homer and the Ulysses of Dante, believes that "both are in defiance of the ancient prohibition, slaying the ancient god of the Limit."[10] Jason's task is similar to that of "double Odysseus" (Homeric and Dantean). In book 2 of the *Argonautica*, he confesses his fear: "As it is I am in constant terror and my burdens are unendurable; I loathe sailing in our ships over the chill paths of the sea, and I loathe our stops on dry land, for all around are our enemies."[11] Later, in book 4, the narrator reiterates this feeling of abandonment in the face of the infinite: "They had no idea whether they were moving in Hades or over the waters. They handed over their hopes of return to the power of the sea, helpless to control where it might lead them."[12] Odysseus, Jason, and all of those who, by their shipwrecks, their voyages, and their explorations of uncharted space, confront the still empty or the unformed, travel into the void. As Jean-Pierre Vernant asks, "What is the Void? It is an emptiness, a dark emptiness where nothing is visible. A realm of falling, of vertigo and confusion—endless, bottomless. That Void seizes us like the yawning of an immense gullet where everything is swallowed up by murky darkness. So at the start there is only that Void, a blind, black, boundless abyss."[13]

Perhaps this gap has begun to be filled in by narrative. Sometimes it is narrative that precedes the place, that announces the emergence of a still-nonexistent space. Odysseus meets Tiresias in the underworld to learn his fate and understands that he will end his days in a country where salt is unknown. Homer did not color in this place, but others did. Jason extracted the Argo from the fatal sands of Libya after receiving aid from three women who unveiled the space before him, guiding him to the lake of Triton. Much later, when the Mediterranean had been surveyed through and through, narrative continued to anticipate places. In Achilles Tatius's second-century Alexandrian "novel" *Leucippe and Clitophon*, Callisthenes tries to track down the beautiful Leucippe. To find her trail, he must decipher an oracle: "There is an island city, its descendents named of a plant, / Joined to mainland by both causeway and strait, / Where Hephaestus enjoys possession of grey-eyed Athena; / Thither I bid you bear sacrifices to Heracles."[14] The strategist Sostratos interprets the oracle's message for Callisthenes: it is a city where such a plant grows (the palm of the Phoenicians), a city that is terraqueous and represents the struggle between the fire of Hephaestus and Athena's olive tree, because there ashes are used to fertilize the trees. This city is Tyre.

The description of the place does not *reproduce* a referent; it is discourse that *establishes* the space. The oracle and omen anticipate the reality of things. The process evolves in the strange *in-between* where we move from the localization of mythic places to the mythification of proven reality. By means of plot, ancient man sought to control the fabulous, and so to control his fear or panic. When Jason, Orpheus, and their companions cross the Symplegades, the clashing rocks are still moving, opening a void to engulf any who dare to approach them; after they pass, the Symplegades freeze. In such a narrative, the prehuman, even monstrous, spaces are cast in a stable and reassuring matrix to be grasped in human terms. The *Odyssey*, like the *Argonautica* and a significant portion of Greek literature, is not interested in the referent when it unleashes its narrative. The landscape is the result of poetic creation and of situations, not the other way around. Therefore, looking for Odyssean places on a current map is not only anachronistic but contradictory: Odysseus draws a map through discourse; he draws a map made entirely of his words, not of referenced places. In a beautiful essay on Homer, Alain Ballabriga notes a peculiarity of Greek geography: "The archaic cosmography ignores real nautical routes. The place-names are situated in relation to one another in almost an ideally straight line."[15] In other words, the cosmography of origins does not seek to reproduce the configuration of places on a more or less mimetic map. It arranges locations according to the order of the sentence. It is the word that creates the place. Thus Ortygia, or Syracuse, on the eastern shore of Sicily, can be farther from Greece than the western part of Sicily: it is sufficient to generate a longer string of words than Trapani. Reading the *Argonautica*, one takes part in a vast enterprise of geographical construction (in every sense of the term): Jason and the Argonauts organize places like pearls on a string from the poet's words. They follow the course of the rivers rather than the extensive sea, perhaps because the river is a long, liquid sentence. One also encounters this concept in much more recent descriptions of the world, even after the beginning of the Christian era. In the second century, at the time of Hadrian, that great eater of imperial space, Dionysius of Alexandria had prepared a *periegesis*, a macroscopic description of these lands inhabited. Dionysius probably had not been a traveler, or even a cartographer: he traveled the world through the mind, through the text, through a text that he wrote in the form of inventory. The connection between text and place is close here; it passes through the power of speech, which creates spaces. Christian Jacob asks the crucial question: "But how, with only the resources of language, can we see a space?"[16] There are many answers. In general, Dionysius, like all *periegetes* of antiquity, not only described the place as it was or should have been but also reproduced his own literary image. The shores of the Black Sea are such that they were sung by Callimachus or Apollonius of Rhodes. In other words, Dionysius does not care about the geographical referent: if there is a referent, it is literary, dependent on a poetic convention. As Jacob says, "Scientific geography cannot regulate the spaces of myth: for even by criticizing or negating them, this still grants them their place. It deconstructs them, transposes them, systematizes them. By this geographical reading of mythology, we actually proceed toward an archeology of the inhabited world, one inscribes memory (and not fiction) in reality, and confuses the present time with the ages."[17]

Multiple literary devices may be employed. Dionysius—like most Greek geographers, from Pseudo-Scylax to Hecataeus of Miletus, from Herodotus to Eratosthenes of Cyrene and Strabo—returns to the figure of analogy or metaphor whenever that which is described does not correspond to any geometric figure. He also forms a bridge between the map and writing: the sentence holds cartographic signs, according to a process of ekphrasis. Like many of his contemporaries, Dionysius imagined a flexible temporality that included both the novelties derived from voyages of discovery and archaisms from his fidelity to myth. In general, the referent never enters his mind. The cleavage between geography and literature had not yet been made; on the contrary, geography and literature mutually supported one another. Ballabriga wondered about this: "Why have the Greeks and others in the Mediterranean, continued to sail in both the known and the enchanted seas?"[18] Clearly, the referent only began to emerge from the time when space assumes a particularly ideological, monological character. One thus points to Rome, the Rome for which (as Raymond Chevallier puts it) "space is a chaos to organize, to police, to urbanize, a field open to pacification and Romanization," and whose ultimate goal is to make "the territorial universe into a single city."[19] But the first intrusion of an extratextual referent into the discourse of space appeared much earlier. The *Odyssey* itself is suspect. According to Valerio Massimo Manfredi and many contemporary Hellenists, the first Odyssey was anchored to the east. The situation of Circe's island at the easternmost extreme of the Greeks' known world is a rare indication of this primitive "orientality" that has survived in the story. Before being fixed, the text would be purged of most of these oriental references, becoming progressively occidental. This would fit into the logic of *exokeanismos*, of the translational movement to the west—toward the River Ocean—that characterizes the entire Greek imagination when confronted with the auxesis, the expansive growth of the world. This Westernization accompanied the Ionian and Tyrrhenian colonization initiated by the Greeks. According to Manfredi, those known as the Euboeans are assigned a new connection to the text of Homer: "Odysseus's itinerary seems to draw a map of the Euboean archaeological sites on the road to the West."[20] With the Euboeans, Odysseus finds Circe near Rome (Capo Circeo), and not in the deadly depths of the Black Sea. The connection between the imaginary and ideological referent has not ceased to assert itself ever since. Other texts, less famous than the *Odyssey* or the *Argonautica*, would establish links between Ulysses and a hero whose fame increased alongside that of Rome, namely Aeneas. And what do you think happened? Odysseus was made to pledge allegiance to Aeneas on the soil of Italy when Greece ceded its Mediterranean primacy to its western neighbors. Odysseus was overshadowed by Aeneas before being relegated to the eighth circle of hell by Dante . . . because he betrayed the trust of the Trojans, ancestors of the Romans and thus also of the Italians.

In going over these examples, it is easy to show that the purity of discourse is all the more mythical. The fact remains that the relationship of Odysseus, or Ulysses, to the early colonizers was without a doubt calculated to ennoble the literature. For it is, as Manfredi notes,

> a relationship of direct subordination, in the sense that the promoters of the legend of Ulysses, or of other heroic traditions, are themselves the protagonists of the great Hellenic migration. In other words, sailors, merchants, adventurers, and explorers, in order to allay the anxiety of repeatedly facing the unknown, plan their routes according to their mythical precursors, their gods and heroes. The first navigator to conquer the Straits of Messina is actually the second to go through this stretch of the sea, because he has already projected before him the ghost of Odysseus, vanquisher of Scylla and Charybdis, a ghost who becomes a *genius loci*.[21]

The specter of Odysseus is part of the dawn of the referent. Literary heroes precede the navigator to the remotest areas of the world, just as the imaginary advances ahead of the real. The referent is conceived and designed according to discourse. The world is still relatively empty. From dawn to dusk, the day is long, and the hours are rich. It should be said that the specter was still hovering around the caravels of Christopher Columbus—not only the ghost of Odysseus but also that of Marco Polo, since Columbus was heading toward India and not toward an America that remained to be discovered. "A narrative never wells up from a single, original source," says François Hartog wisely, "it is always entangled with some other narrative. The ground covered by the traveler's tale or narrative is also covered by other narratives: before the wake left by the discoverers of the Pacific was turned into writing, it was already overlapping a trail left by the written narratives of their predecessors. When Christopher Columbus set sail, he took Marco Polo's book with him."[22] Odysseus alone was deprived of the precursor's narratives; he moved between the human and the nonhuman, the place that the text itself was fabricating. Jason was better off: he had Orpheus, a poet and lyre player. The testimony of others was always close at hand in the writings of those bearing witness to spaces never before crossed, as is later verified in Tasso's *Jerusalem Delivered* and *The Lusiads* of Camões. From Tasso to all others, literature continued to anticipate geography. Since Verne and Conrad, the ghost of Odysseus has become more discreet, as the last blank spots were colored in on world maps. From the still-empty world of Homer follows the too-full world of postmodern literary geography.

Today the writer always comes in second place: the writer is always preceded by those who have fixed the referent, who are sometimes themselves writers. How can one write a line on Lisbon without looking through the spectacles of Fernando Pessoa? The world seems as full as an egg. Perhaps the world is not round by chance. This is the condition for most authors in the modern or postmodern era. Nevertheless, this overdetermination caused by a ubiquitous referent sometimes leads to a liberating effect: no longer able to fill the empty spaces as in Homer's time, writers will empty the too-full world today. And, consequently, they will begin to play with those points of reference that are considered excessively stable or overcoded. Roudaut offers an elegant commentary on this phenomenon: "The inventory of the world, the mapping of its surface, from Timbuktu to Tahiti, marked the end of all hope. The pilgrimages and voyages to the Fortunate Isles have the same goal: to find for this life a haven of grace. When the hope of paradise is banished from this life, and when we are irredeemably doomed to fail, then, like a collective dream that would take this roundabout way to speak, the image of an imaginary city emerges in the description of real life, engaging in a reversal of signs of this world and of the beyond."[23] In any event, this is a domain in which the reenchantment of space according to old Odyssean methods seems more natural: it is occupied by fantasy literature and science fiction, which generate an enthusiasm that would be astonishing if it did not reflect the unrestrained need of the postmodern to move beyond realism, realia, and constraints of the referent. According to Brian McHale, "science fiction . . . is to postmodernism what detective fiction was to modernism: it is the ontological genre par excellence (just as the detective story was the epistemological genre par excellence)."[24] The new *Odyssey*, which takes place in 2001, is accomplished in *space*. And as noted by Manfredi, Dante's verses on Ulysses are written on the launch pads for rockets at Cape Canaveral, while the spacecraft launched toward the sun in October 1990 is called *Ulysses*. And what about the spaces behind the stories of Tolkien, of Lovecraft, of Ende, and so many others? When the author seeks to detach himself from the real, does he necessarily produce antirealist literature? Is mimesis always based on fidelity to appearances? All literature is destined to reflect the major preoccupations of the epoch, whatever the conditions—however more or less "realistic"—of their expression. We are far from the spectacle that Stendhal saw or thought he saw in a mirror carried on the high road. But times change, though the postmodern may be less distant from the ancient than it seems. Still, in those fields that study the relationship between reality and its representations, one of the great debates concerns the inscription of the text in space, or of space in the text: is literature connected to the real by the space it represents? In its spatial dimension, does the text have a referent in the so-called real world?

Reality, Literature, and Space

With the increasing complexity of temporality in the twentieth century, along with the parallel weakening of historicity, there emerges a spatiality more stimulating than that of the positivist era: these are phenomena that deeply affected perceptions of reality in the recent postmodern decades. As long as time remained a river flowing quietly through a monologic history, reality dissociated itself from all forms of fictional representation of the world. But time is finally out of joint, and the river forms a swamp. The perception of reality has become as complex as determining its spatiotemporal coordinates. Reality engages literary discourse, which extends to all representational arts thought of as fictional, in a dizzying spiral. The relations between reality and fiction have been the subject of substantial consideration. In postmodernity, the gap between the world and the text has been significantly reduced, while taking a somewhat baffling form. The distinction between real space and represented or transposed space has blurred. In an essay exploring the Buddhist perspective on space-time, David R. Loy confesses a perplexity that seems to be shared by a majority of his contemporaries: "What is the 'real space and time' in which our culture lives? A hundred years ago it would have been easier to say, but the twentieth century has complicated things."[25] The century that just ended, a period marked at its beginning by the theory of relativity and at its end by postmodernism, has troubled many certainties.

In the traditional scheme, the relationship between the real and its representation is articulated around two complementary principles. The first establishes that reality is so distinct from its representations that the question of a hierarchy among them does not arise. In other words, the representation never replaces the real. As McHale points out, "Among the oldest of the classical ontological themes is that of the *otherness* of the fictional world, its separation from the real world of experience."[26] The second principle makes representation ancillary to reality. The representation points to the real according to a scale that includes relations alternately extensive (baroque) or narrow (realism, naturalism, etc.). In a postmodern environment, are these principles are still applicable?

Let us mention only the fictional representation of the world in order to avoid entering into another fiery clash between literature and literariness;[27] rather, let us start by questioning the validity of the second principle. Is representation always in the service of reality? Does the world necessarily appear in fiction, whatever the modalities of the latter? In my opinion, the answer is simple: yes. In *Chronicles of My Life*, Igor Stravinsky remembers a funny and instructive anecdote. In 1917, wanting to cross the border between Italy and Switzerland, he was stopped by customs because he had in his luggage the first of three portraits that Picasso would paint of him. Customs accused him not of receiving stolen goods but of espionage. They had mistaken this portrait for a military map! We would say that the picture was not realistic, because after all such a mishap would not have happened if Stravinsky had lived early enough to have his portrait painted by Velasquez. But, like customs, we would be wrong: Picasso, as well as Velasquez before him, both reproduced reality. The essence of the relationship cannot be disputed; rather, the brouhaha concerns the distance separating the commonly perceived reality from the modes of its representation. Picasso had simply broken with the naturalist poetics of a Zola. The analogy between the world as we experience it and its representation is less and less meaningful. But in any event, representation reproduces the real or, better, an experience of the real. For we must not forget that human space only exists in the modes of this experience, which, now becoming discursive, is the creator of the (geopoetic) world. Any work, no matter how far from sensed reality, as paradoxical as it seems, is part of the real—and, perhaps, participates in forming the real. Unreal realism is therefore an option, only just a bit more disconcerting than other postmodern processes.

As for the first principle, which establishes the real as an unbreakable icon, its survival is problematic. By 1905, in postulating space-time and dimensional plurality, the first theory of relativity undermined the good authority of a positivism that had affirmed Euclidean and unitary coordinates of the world. Since then, everything has accelerated. And the consequences are tangible: the gap between reality and fiction has narrowed; for some, it has been filled in. In his *Dialogues* with Claire Parnet, Gilles Deleuze says that "pure virtuality no longer has to actualize itself, since it is a strict correlative of the actual with which it forms the tightest circuit. It is not so much that one cannot assign the terms 'actual' and 'virtual' to distinct objects, but rather that the two are indistinguishable."[28] It is certainly not easy to grasp what Deleuze means by "virtual" and "actual." In *The Fold*, he opposes actualization (of the soul) and virtuality, on the one hand, to realization (in matter or body) and possibility, on the other. To those who would accuse Deleuze of superficiality, one might offer this lovely response by Jonathan Culler: "If serious language is a special case of the nonserious, if truths are fictions whose fictionality has been forgotten, then literature is not a deviant, parasitical instance of language. On the contrary, other discourses can be seen as cases of a generalized literature, or archi-literature."[29] Not only is literature correlated with reality through language, but the real and its discourses are incorporated into literary discourse. The reduction of distances, or even the reversal of polarities, between the real and the literary is not merely a matter for philosophy. In an article devoted to the study of some works of Michel Tournier, Botho Strauss, and Peter Handke, Peter Bürger argued that postmodern writing has resulted in the "derealization of the real."[30] But caution is called for! The idea of combining fiction and reality seems excessive, because it would inspire that kind of hyperrelativism that comes from a poorly understood postmodernism. In its extreme consequences, it would then be indifferent to a minimal ethics of preserving the category of truth and the tragic dimension of our society; truth would be colonized by fiction and any axiological hierarchy abolished. The risk would occur if the reconciliation between reality and fiction deprived reality of its verifiable character, if (fictional) textuality "derealized" the world into absurdity. This is not the case, of course: the writer is neither unconscious nor incompetent.

Reality has an essence that fiction cannot subsume. Pierre Ouellet eloquently summarizes the oscillation between reality and image, between *factum* and "fictum," in his *Poétique du regard*: "This opening, this game, creates the 'window' of which all images consist, through which one can watch the world that it neither re-presents nor actually realizes, but de-presents and un-realizes—'tearing' the continuity of reality, so that at the same time it partakes of the imaged thing, in order to appear in this tear, within its borders or strict limits of the unrealizing order that it forms, the 'world image' where the *fictum* and *factum* phenomenologically coincide, without ever losing their ontological distinctness."[31] But now for a change of register. In *Out of This World*, Graham Swift has managed to portray the status of representation and, therefore, that of the writer. The

British novelist has imagined an American corporal who in 1945 participated in the liberation of the concentration camp at Nordhausen, where prisoners who were too weak to work on the construction of the V1 and V2 rockets in the tunnels of Dora-Mittelbau were sent. Instead of facing this spectacle head-on, the young soldier circulates around the graves, his eyes staring through a camera without film. It is understood: he needs to mitigate the impact of the horror by using the camera as a filter. Despite this paltry subterfuge, the images of the place mark his life. If he had put film in his camera, perhaps he might have captured his memories in a photographic medium, a re-presentation. Instead, his memory keeps bringing back to him the images he had pretended to filter, and they remain forever engraved in his heart, as vivid as the fateful day when he entered the camp. Swift's character is much like the writer, but with one main difference. Faced with the tragic, the corporal tries to re-present reality in order to maintain a minimum distance. The writer does not choose to do so: the writer gives this attitude a rationale, for "art," which would spare him any real contact with the facts. For the corporal as for the writer, the lesson remains the same: the approaches to the real are innumerable. The corporal could—should?—get rid of his fake camera. For his or her part, the writer, whose story will always be relayed by fictional discourse, never abandons this screen. Whatever the level of representation, reality is invariably the referent of discourse. We cannot interfere with the real directly unless we get rid of the last safeguards and hastily equate postmodernism and absolute relativism.

The distinction is between the phenomenological and the ontological. For Lubomír Doležel, the narrative modes of the fictional world are governed by a number of operators borrowed from formal logic: alethic, deontic, axiological, and epistemic operators.[32] According to Doležel, these are all are unique to the world of fiction. From my point of view, some are not exclusively so. A hierarchy seems warranted. The principle of heterarchy (à la Douglas Hofstadter) is intrinsic to the fictional world (as long as it is isolable), but extrinsic to the relationship between reality and fiction. Thus some operators are independent of reality and relate to the essence of postmodern literature. This applies to alethic operators, which establish the categories of the possible, the impossible, and the necessary. These operators find a free and open field in the fictional world because they do not cause logical contradictions (as Doležel argues).[33] This extends to epistemic operators, which cover the known, the unknown, and the believed, and to quantitative operators, which distinguish between some, none, and all. But deontic and axiological operators escape beyond the solely fictional world, unless strictly circumscribed (as Doležel would have it). From my point of view, the deontic categories of permitted, prohibited, and obligatory are placed next to the axiological categories of good, bad, and indifferent. They belong to the core of any intangible cultural convention, to ethics.

If one considers that fiction can have an impact on reality, that there is an interaction between the referent and its representation, it seems to me essential that the issue of ethics is raised, though not resolved. It is not incompatible with a postmodern approach to text and reality. Peter Middleton and Tim Woods, in *Literatures of Memory*, devote a whole chapter to the ethics of historical fiction in the postmodern regime. After noting the "intense ethical anxiety" that has marked our era, they reach this conclusion: "The distance between epistemology and ontology, or between historical knowledge and literary fiction could be negotiated only by some kind of moral practice, although a morality of tradition or universalizing precepts is insufficient for the textual conditions of late modernity."[34] This is one of the new challenges facing contemporary theory, particularly postmodern theory. Of course, this imperative applies equally to studies of time and history in contemporary narratives as well as to the transposition of space in the narrative, because space too is human: *all too human*, like time and history. If a relationship of strict equivalence between reality and fiction is inconceivable, their increasing proximity is nonetheless clear. The world and the text are less distant than in the recent past. As McHale puts it, "this is precisely the question that postmodernist fiction is designed to raise: real, compared to what?"[35] McHale here asks a fundamental question that literature formulates regularly. Where is the referent of the fiction? What is it? What is its status? In a context in which a strict hierarchy between reality and fiction is questioned, the excursions between them range from one level to another. McHale speaks of the interpenetration between reality and its representation (heterocosm) or even of the "flickering effect."[36] McHale also mentions Roman Ingarden's idea of "opalescence." Thomas Pavel has also referred to this as a mixed "ontological landscape."

This whirling approach, (to enthusiastic spirits) or daunting (to those more skeptical), has emerged in contexts other than literary. In *L'impossible voyage*, Marc Augé has ventured into several of the French temples devoted to the "in-between" of the real and the fictional: Disneyland Paris, Center Parcs in Normandy, Mont-Saint-Michel, and the L'Oreal factory in Aulnay-sous-Bois. In the tropical bubble that humid Normandy shelters, Augé explodes, "There was a time when the real clearly distinguished itself from fiction, when you could be scared by telling stories but know that they are invented, when one could go into specialized and well-defined places (amusement parks, fairs, theaters, cinemas), in which fiction imitated the real. Today, imperceptibly, the opposite is happening: the real copies fiction. The least monument of the smallest village is illuminated to look like a decoration."[37] The notion of the simulacrum, as Baudrillard has elaborated throughout his work, conveniently explains what happens in the high places of the society of the spectacle on display in Normandy, Paris, and elsewhere. But Augé is more radical than Baudrillard:

"The expansion will not stop until the day when the entire developed world has become fictional, amusement parks that can no longer reproduce reality, that is to say fiction."[38] Leaving France for the United States, Augé finds the same impression in New York when observing the adjustments made to Times Square, Fifth Avenue, or Central Park: "We thus come full circle, from a state where the fictions feed the transformation of the imaginary into the real to a state where the real attempts to reproduce the fiction." Augé concludes, "In urban space, and in social space in general, the distinction between reality and fiction becomes blurred."[39]

Augé's observations are nearly the same as those Soja records in *Thirdspace*, in which the postmodern geographer offers a textbook example: Orange County, which is southeast of Los Angeles and includes John Wayne Airport, Anaheim, Disneyland, and the Nixon Library. At Yorba Linda, his birthplace, Richard Nixon grew up in a rural environment during childhood; but later on he actively assisted the transformation of Orange County into a haven of real estate based on the idealized image of California. This stereotypical representation of California was that of Hollywood and the sitcom, as well as all the advertisements of Malibu beaches. Soja carefully examines the various phases of this dual process of construction—real estate and marketing—to reach the same type of conclusion as Augé: "Under these transcendental conditions, it is no surprise that image and reality become spectacularly confused, that the difference between true and false, fact and fiction, not only disappears but becomes totally and preternaturally irrelevant."[40] The plan of Orange County finds itself extended to many different images—or expectations—in literature and film. Thus in *The Stepford Wives*, Ira Levin's satirical novel, transposed to the screen twice (by Brian Forbes in 1975 and Frank Oz in 2004), Connecticut is home to a seemingly ideal suburban town, Stepford. But the pursuit of bourgeois comfort and its hackneyed stereotype eventually banishes all humanity from the place, cutting its ties to the real world. The women of Stepford, or rather the wives of Stepford, are "really" robots, because only robots meet the criteria of programmed perfection in which any variation from the norm is excluded. Dehumanization and absolute derealization often go hand in hand.

Orange County is emblematic of the epoch of the simulacrum. Soja theorizes about the tendency to transform real space into an imaginary place, using the example of Los Angeles, a city that, according to a famous slogan, is really "seventy-two suburbs in search of a city." Drawing on Lefebvre's terminology, Soja looks at "real-and-imagined" (or perhaps "realandimagined"?) places.[41] These are mixed spaces that float between several levels of conception and representation, apart from any stable ontology. The divide between reality and fiction is minimal, and it is reasonable to ask what remains of the traditional "reality" there. But at the risk of repeating myself, I add that the real incorporates both the "facticity" of a Disneyland or an Orange County and the "reality" of the (formerly) working-class suburbs of a Sheffield, England or a Lille, France. It is the *perception* of this "reality" that is "unreal." And postmodern literature best suits this new version of reality, this "derealized reality"; indeed, literature is perhaps the best option for reading this new world, by virtue of its very fictionality. McHale has highlighted this new form of seemingly paradoxical mimesis in a section whose title ("How I Learned to Stop Worrying and Love Postmodernism") pays homage to Stanley Kubrick's comic masterpiece, *Dr. Strangelove*. McHale quotes Gerald Graff: "Where reality has become unreal, literature qualifies as our guide to reality by de-realizing itself. . . . In a paradoxical and fugitive way, mimetic theory remains alive. Literature holds the mirror up to unreality. . . . its conventions of reflexivity and anti-realism are themselves mimetic of the kind of unreal reality that modern reality has become. But 'unreality' in this sense is not a fiction but the element in which we live."[42] We return to my own premise: whatever its form, literature—like all mimetic art—is always a representation of an infinitely plastic real, in which the seemingly obvious "reality" constitutes only one position among others.

Between the Pavement and the Page

Space oscillates between reality and fiction, but the levels are not always discernible. According to some, fiction even takes precedence over reality. But this is an aporia. The real absorbs all configurations of representation, even those that seem to encompass modification of its structure, or, in other words, fictions. The real is always the terminus ad quem of representation. At this stage, it seems necessary to explore the thing that ensures a smooth transition between reality and representation, namely *narrative*. (There are others, of course, as not every transition can be formulated or formulable by stories.) In the absence of a strictly established hierarchy, postmodern narrative captures the world, uninstalls it, and re-presents it or re-worlds it at will, all while preserving its functional quality, its real essence. This is true not only for fiction but also for other categories of narrative for which the representation of the real is a goal. Hayden White, one of the leading historians of the last generation, has adopted this postmodern logic in his examinations of historiography.[43] Soja summarizes White's position in *Thirdspace*: "For White, history is about 'the real world as it evolves in time,' but as he also notes, 'it does not matter whether the world is conceived to be real or only imagined; the manner of making sense of it is the same.' In this way, White opens historiography and the narrative discourse to 'fictionalization,' to a poetics of interpretation that draws from literature and literary criticism to represent a real world that is simultaneously real-and-imagined."[44] Not only is history implied here, but so are geography, the social sciences, and the "hard" sciences, as well as the humanities, or any other discipline that attempts to offer an explanation of the world. Or a "reading" of the world. In a cultural context in which the real and the imagined are no longer always divided and sometimes come to revolve around each other (i.e., Soja's *real-and-imagined*), literature is also a point of access to a decanonized reality, one open or reopened to narrative.

The major difficulty lies in the fact that the relation of fictional text to the world of reference has been hotly debated by a generation of literary theorists. Thus it happens that mimesis is seen as false. There is no text outside the text! Jacques Derrida's famous slogan (from *Of Grammatology*) merely sanctions a gradual detachment from the reality that, in France, found interesting affiliations with the *nouveau roman* or with the unrestrained productions of the Oulipo writers, Queneau, Perec, Roubaud, and others. Recently, however, the text has begun to commit to the outside. First came parody, using methods of hyperrealism (from the pinball machines of painter Charles Bell to the automobiles of writers like Michel Deville and René Belletto); then it happened more discreetly. It is possible that the 1990s sanctioned the return of the real in literature. It is as if the illusion of referentiality had ceased to be illusory, at least for literary theorists. It seems that the last decade of the millennium marked the beginning of a new phase of postmodern derealization: the conquest of the real by the literary, and thus also a certain fictionalization of the real. Some herald the death of the novel; others, more baroque, envision its triumph as the real is engulfed. Therefore, one enters into an indistinct zone separating the somewhat realistic literary from a *literaturized* real.

It will come down to walking the streets of Paris, Berlin, Prague, Milan, or Dublin. In their absence, one could take the streets and boulevards of one's hometown, large or small, urban or rural. But it has never been for only one person to do: thousands, hundreds of thousands, millions of citizens have preceded him or imitated the task. Tourists, infinitely many in some cases, also perform this function. It is not only flesh-and-blood people who take these walks. Literary texts are full of characters who roam the streets of Paris, Milan, and elsewhere. In *The Betrothed* by Alessandro Manzoni, Renzo searches for Lucia while wandering around the streets of the Duomo of Milan; he then enters the *Festa del Perdono* lazarette, his itinerary adopting the logic of the map. The unquiet and contemporary heroes of Andrea De Carlo and Andrea G. Pinkett crisscross the Lombard capital from side to side, mentioning (sometimes using an interposed narrator) the places that punctuate their journeys. The Milanese, and sometimes tourists, know the corso di Porta Vittoria or the corso Vittorio Emanuele: the Milanese police, detectives, and criminals of the *giallisti* (authors of thrillers) do as well. This raises another question: What is the difference between the Milan that the potential reader on the street describes with varying degrees of enthusiasm to his or her usual interlocutors and the Milan that the reader knows *through* Manzoni's *The Betrothed* or through the latest mystery novel by Pinkett? For some, the answer is obvious: there is no relationship between the two models of representation, because the Milan of Manzoni or Pinkett is a city of paper, while the Milan of the sightseer unfolds before his or her own eyes. And this is so, even if what the reader sees is on another piece of paper—a postcard, for example. We can then make a backhanded sketch of some of the connections between the referent and representation. Examples abound of such peremptory effusions in literary theory, which is often based on philosophy and, in this case, on the language of Charles Sanders Peirce and Ferdinand de Saussure. Here is one, among countless others, from a book by Michel Picard: "The Dublin of Joyce is not Dublin, the Nancy in *Lucien Leuwen* was never Nancy."[45] Duly noted. But such an assertion, if it reassures both the literary critic and the geographer about the specificity of their respective fields, is premature: one finds that, if Stendhal says Nancy, he is probably thinking of Nancy. Let us add a grain of salt to this story. In *The Red and the Black*, the author chooses to establish the city of Verrières, which is imaginary—or almost: the model is Besançon. If Nancy had not been the geographical Nancy, it would have been enough to change its name to elide any connection with an obvious referent. This is what Stendhal did with Besançon. If it proves too simplistic to deny any association between the city represented in literature and the city described in the geographical atlases, the fact remains that this connection is extremely problematic.

In *Le voyage, le monde et la bibliothèque*, Christine Montalbetti has engaged in a careful study of this connection, and concludes that the links between the text and the referent cannot be sustained. The principle is established from the outset: "There is, in any referential enterprise, something that would be impossible."[46] Leaning in the direction of Picard, she notes that the Saint-Brieuc of Jean Echenoz, in *Les grandes blondes*, is not Saint-Brieuc. One could define God in two ways: either God is X (or Y) or God is not X (or Y). In the first case, the definition is apophantic; in the second, it is apophatic. By denying any link between the fictional town and its referent, one will eventually develop an apophatic geography of France. One can never know exactly what Nancy or Saint-Brieuc are, but at least we know what they are not. The impossibility that Montalbetti argues for is explained by the separation of writing and its object, a separation that is the basis of the "referential project" and establishes "a structure of confrontation" between reality and the text. It postulates the heteronomy of speech and of the world, resulting in the inability of writing to reproduce the world. Therefore, "only fictional speech is possible, since the question of conformity does not arise."[47] We return to the situation of structuralism: the arbitrariness of the sign, the autonomy of the text with respect to the real, the pure autoreferentiality, the absence of any involvement of the text in the world, or the simple homonymic relation between the two instances. According Montalbetti, "where the storyteller believes in identifying the material space that he surveys in an epic or novelistic place, where a fragment of reality itself seems to function as a scene, where in order to name characters he has recourse to the onomastics of fiction, he neglects the homonymic dynamics behind the unfolding scenery, and fails to exert minimal prudence in sealing off fictional spaces from those that distinguish real spaces."[48] To better illustrate this, Montalbetti then imagines three types of complexes, embodied by three figures for whom the separation between reality and fiction has blurred too fast: Victor Bérard, Don Quixote, and the projectionist Buster.

In *Les navigations d'Ulysse*, a work first published between 1927 and 1929, Victor Bérard tells of his attempt to trace the route of Odysseus, navigating his own boat based on "information" provided by the *Odyssey*. The quest was certainly something rather ridiculous because Homer's geography does not correspond to ours. In comparison, locating the site of Troy (as Heinrich Schliemann claimed to do) was much easier . . . as long as he had really discovered the scene of the *Iliad*. For Montalbetti, Bérard's complex consists in "acting as though fiction, somehow, had taken place in the physical world."[49] But as we have seen, such a distinction had no meaning in the (blind) eyes of Homer. Montalbetti here engages, I think, in the same excesses as Bérard, but taking the opposite side: she ignores the fact that reality is entangled with fiction, while Bérard got carried away with the idea that fiction favored reality. Don Quixote's complex was caused by the erroneous substitution of fictional phrases for real ones and by fictionalization of the referent: "What is at stake, in the complex of Don Quixote, is how referential writing always attempts to measure its object, by providing a formulation more readable, more literary, more coded, but that, borrowing from the register of fiction, is an alteration of the object that it had tried to represent."[50] The Knight of La Mancha is often called upon to account for the relationship (or lack thereof) between the real and the fictional. For Pavel, Don Quixote is the victim of an "ontological stress" caused by his inability to evolve within an ontologically determined landscape. Don Quixote is a kind of precursor of postmodern oscillation. There remains the complex of the theater projectionist Buster (Keaton), who steps onto the screen in the film *Sherlock, Jr.* This poetic crossing-over corresponds to a new transgression of boundaries between reality and fiction: "In the dynamics of this complex, it is no longer the fictional hero who leaves his improbable mark on the real lands, but the referential character who wanders into fiction."[51] We see that these "complexes" can be treated. Moreover, Montalbetti has given us the key to the analysis, but without using it herself: "the narrative unfolds in parallel spaces."[52] Such parallel spaces have been formalized in the theory of possible worlds, discussed further later in this chapter. But we have already noted that where a parallel relationship exists, the lines do not cross, but they situate themselves in relation to one another. Regardless of the nature of this link, however tenuous, it merits its existence.

Montalbetti paid tribute to the structuralist framework developed by Gérard Genette, but this tribute seems late. In 1997, could one still ignore the theories proposing the blurring of the boundaries between reality and fiction? With Pavel's *Fictional Worlds*, we can definitively break with structuralism and its autotelic logic. Similarly, we may have broken from what McHale describes as a "nostalgia for unproblematic mimesis."[53] It is therefore not surprising that the first chapter of Pavel's book has a title like a manifesto: "Beyond Structuralism." After denouncing the "textolatry" of Derrida and other architects of the break with the *hors-texte*, Pavel writes, "A debate began to develop which showed that the neglected topics of literary reference, fictional worlds, and narrative content can be addressed from a new, unexpected angle. It suggested that formal semantic models and, more generally, rapprochement to philosophical results in the domain of fiction can provide for better accounts in various areas of narratology and stylistics."[54] Pavel was not the first to speak in these terms. He was preceded by Umberto Eco, who expressed similar views in *The Role of the Reader*, as well as by such heirs of the Prague Circle as Doležel and Benjamin Hrushovski.[55] For Pavel, two extreme relations between text and reality are considered: segregation, which involves isolating the text as a mere product of imagination; and conversely, integration, which claims that "no genuine ontological difference can be found between fictional and nonfictional descriptions of the actual world."[56] Regarding the possible study of the relationship between Dublin *in itself* and the Dublin of Joyce, one will adopt one attitude or the other, with nuances. Everything depends on the degree of intensity that we assign to the model: its existence may, according to Pavel, take on a symbolic character, and therefore be more or less "weak." Just as there is a Dublin subject to the gaze of the visitor, there is a symbolic Dublin with less anchorage. It is the Dublin of works of fiction. To a different degree, it could be the Dublin of all versions transmitted through discourse (which may or may not have fictional status), and therefore through a subjective enunciator. Here we see clearly that Pavel's speculations are closely related to the *pensiero debole* of Vattimo, Rovatti, Eco, and the whole postmodern school, which opposes *pensiero forte* constructed on the positivist model.

The Theory of Worlds

One of the most effective ways to examine the coupling of reality and fiction is to question the number—and especially the nature—of worlds in which the connection is included or to which it refers. In doing so, one enters a totally unreal world that is subject to a uniquely fictional code. One enters a second, third, or plural universe: the world of simulation, of make-believe. The rules of the game are set forth immediately and clearly. In terms of representation, is the world homogeneous, and does it contain all the real and the fictional? Or is the world divided into multiple worlds that form a heterogeneous universe? In *Heterocosmica*, Doležel has compiled a detailed inventory of different models that unite the world or worlds and their formal interactions. He distinguishes models with one world from models with several worlds—the most popular model is without a doubt the one that points to the plurality of worlds. Eco had already formed a working definition of "possible world" in *The Role of the Reader*, and Eco was one of the first to introduce the concept in Europe (after Wittgenstein and some of his precursors):

> (i) a possible world is a *possible state of affairs* expressed by a set of relevant propositions where for every proposition *p* or *~p*;
> (ii) as such it outlines a set of possible *individuals* along with their *properties*;
> (iii) since some of these properties or predicates are actions, a possible world is also a *possible course of events*;
> (iv) since this course of events is not actual, it must depend on the *propositional attitudes* of somebody; in other words, possible worlds are worlds imagined, believed, wished, and so on.[57]

The fictional world, which is a possible world, thus corresponds to a world developed outside the processes of actualization that characterize the real world. The fact that the world emerges without any need for actualization does not, however, imply that it is incompatible with the real world. As Eco points out, "A fictional text abundantly overlaps the world of the reader's encyclopedia."[58] What remains to be seen is how the two worlds (real and fictional), or the two versions of the same world (real-and-fictional) are compatible with the encyclopedia of the audience.

Many theorists have opted for the heterogeneous. Their research tends toward the same goal: to show the composite nature of the world and of any relationship to a referent. The unity of the world is often found to be the result of an oversimplification, because everything interacts with its environment and all relations are dynamic and diverse. Doležel asserts that "the semantics of narrative is, at its core, the semantics of interaction."[59] This general and permanent oscillation has been distilled by Even-Zohar into the idea of the *polysystem*, according to which emphasis should be placed on the labile relationship that unites the text and the referent, which is no longer an absolute but merely a point of departure. For Even-Zohar, the referent becomes the "realeme," a kind of transposable benchmark, in a context of variable and non-Euclidean geometry. What Even-Zohar calls the realeme sometimes takes other names.

In Doležel, the ensemble of realemes constitutes a protoworld, which forms a constellation of "heterocosms," or possible worlds. Since, for Doležel, the border between reality and fiction tends to disappear, we can see the strong similarities between this approach and the theory of intertextuality: the protoworld is a kind of hypoworld around which are organized the hyperworlds, or—to use the language of pastiche from Genette's *Palimpsests*—a source world that produces derivative worlds. McHale, when he evokes the passage from one world to another (transworld), speaks rather of the *zone*. The zone is for him a heterotopic space where alethic operators structure the narrative according to an autonomous logic. For Pavel, heterocosms are "ontological landscapes." This means that the ontology is exclusively considered within the fictional world. But Pavel relativizes this specification by introducing a new polarity, namely the relationship of the center to the periphery: "Taking the division of the ontological space into central and peripheral models as a very general formal organization of the beliefs of a community, we may localize fiction as a peripheral region used for ludic and instructional purposes."[60] Fictional worlds are distant planets that orbit a star, a star that would correspond to reality.

These approaches are all tied to the theory of possible worlds, which (after Leibniz and his monads and, more recently, Wittgenstein and states of things) has passed through formal logic under the name of "modal semantics," before finding applications in literary theory with Nelson Goodman[61] and other theorists in the 1980s. This is how Andrea Carosso, in the introduction to the Italian translation of Pavel's *Fictional Worlds*, describes modal semantics: "Modal semantics integrates the levels of reality that emerge from our statements and questions in a way that can scientifically explain the coupling that commonly occurs in discourse between things belonging to the real world and things that are foreign to it."[62] This rejoins Doležel for whom the actual or material world is likely to generate an infinity of possible worlds that do not necessarily involve an inherent ontology of the real world. They could be mathematical models or logical formulations, which only require philosophical interpretation. According to Saul Kripke, in a phrase Doležel is fond of quoting, possible worlds are postulated; we do not discover them with a telescope. In literature, which at times draws inspiration from the scientific sphere, fictional worlds are, according Doležel, a particular category of possible worlds. They are aesthetic artifacts constructed and maintained through fictional texts. Doležel then lists the main characteristics of these possible worlds. They are possible, not actual (or realized) states of things, probabilities rather than a universal principle to which they would necessarily apply. In a novel, Napoleon may die someplace other than Saint Helena and do something other than attack England (to use an example popularized by David Lewis). Fictional worlds are infinitely varied, and only *compossibility*, which is an organizing principle that governs the fictional world, is required. Napoleon may die somewhere other than Saint Helena, but he cannot die in two places at once without some formal (literary) process. Possible worlds are incomplete. They may have a homogeneous or heterogeneous structure. Finally, they result from the textual poiesis. Doležel ends this theory's prologue by saying that one only has access to these worlds through semiotic channels.

The one-world model has had famous supporters, like Bertrand Russell, who in his *Introduction to Mathematical Philosophy* notes that there is only one world, the "real" world, and that Shakespeare's imagination in writing Hamlet is part of it (the example Russell uses).[63] All levels of reality and fiction thus refer to the same nodal point. On this basis, there would be no reason to separate the different levels of representation of Elsinore castle. Doležel does not forget Saussure, whose self-referential theory is, however, not very useful for the study of fictionality, at least according to Saussure himself (and I give him the benefit of the doubt). More interesting are the speculations of Gottlob Frege, for whom fictional utterances are neither true nor false, but move through two types of language: one cognitive (referential) referring to *Bedeutung* (or the denotation of an entity in the world) and the other poetic (pure meaning) referring to *Sinn* (or the mode of designation). These terms, developed in the late nineteenth century, disclose the existence of *one* world that is described using two complementary languages. According to this view, there would be a referential Dublin and a poetic Dublin, or more precisely, a Dublin that is by turns referential and poetic. We may conclude this quick overview of Doležel by mentioning Kendall Walton and his "fictional pragmatics," according to which, on the model of child's play, fiction is a pure make-believe, constitutive of a world where the reader or player engages in a symbolic journey of reading by projecting his ego. This activity has the gift of bringing fictional territories into relation with those of the referential world. According to Pavel, "the fictional ego examines the territories and events around him with the same curiosity and eagerness to check the interplay between sameness and difference, as does any traveler in foreign lands."[64]

The theory of worlds is obviously interesting for the analysis of literary representations of space. Are literary space and "real" space better understood in a model of plural worlds, or in a model of only one world? The debate is far from over. Without a doubt it is aporetic, like everything that is part of the hermeneutics of the world or a "metaphysics of fictional objects."[65] It is not my intention to add my two cents to this debate that is obviously destined to continue. After all, my problem is limited to this simple question whose treatment is complicated: Is the space represented in literature cut off from what is exterior to it (as argued by the structuralists) or does it interact with the world outside the text? If the latter, then real spaces and fictionalized spaces coexist on the basis a common referent. In addition, I do not lose sight of the fact that literature can act upon the real world, conferring an ethical responsibility on those who produce it. Therefore, although the model of plural worlds is fascinating, it seems inappropriate to adopt it without nuance, because the real world is usually placed on the same plane as the fictional worlds. This is especially true in David Lewis's theory of *modal realism*,[66] which promotes a dedifferentiation of the worlds, where all possible worlds are as real as the actual world. Although Lewis's influence has been attenuated, the principle continues to underlie most of the illustrations of this theory, which, inspired by formalism, continues to isolate the fictional world. From my point of view, a model of a single world could be sufficient to shed light on the relationship between referential and fictional spaces, but this world should be heterogeneous. It should establish within itself a communication between the real and the fictional, so that they are neither completely separated nor totally conflated. It should also reflect a sense of openness, permitting contact between the two spaces. We have to keep in mind that liminality is the threshold (limen) and not the border (*limes*): the threshold presupposes free crossings, unlike the border, which can be sealed.

The threshold between the kinds of space could present two distinct natures. The first would be metonymic and would establish a contiguity between reality and fiction. This scheme would be a one-world model. The threshold would then be *bifrons*, like Janus. If we wished to reestablish a hierarchy, we could even consider moving from metonymy to a *mise en abyme*, extreme metonymy, and consider that the real contains the fictional at the level of the metareal (as with Genette's idea of the *metatextual*). In this case, it seems appropriate to introduce evidence relating to another theory, that of the *interface*, which also involves the possible world of the simulation. Launched by Ted Nelson in 1965, this theory has been developed by researchers such as George P. Landow, Jay David Bolter, and, more recently, Alessandro Zinna, in the particular context of studying the relationship between traditional writing and writing for information technology. The key concept of the theory of the interface is "hypertext," which corresponds for the most part to a network of documents linked via material and informational interfaces. According to Zinna, "hypertextualization, then, is a linear or multilinear succession of parts that are the result, depending on the case, of a textualization or a syncretization of elements, that is to say, a succession of simple elements or complex units."[67] Here we see a global interactivity, seamless, whose principle is the rearrangement (or montage) of heterogeneous elements brought together by an interface. Also according Zinna, this montage is a topological arrangement of components as well as their synchronization. Furthermore, "disposition and timing are based on different forms of *congruence, coherence,* and *cohesion*."[68] Indirectly or not, it refers to the types of relationships that unite the world of reference and the possible world. But in this case, connections are made in a mixed environment, both material and immaterial. Continuing his examination of forms of contact between the different parts, Zinna further notes, "The liminal thresholds of each element are likely to give rise to patterns of relation by juxtaposition, superimposition, connection, and blurring of the border thus presented."[69] Several figures can be imagined: establishing a distance with an intercalary element, making contact through delimitation, or making contacts through degrees of superposition.

Without further examination of this theory, we can advance a hypothesis: the representation of the referential world (and of so-called real spaces) in fiction engages in a process of interactivity between instances of heterogeneous nature brought together in the same world through an interface. The interface is also the means of connection between the elements of this world. This approach is something like the concept of the *fold*, developed by Leibniz in his theory of monads, and taken up by Deleuze in his book on Leibniz. The fold was at the intersection of body and soul, just as it is now at the juncture of reality and fiction: "To the degree that the world is now made up of divergent series (the chaosmos), or that crapshooting replaces the game of Plenitude, the monad is now unable to contain the entire world as if in a closed circle that can be modified by projection. It now opens on a trajectory or a spiral in expansion that moves further and further away from the center."[70] The postmodern world, of which Deleuze is one of the most prominent theorists, is in the process of expansive mobilization. The threshold is also subject to this global instability. The interface suggests a definition of this threshold that separates and unifies those insubstantial, almost unnoticeable, spaces. I consider the interface a non-surface and thus a line for instant communication between real and fictional. But there is a second way of understanding the threshold. If it has a metonymic nature, it is logical to assume that it can also adapt to the shape of the metaphor. Metaphor is displacement (*metaphora*); it is projection. It is an entity of "as if," of make-believe, of simulation. It supposes a minimal distance between instances; it introduces a cushion that makes the threshold less permeable without closing it entirely. The threshold here would be distended, its liaisons polymorphic. This scheme would be consistent with a model of many possible worlds in which each world would find a distinct place in a constellation of variable geometry. Oscillating in an ever more precarious way at a distance from the referential center or from the ensemble of realemes, the uncertain liminality of the interface is the terrain where fiction and reality engage in their role-play.

Referential Oscillations

The fictional place takes part in a variable relationship with the real. Its geography assumes a mixed status, exactly like the history reproduced in the "historical novel." In the early twentieth century, Alexius Meinong attempted to construct a "theory of objects," also strongly criticized by Russell, for whom it was too radical: "In such theories, it seems to me, there is a failure of that feeling of reality which ought to be preserved even in the most abstract studies."[71] According to Meinong's theory, each object is defined by a certain number of properties, and each set of properties corresponds to an object, whether it exists or not, whether it is possible or not. In other words, an object appears both in its present reality (it *exists* at that moment, strictly speaking) and in its potentialities that can be actualized at some other point (it *subsists*). Each object is assigned a certain coefficient of "reality." Clearly, if it is already real in the classical sense, the object reveals more potentialities that remain to be realized. What is the application of such a theory to fiction? In a way, the answer was given by Jorge Luis Borges, who cites Meinong in *Ficciones*. Following Meinong's principle, the Uqbar civilization in Mesopotamia invented Tlön, a theoretical civilization. But metaphysicians of virtual Tlön do not care to make their world real: "They know that a system is nothing more than the subordination of all aspects of the universe to some of them."[72]

Terence Parsons revisits this strange theory that attributes to nonexistent things an existence, albeit a virtual one. He distinguishes between nuclear, identifying predicates (e.g., goldenness, detectivehood, and mountainhood) and extranuclear, nonidentifying predicates that include ontological, modal, intentional, or technical properties. Fictional objects are provided with the nuclear properties that we attribute to them, but only in the fictional world that integrates them—the modalities of this inclusion relate to the extranuclear. As a consequence, the nuclear qualifies a fictionality that the extranuclear clearly decouples from the real. Pavel mentions the example provided by Parsons: Mr. Pickwick is nuclearly an Englishman who observes the human condition, but he is extranuclearly a character from a novel by Charles Dickens. To better isolate the objects of fiction, Parsons also makes distinctions among *native objects*, which are characters or objects original to a story; *immigrant objects*, which are imported either from the real world (like London) or from another text (Quixote, Iphigenia, and so on); and *surrogate objects*, which are substitutions that capture real referents in order to transform them (thus, surrogate objects would include, according to Parsons, the Paris of Balzac). Regarding the study of representations of space, this causes a flutter: Would Paris be an imported object or a substituted object? Pavel summarizes the situation in this way: "Of course, taking Paris in *La Fille aux yeux d'or* as a surrogate object is mutually exclusive with considering it an immigrant object. The decision is determined by our views on mimesis and realism as well as by our knowledge about extratextual entities."[73] This depends in particular on the effect that borrowing from reality has on the economy of the text. Extending the argument to the status of the character, Parsons notes that Napoleon appears fleetingly and in the distance in *La fille aux yeux d'or*: he is an imported object. But Richelieu plays a role in *The Three Musketeers*, so why is he a substitute? As Pavel notes, one is brought back to the clear separation between reality and fiction, between the referent and its representation. In its (apparent) simplicity, Meinong's theory had avoided this kind of distinction. For if the city of Paris is an "object" actualized in the real world, its virtualities are not subsumed under the referent. Paris exists virtually in the proliferation of fictional representations by which it is apprehended. Let us hear once more from McHale, who has posed the problem aptly: "People such as Napoleon or Richard Nixon, places such as Paris or Dublin, ideas such as dialectical materialism or quantum mechanics . . . are not *reflected* in fiction so much as *incorporated*; they constitute enclaves of ontological *difference* within the otherwise homogeneous fictional heterocosm."[74] One then asks oneself about the type of relationship that these enclaves have with the referent, about the specificity of virtual representations with respect to the real model (the real remaining a model).

The literary *place* is a virtual world that interacts in a modular fashion with the world of reference. The degree of correlation between one and the other can vary from zero to infinity. Several authors have attempted to classify the type of link that fictional space maintains with referential space. According to Earl Miner, there are three fictional places: the *common place*, which makes no reference to the "real world" referent; the *proper place*, which refers to a known place in its existing location; and the *improper place*, which refers to a nonexistent place whose valence is often metaphorical (like heaven, hell, etc.).[75] In a similar manner, Lennard Davis has also identified three types of fictional places, but distributed differently: the *actual place*, such as Paris in Balzac; the *fictitious place*, such as George Eliot's Middlemarch; and the *renamed place*, such as F. Scott Fitzgerald's East Egg or West Egg (fictional names for real places in Long Island, New York).[76] Miner's typology is applied to a corpus ranging from Dante to Spenser, while Davis also includes nineteenth- and twentieth-century authors. Transcribed space may have no referent at all; it may instead seek to appropriate for itself a series of given realemes. For instance, if we look at Calvino's invisible cities, we readily admit that they remain separated from any referent, even though they are supposed to be an inventory of places in Kublai Khan's empire as compiled by Marco Polo.[77] The same applies to all explicitly imaginary spaces of literature. But if the referent is manifest, new variants appear. In *Les villes imaginaires dans les littérature française*, Roudaut tried to distinguish two types of cities with respect to the referent: those that dissimulate and those that do not. In the latter case, the examples are many; we understand that Milan, Nancy, Dublin, and Paris are cities for which people know what to expect. As Roudaut says, "The name of Rouen alone provides all the necessary information."[78] But we must be careful here: sometimes the author manipulates appearances. The representation may have a (certain) level of conformity with the referent; it can also play with it, play with the reader and with itself. In turn, I propose that we retain three types of couplings, which adapt to postmodern evolutions of fictional spatiality: homotopic consensus (knowing that pure conformity is a trick), heterotopic interference, and utopian excursus.

Homotopic Consensus

Whereas a correlation between the referent and its fictional representation is possible, we still have to establish the terms of the links between them. We first ask what allows them to come together. In a study of intertextuality, the titles of parallel works represent a vital clue; it is the same for places. When a work is named in relation to a real world referent, it is what Kripke calls a "rigid designator"[79] (here, the place-name) or what Pavel characterizes as a "cluster." Since this relationship already exists, it is not a construction ex nihilo, but rather a reconfiguration of a realeme, the formatting of one or more of its potentialities. Note that the opposition between construction and reconfiguration, applied to space, evokes the distinctions that Paul Ricoeur in *Time and Narrative* makes between *prefiguration* (or the presentation of raw referent), *configuration* (the fictional arrangement of the referent), and *refiguration* (the fictionalized referent). Spatiality and temporality are inextricably linked, but this we already knew. When Balzac represents Paris, or Dickens London, or Döblin Berlin, or Dos Passos New York—or when Umberto Eco represents Paris, Jacques Roubaud London, Jean-Philippe Toussaint Berlin, or Kafka New York—in all these cases, and many others, a relationship is established between Paris, London, Berlin, or New York and their respective literary representations. For all the authors mentioned here, the relationship is marked by a homotopic consensus. In other words, the virtual properties expressed through the narrative will be added to the progressively actualized properties of the referent.

Verisimilitude is a necessary criterion. Homotopic consensus supposes that a representation of the referent emerges from a series of realemes and that the links between them are manifest. In *Short Letter, Long Farewell*, Peter Handke's anonymous protagonist travels coast to coast, across the United States. In a suburb of Saint Louis, Missouri, he is hosted by a couple of painters, who paint movie posters and historical landscapes. In their opinion, this art should be as least "artistic" as possible. Each landscape must necessarily refer to a historical moment, in a framework that has been established by and in the collective memory. This logic is pushed to its extreme: "The painter was also unable, as I discovered, to conceive of sketching anything that did not exist: his landscapes had to be exact imitations of real landscapes, the people in them had to have really lived, and they had to have done what they were doing in the pictures."[80] He refuses, for example, to represent the Battle of Little Bighorn, because, since there were no survivors, there is no eyewitness account of the rout. At that moment, the protagonist, who is Austrian, remembers that he had never seen images of fantasy in America, but always reproductions of historic moments. This situation is an extreme case, but most narratives that represent an existing place in the protoworld almost always conform to the referent. Thus "realism," although resisted in a lot of ways, remains the dominant system of representation.

But this does not preclude the range of freedom that exists between the narrative's desired goal of conforming to the real world (the "geographic narrative"?) and the consensus sought by deliberately fictional narrative. Examples illustrating this premise are numerous. Santa Lucia di Siniscola, a small resort located on the eastern coast of Sardinia, just below the Costa Smeralda, is little known to tour guides, but it has had astonishing literary success. D. H. Lawrence, Albert t'Serstevens, and André Pieyre de Mandiargues have all described the tower, which is probably the place's only curiosity. For Pieyre de Mandiargues it is square, for t'Serstevens it is round, and for Lawrence it is doubled! In "reality," the tower—singular—was built in the seventeenth century by the Aragonese. Thirteen meters high, it is round. T'Serstevens had inserted his description in a travel narrative, as Lawrence had done before him; Pieyre de Mandiargues had set *Le lis de mer* in this locale. This question of genre is not of great importance (although one would expect a more accurate depiction of the referent in a travel narrative). According an ancillary status to literary narrative would be disastrous. I repeat my point articulated earlier, that fiction does not mimic reality, but that it actualizes new virtualities hitherto unexpressed, which then *interact* with the real according to the hypertextual logic of interfaces.

Ricoeur evokes this in his idea of the *quasi past* of fiction, which he characterizes as "the detector of possibilities buried in the actual past."[81] It seems uncertain that the virtual is included in the actual past; the virtual seems to escape time altogether: it is a past not spoken and also an unspoken future. Whatever the case may be, the relation of quasi past to actual past also refers to that of fiction to reality: fiction detects possibilities buried in the folds of reality. Every time the fictional representation is of the homotopic type, there is a risk of confusion between the referent and its representation. In the framework defined here, that of claimed verisimilitude, there is compossibility between the referent and the representation. In other words, the virtual properties expressed by the fictional text would not be opposed to the actual or realized properties in the sphere of the referent. But, as Pavel points out, "it makes a serious difference if we postulate that possible worlds must have the same inventory of individuals as the real world, or if we allow worlds accessible from ours to contain fewer individuals or more."[82] One can see that the referent and representation may not be compossible. The interface between them may become opaque, blurring the lines connecting them.

Heterotopic Interference

The rigid designator constituted by the name is an indicator, but one that can be misleading, just like a title. In a well-known joke, which has been the subject of analysis,[83] a visitor to an art exhibition in Moscow discovers an intriguing painting. Titled *Lenin in Warsaw*, the painting shows Madame Lenin sharing her bed with a young executive of the party. The perplexed visitor then asks why the painting is so named if Lenin himself is not in it: "Where's Lenin?" His interlocutor responds, "Lenin is in Warsaw." Why should one assume that Lenin would be in this picture, while his wife is depicted cavorting under the sheets? Where is Warsaw? Is he going from Warsaw to Moscow? Moscow to Warsaw? In fact, the visitor mistakenly condenses the present into a single and same place; it escapes him that two different people can be conjoined (so to speak) in Warsaw and Moscow, even if their activities are very different. But it also happens that Warsaw and Moscow overlap in one place. Hypothetically, a city can hide another. In *Bastogne*, Enrico Brizzi superimposed Bologna upon Nice in a novel whose title refers to a Belgian city. Nice is deprived of the Bay of Angels, of the sea, of everything that makes Nice Nice, in fact, in favor of a more urban setting evoking that of Bologna. On the back cover, the author claims to have been born in Nice in 1974. Thus Nice remains Bologna until the end . . . or perhaps not. Internet sites devoted to the author are divided, some saying that Brizzi was born on the Riviera, others saying he was born in Bologna. The storks are lost; romantic places overlap.

The example provided by the novel (and biography) of this Italian "young cannibal" is part of what I would call *heterotopic interference*. When such interference or blurring occurs, the connection between reality and fiction becomes precarious. The referent becomes a springboard from which the fiction launches itself. One might see the referent and its representation entering into an impossible relationship. In *The Fold*, Deleuze distinguishes the *incompossible* and the *impossible* by saying that the former corresponds to a vice-diction and the latter amounts to a contradiction. *Vice-diction* is the mode of utopia. But in this case, it is indeed a contradiction that we are dealing with. Nice and Bologna are not interchangeable. If the spatiotemporal framework of a work is consistent in itself and for itself, and not contradictory, it can still fail in explicit referentiality, becoming a contradiction, a heterotopic space. In *Two Gentlemen of Verona*, Shakespeare transformed the eponymous city into a seaport. Perhaps it was a simple mistake, or perhaps a sign of disdain for the contingencies of real geography. In any event, Verona is not on the shores of the Adriatic, just as Nice does not extend to the interior of the country. When Anna Maria Ortese titled a novel *Il Porto di Toledo* (*The Port of Toledo*), this was no mistake, as she proclaimed the total autonomy of the fictional world with respect to the so-called real world. Indeed, autonomy is relative here, since Toledo is the name of a central district of Naples, around the great thoroughfare, the Via Toledo. But that hardly counts, because, just as Ortese wished, we establish a rough equivalence between the lofty Castilian place and this Toledo. It must be said that this was not the great novelist's first such attempt: earlier she had written *Il mare non bagna Napoli*.

Let us pause here to consider the extensive character of the incompleteness of the world (as in Homer) in order to better see the intensive saturation of the world (in postmodern writing). One begins to furrow new and alternative seas, like Odysseus in his time. The difference then lies in the texture of these seas. Homer had sent his hero on adventures into the farthest reaches of a known world; the postmoderns move their characters in heterotopic worlds, in which the referent is connected in a generally playful way—such that we could have a "port" of Toledo, for instance. The contact of these worlds engenders a defamiliarization analogous to Odysseus's bewilderment when faced with a monster that disrupts the formerly familiar Mediterranean. Yet, although they ought to be incompatible, these spaces are coextensive with each other, or else Aeolus and Polyphemus could not inhabit the same world with Penelope and Nestor.

The modes of this impossibility have been studied in postmodern criticism. In *Postmodernist Fiction*, McHale identifies four strategies of interference between the referent and its representation: juxtaposition, interpolation, superimposition, and misattribution.[84] *Juxtaposition* is used to link known but incongruous spaces: for example, to move from France to Italy, we cross Norway. But this is not all that interesting for literary studies. By the process of *interpolation*, one introduces a space without a referent into the heart of a familiar space. This is what happens with the Poldevia of Queneau, Roubaud, and a few others,[85] a fictional kingdom located somewhere in Central or Eastern Europe, as well as the Ruritania of Anthony Hope, and the Syldavia and Borduria of Hergé, and so on. Interpolation operates, in short, by including a nonreferential space in a much broader space that is referential: Poldevia and Syldavia in the Balkans, Faulkner's Yoknapatawpha County in Mississippi (or more generally "The South"), or the Syrtes of Gracq. In *Le rivage des Syrtes* (in English, *The Opposing Shore*), numerous disturbances of referential space interfere with the reader's orientation. According to Sylviane Coyault, "the novelistic topography here takes part in a real geography, as Syrtes corresponds to the actual Libya; but the directions south/north find themselves inverted, so that the shoreline rather suggests southern Europe. On the opposing shore, Gracq places the hereditary enemy, Farghestan; the place is not really a city on any map, but the toponyms come from existing names (i.e., Farghestan = Pakistan, Turkistan)."[86]

Superimposition, McHale's third strategy, causes the telescoping of two familiar spaces, which generates a third space deprived of any real referent. Just imagine the copresence of the Eiffel Tower and Big Ben in the same city. McHale gives the example of William Blake's *Jerusalem,* in which the poet superimposed British counties and territories onto the tribes of Israel. McHale also mentions Guy Davenport, who, in *Da Vinci's Bicycle,* has coupled the Toledo of Castile—yet again!—with Toledo, Ohio.[87] The duplication of European referents by American pioneers has provided fodder for many literary games. When the Tunisian writer Abdelaziz Belkhodja imagined the action of a detective story, alternating between the ruins of Carthage and an American Carthage, he could choose from nine homonymic places, from Arizona to New York; he chose Carthage, North Carolina. Joyce engaged in a similar process in *Finnegans Wake,* in which he superimposed the Dublin in Georgia, one of eight American Dublins, onto his native Dublin and eventually transformed the Irish capital into the city of the double.[88] But perhaps the best known example is from a film by Wim Wenders, *Paris, Texas.* When Travis (played by Harry Dean Stanton) asks his brother Walt (Dean Stockwell) if he has ever been to Paris, he says no, because he never crossed the Atlantic. Travis then shows Walt a photograph of Paris, *his* Paris: a vast, arid terrain located in the northeastern part of Texas, home to approximately twenty-five thousand people. This town boasts "the second largest Eiffel Tower in the second largest Paris." Indeed, their father's favorite joke was to say that he lived in Paris, then wait a few moments before adding Texas.

There remains a fourth process, *misattribution,* by which one accords an impossible (or at least unlikely) quality to a known location. We have already seen this in Shakespeare (Verona), Ortese (Toledo), and Brizzi (Nice). In an example given by McHale (and Doležel), Ronald Sukenick's novel *98.6,* with its jungle in the heart of Israel, abolishes automotive traffic and reintroduces ancient caravans. Sukenick explains the principle of his novel in a metafictional intervention: "Here in Israel the extraordinary is run-of-the-mill. We are capable of living in a state where certain things that have happened have not. At the same time they have."[89] These various processes are all ways in which the postmodern writer tries to free himself from the yoke of a referent deemed too intrusive. Since the *nouveau roman* and especially since the work of the Oulipo group, we know that one of the tenets of the contemporary moment is to accept, even encourage, this game playing with the constraints of reality. We write better *against* them.

McHale's typology can be refined. Strategies such as transnomination (or *unnaming*) or anachorism seem admissible. *Transnomination* occurs when the author situates the action in a place whose referent is explicit (or named) before undoing the ties that bind it to its representation. In this case, the represented place oscillates between realeme and refutation. Jean Grenier tried to explain this principle in *Islands*: "What is important is to view India not such as she *is* according to Europeans or Indians, in any case an absurd ambition. India must be seen according to the same bias which ruled the way Corneille and Barrès viewed Spain. And in considering India as an *imaginary country* we will come closer to her reality. I would not wish to consider her in any other way."[90] In this case, it is the opposite of homotopia: instead of aiming at verisimilitude of the representation, it deprives the referent of its autonomy, its status as a "model." Illustrations of this strategy are not uncommon. In an epigraph to *The Wages of Fear*, Georges Arnaud warns the reader, "Topographical accuracy is not to be looked for in this book. The Guatemala of the story does not exist. I know; I have lived in Guatemala."[91] The story therefore oscillates inasmuch as the referent is both displayed and evacuated. Henri-Georges Clouzot, who in 1953 made the film version of Arnaud's book, was content to transpose the emblematic town of Las Piedras to the Camargue, without further ado. What is so interesting about this strategy of transnomination? It can be a small and playful bit of theft, or it may be more profound. In his play *Andorra*, Max Frisch stages a parable about anti-Semitism involving local residents of the eponymous place. The young Andri passes for a Jewish boy raised by a local teacher. Andri and Barblin, daughter of the teacher, fall in love and want to marry. The teacher refuses to allow it, but the reasons for the refusal are ambiguous. In fact, Andri was the child of an extramarital relationship that the teacher had with the Señora, a citizen of the powerful neighboring country that eventually invades Andorra. Would the teacher permit the marriage if, instead of the half-brother of Barblin, Andri was actually Jewish? Doubt is hardly allowed, as anti-Semitism has become visceral among the nobles of Andorra. Why has Frisch transposed the action to Andorra, whose name refers to the Pyrenean principality? Perhaps because it is based on a real fact. But his depiction of Andorra bears little relation to the referent: it is certainly a mountainous country, in the process of becoming a republic, but this is intended to mislead the spectator. And indeed the highlight of the play sweeps past the uncertainties: Frisch cautions that the fictional Andorra has nothing to do with the state of the same name, nor with another small mountainous state. Although, as a Swiss native, Frisch would perhaps have preferred to remain neutral, the choice of transnomination retains a real political significance.

In his author's note to *Conversations in Sicily*, Elio Vittorini was quick to point out that Sicily did not exist, or at least that, "just as the protagonist of these Conversations is not the author, so the Sicily in which his story takes place is Sicily only by chance, because I like the sound of the word 'Sicily' better than 'Persia' or 'Venezuela'"; this was chiefly to thumb his nose at fascist hierarchies.[92] It is true that Vittorini's Sicily was more perilous than Frisch's Switzerland. In 1974, on another continent, Robert Kroetsch arrived at the following conclusion: "At one time I considered it the task of the Canadian writer to give names to his experience, to be the namer. I now suspect that, on the contrary, it is his task to un-name."[93] For Kroetsch, as for a whole host of postcolonial writers, referential space is overnamed, saturated with names and with reprehensible realemes; space must be transnominated in order to find a new purity. Transnomination may be a way to fight against the saturation—here the ideological saturation—of the protoworld.

All of the strategies listed thus far blur the simple spatial relationship between referent and representation. But one can also imagine an interference in which the spatial referent is out of step with the temporal standard of measurement. This process is generally retrospective. The author makes a spatial reference in a temporal context that is not historically accurate. We speak of an anachronism but with respect to space, an *anachorism,* which Soja calls an "inappropriate location in space."[94] Thus, in *The Dog King,* Christoph Ransmayr organizes an area without a specific referent, but we guess quickly that this is his native Austria. A war, the Second World War, seems to extend indefinitely, at least well after 1945, in a kind of no man's land where the geology supersedes geography. Gracq had done something similar in *The Opposing Shore,* as noted by Coyault: "Geography blurs historical landmarks and allows the telescoping of at least four periods: the Roman Empire, the Middle Ages, the year 1000, and the twentieth century. Indeed, the author also draws on the 'phony war' of 1939 and the Cold War between the Eastern bloc and the West."[95] When this decoupling carries into the future, one enters into a different regime: that of utopia. We might mention the Los Angeles of 2019 in Ridley Scott's *Blade Runner,* or Franklin J. Schaffner's New York in *Planet of the Apes,* or perhaps the world of Steven Spielberg's *Artificial Intelligence,* and so on. In all these cases, the rigid designator indicates a metropolis that the reader or viewer knows, but now set in the context of an unknown time; one enters the realm of vice-diction. The narrative invalidates any realeme; it sets up a fictional world that reality does not really contradict or has not always contradicted. When, in 1981, John Carpenter made *Escape from New York,* he did not think that the scenario imperiling the life of the President of the United States in 1997 would be impossible. Fortunately for Bill Clinton, by 1997 events had taken a different turn. As for Los Angeles in 2013, as imagined in Carpenter's sequel, *Escape from L.A.,* we will have to wait a bit before we know whether the city will *really* be a penal colony established by a new right-wing government.

Utopian Excursus

After homotopia and heterotopia, we arrive at utopia, whose definitions abound. Utopia is a nonplace, or *ou-topos,* with no rigid designator and not pointing to a referenced space of the world. From a generic point of view, a broad definition has led to a varied typology, incorporating nearly all imaginary places.

They range from eutopic utopias of the ideal city (e.g., *The City of the Sun*) to pure dystopia (e.g., *Nineteen-Eighty-Four*), from science fiction to heroic fantasy to variations of fantasy whose creation of alternative worlds and spaces merits special attention (e.g., *The Lord of the Rings* or *The Neverending Story*). Eco has identified several types of science-fiction worlds: allotopia, utopia, uchronia, metatopia, and metachronia. This taxonomy covers both time and space. To summarize, we could say that *allotopia* portrays a world that is different from the one we are accustomed to (e.g., with talking animals, enchanted fairies, etc.) and replaces it. It is sort of a science-fictional version of the referential interference that McHale calls superimposition. In *utopia*, as Eco uses the term, "one can imagine that the possible world that is described is parallel to ours, but exists in a place that would normally be inaccessible."[96] No longer having a stable link to a real referent, utopia can articulate the representation of another possible world, which in principle is the paragon of all virtues (when it is eutopic). As for *uchronia*, it imagines "what would have happened if what really did happen had happened differently."[97] Eco gives the example of a Julius Caesar not assassinated on the Ides of March. Uchronia, or alternative history, retains a link with the referent and approximates anachorism, as I mentioned a little earlier, in which space is subjected to a process of temporal displacement. For their part, *metatopia* and *metachronia* place the possible world created within the narrative in a future phase of the real world today. We can see this in the cinematic illustrations mentioned previously and in whole swaths of traditional science fiction. These forms also incorporate all the stories—not necessarily science fiction, fantasy, or utopia in the classical sense—that are homotopic if they point to a known referent in the real world or heterotopic if they play around with that referent, but that are neither one nor the other because they designate a nonreferential space in a "realistic" context itself deprived of a referent. We find a number of these spaces in Alberto Manguel and Gianni Guadalupi's *Dictionary of Imaginary Places*, among them the Freedonia that the Marx Brothers depicted in *Duck Soup*; an actual, but presumably unrelated, "Republic of Fredonia" existed for a little over a month in 1826, when Anglo settlers of East Texas (now Nacogdoches) declared independence from the Mexican authorities.

Whereas homotopia implies a compossibility between referential space and its fictional representation, and heterotopia sets the two instances in contradiction to one another, utopia activates an incompossibility, one that does not involve contradiction but rather vice-diction: the narrative unfolds at the margins of the referent or around a projected referent in a derealized future. The sense of novelty arising from the implementation of this contemporary spatiotemporal scheme has several channels of expression. In his *Atlas of the European Novel, 1800–1900*, Franco Moretti questions the specificity of places of reference and places without a referent, and he examines the logic proper to each. After analyzing a Jane Austen novel, he finds that "happy endings" often occur in imaginary places, whereas the complications if the lives of the characters occur more often in "real" places. This conclusion is certainly debatable, but Moretti is prudent enough to avoid begging the question; his analysis is based on plentiful readings and statistical data. In fact, Moretti does not merely identify the different types of relations between represented space and spaces of reference, or the absence of relations between them; he proposes an ontological *distinguo* among different literary spaces. In general, the spatial ontology in the world of fiction is based on its intrinsic polarities: top and bottom, circular or linear, and so forth. In this case, although it continues to evolve in a strictly fictional world, one establishes a link between the utopian (imaginary) representation and the homotopic or heterotopic (real) representation. One can stage this confrontation further by coupling real space and fictional space, as I will attempt to do in the following chapters.

CHAPTER 4

Elements of Geocriticism

A Geocentered Approach

Most issues of spatial analysis in the field of literature focus on the individual's point of view, which, depending on the genre, is the author's or a fictional character's point of view. One might call this an egocentered analysis, since discourse on space is made to serve the discourse on the writer, who becomes the ultimate object of critical attention. For example, only in some of its paradigms does imagology reserve a place for the realeme when examining the representation of a place by a given author. But ultimately, the egocentered logic prevails in imagology because the interpretation of the work, and not of the place, motivates the critical efforts. What is imagology, and what is its contribution to the field of spatial studies? In response to the first question, Jean-Marc Moura provides a succinct definition: it is "the study of representations of the foreign [*l'etranger*] in literature."[1] In fact, this enterprise moves beyond the scope of literature; it requires a grounding in anthropology, sociology, or history. Interdisciplinarity is a sine qua non of imagology. The emerging images produce, according to Daniel-Henri Pageaux, "an awareness, however small it may be, of a Self in relation to an Other, of a Here in relation to an Elsewhere. The image is thus the expression, literary or not, of a significant difference between two orders of cultural reality."[2] We are again confronted with the notion of deviation—this time, however, one that applies not to the relationship between the realeme and its representation, but to the differential relationship between the looker and the looked-upon, between the gazing culture and gazed-at culture. Imagology examines how an author apprehends an environment that is unfamiliar. In considering the clash between the culture that looks and the culture that is looked at, one may examine the representation of space a bit more. But imagological space has a nature of its own. It is not a self-image, since, by definition, it is seen through the eyes of a third party. Space is put into perspective, captured in a "heteroimage": it becomes the place of an otherness that can diminish without truly being overcome. In its imagological conception, space is the space of travel, a viatic space. By the same token, because it is exotic, in the primary sense of the word (meaning "outside"), it is strongly affected by stereotyping. Imagology is therefore hesitant to take into account the referent. As Moura explains, "removing the problem of the referent, [the imagologist] works on the premise that productive imagination (re)creates the foreign through literature."[3] The imagologist prefers to begin with an egocentered plan, built around the views of the author or character (or groups of authors or characters) and their reactions, judgments, and so on when faced with other spaces and their inhabitants. This work is therefore intrinsic to literature. In the end, the imagologist evades the question of the relationship between written space and the referent.

In literature as in other mimetic arts, almost all studies of space tend to limit representation to a field in which the real *in itself* is set aside. Generally, one does not pose the question of the referent, or one finds it better to avoid it. It is true that the correlation between literary representation and geographical referent is understood in a variety of ways. In theories that refuse to connect extrinsic reality and the intrinsic world of narrative, the relationship between the two is uneven. The text, reduced to an ancillary condition, would be judged by how well its representations conform to the modeled reality, such that representation remains a slave to reality. Literature would be subject to reality, so that literary studies would become the random tool of a third discipline that would open it up and steal its soul. However, at the interface of world and text, events take place that are more complex and ambitious (for literature) than merely serving the interests of reality. A rebalancing of the world and literature could even lead to a reversal of the trend (as I will discuss more broadly in the next chapter). The fictional representation of space is likely to exert an influence over the "real," the "reality" of which has been weakened in the postmodern era. In this context, geocriticism finds a place to be most original.

Unlike most literary approaches to space—such as imagology, ecocriticism, or geopoetics (à la Kenneth White)—geocriticism tends to favor a geocentered approach, which places *place* at the center of debate. So, for example, rather than focusing its attention on Lawrence Durrell, the British *author* writing stories whose action is set in a place called Alexandria (in *The Alexandria Quartet*), the geocritic endeavors to explore Alexandria, a place under whose aegis are gathered a series of narratives, like Durrell's and, among many others, those of the French traveler Constantin Volney, who accompanied Napoleon during the Egyptian campaign, or those of the Greek poet Constantine Cavafy, the Greek novelist Stratis Tsirkas, or Edwar al-Kharrat, a Coptic Christian writer from Alexandria. Thus the spatial referent is the basis for the analysis, not the author and his or her work. In a word, one moves from the writer to the place, not the other way around, using complex chronology and diverse points of view. Compared to imagology, the perspective is thus reversed. This apparently simple alternative leads to several significant consequences. We begin by questioning the legitimacy of the reversal. Is a geocentered approach viable? Questions about the nature of the links between the realeme and representation become unavoidable. As long as one accepts the principle of a geocentered approach, one is free to employ a methodology that allows the space to be seen from new angle, an angle that resituates the entire field. The geocritical methodology tends to inscribe space in a mobile perspective. But a new perplexity emerges immediately: What should we think of stereotyping and exoticism in the changing environments that geocriticism attempts to describe? These are a few points to which I will need to return.

Imagological study ignores the question of referent; it concentrates exclusively on the *way* that the writer transcribes the realeme. The represented object is effaced in favor of the subject who does the representing. For Moura, the idea of a mirror image versus the "translation's distortion of reality" image reveals a "false problem."[4] This is certainly true if one assigns priority to the perspective of the writer, of *one* writer in particular. This is even true if one considers the referent to be singular, stable, and thus freed from—as if it has ever really been enslaved to—its representations. But so-called real space is polyphonic and navicular; geocriticism confronts a referent whose literary representation is no longer seen as distorting, but as foundational. Based on the evidence discussed in the preceding chapters, we may assume that the referent and its representation are interdependent and interactive. This relation is dynamic, subject to constant evolution. Geocriticism is not confined to the study of the representation of the Other, perceived in a monological environment. If factual space is transformed into an acceptable referent, a relevant benchmark, it becomes a common denominator for a group of writers. In fact, geocriticism actually continues to assign supremacy to the artist, but it no longer places the artist at the center of the universe. Space is stretched to other areas. It becomes the focal plane, a home (which makes it all the more human). Also, the bipolar relationship between otherness and identity is no longer governed by a single action, but by interaction. The representation of space comes from a reciprocal creation, not simply a one-way activity of a gaze looking from one point to another, without considering other reciprocating gazes (as in Eurocentrism, for example). Geocritical analysis involves the confrontation of several optics that correct, nourish, and mutually enrich each other. Writing of space may always be singular, but the geocritical representation emerges from a spectrum of individual representations as rich and varied as possible.

Take the example of Sicily. In the late eighteenth century, the island described by Goethe in *Italian Journey* or Denon in *Travels in Sicily and Malta* was a virgin territory for modern literature. Some travel narratives had begun to form a cadastre, but the island itself, by an unfortunate coincidence, remained free of major writers after the thirteenth century (and the Sicilian School, which invented the sonnet). For Goethe and even more for Denon, the actuality and contemporaneity of Sicily was conjured away. The island seemed always and forever stuck in antiquity. Sicily has since been the subject of narratives by t'Serstevens, Fernandez, and Durrell. It was no longer legitimate for these authors to ignore the present and the literary production of the island. Sicily in the meantime became a space well known through the prestigious works of Verga, Pirandello, and Quasimodo, the last two both Nobel laureates, as well as those of Vittorini, Brancati, Tomasi di Lampedusa, Sciascia, Bufalino, and others. Like Denon, Durrell felt a predilection for antiquity. Like him, he cited the classics, in one passage expressing regret that Stendhal had abandoned Sicily in favor of Rome or Naples in providing a walking guide. But contrary to Denon, Durrell situated this in the *local* literary context: "There would probably have been a good Sicilian candidate also, but our ignorance of the island's letters was abysmal."[5] In an imagological approach, we would record this confession and would move on to the next work of Durrell. However, for the geocritical approach, we can locate this declaration of Durrell's within a network of literary representations of Sicily. It soon becomes clear that the ignorance displayed by Durrell was hardly shared by his peers. Visitors no longer remained oblivious to the flows of Sicilian literature. Similarly, Sicilians (and Sicilian writers) often discover themselves in the look and in the writing of others. Therefore, alterity ceases to be the preserve of a gazing culture, because the latter is itself subject to the gaze of others. All representation is thus treated in a dialectical process. By taking a geocritical perspective, we opt for a plural point of view, which is located at the crossroads of distinct representations. In this way, we contribute to the process of determining a common space, born from and touching upon different points of view. Also, we come closer to the essential identity of the referenced space. At the same time, we confirm that any cultural identity is only the result of incessant efforts of creation and re-creation. This conclusion establishes one of the methodological tenets of geocriticism: *multifocalization* of views on a given referential space.

Another series of elements, by nature conjectural, argues in favor of a geo-centered approach. A study devoted entirely to the point of view of an author or group of authors is of course legitimate. But such critical practices often exclude another approach that, instead of limiting itself to a canon at the heart of the literary field, occupies the borders, examining the interface between literature and the margins. Omitting this interface leads to a posture in which the separation between literature and the world is possible, even sanctioned. This attitude is often that of a Westerner, for whom the literary and spatial universes are relatively stable and distinct, such that they can be clearly demarcated and separated. The split is relativized, however, as the distance from the center grows, as the field of postcolonial studies has demonstrated. Recent decades have witnessed a reconstitution, or even a reelaboration, of spaces not only in the former colonies but also in most countries in Central and Eastern Europe and those nations whose contours have resisted the onslaught of history (in its tragic version, incarnated as colonialism, wars, and so on). In the European context, literary works calling for an alternative geography have proliferated, hence a renewed interest in forgotten parts of the former Austro-Hungarian Empire. Galicia, which now extends to both sides of the Polish–Ukrainian border, and Bukovina, divided between Romania and Ukraine, have aroused the curiosity of many writers and critics recently. If, originally, these countries were political entities, they have reclaimed their fame under the pen of writers. Bukovina has been reintegrated into the European cultural horizon thanks to the renown of Karl Emil Franzos, Paul Celan, Rose Ausländer, Gregor von Rezzori, and others who came from Chernivtsi, the historic capital of the former province of the empire, now elevated to literary heights. Its neighboring Galicia has been the object of similar enthusiasm after it was linked to Joseph Roth and other writers from this region, which had been erased from official maps.

For example, at the heart of Central Europe, a place occupied for centuries by certain unrecognized minorities has recently been highlighted on literary maps. In *Voyages au bout de l'Europe*, Karl-Markus Gauss explored a European *ultima tellus* that extends—or is reduced—to southern Italy, eastern Germany, western Macedonia, the center of Slovenia, and downtown Sarajevo (referring respectively to the Albanian-speaking Arbëreshë people of Calabria, the Slavophone Sorbs in Brandenburg and Saxony, the Aromanians who speak neo-Latin in the region of Bitola, the German-speaking Gottscheens in Kočevje, and Sephardic Jews in Bosnia who perpetuate a form of the Old Castilian language, that of the ancestral city of the former victims of Queen Isabella the Catholic). In Europe over the last few decades, one sees a proliferation of texts of this kind, to the point that a new generic category has appeared on the literary scene: "geographic fiction," which falls somewhere in the range of travelogue, biography or autobiography, and fictional narrative. The milestone of this new genre could be *Danube*, in which Claudio Magris, floating down the eponymous river from its source to its delta, and swimming through the tales that its banks have inspired, has identified a litany of "river" stories in which literature, history, and geography interact on equal terms. New maps were drawn in Europe after the collapse of the Berlin Wall and, on a smaller scale, through the European Union's more or less successful promotion of minorities. Also, in Africa and much of the world, maps have taken new shapes in the wake of decolonization, and similarly, in Australia and parts of the New World, following the belated recognition of the indigenous peoples silenced or put to death by the first generations of European pioneers. All of these phenomena are rather recent, in the light of History (with a capital *H*). Literature remains a vector of counterhegemonic speech deeply rooted in culture and geography. "Writing," says Andrzej Stasiuk, "is the enumeration of names. It is where the thread of life collects the geographical pearls."[6] Of course, along this voyage, the line between the referent and its representation tends to be erased. It is this interface, explained by the cultural evolution over recent decades of postmodernism, that geocriticism intends to explore.

If postmodernism is the seat of a counterhegemonic discourse, it is so in more ways than one. This is because it depicts a weakened reality that grand narratives, in Jean-François Lyotard's sense, find difficult to define. In this somewhat floating environment, the distance between what we call the real and representation (or what would be called the fictional) is reduced. The benchmark loses its visibility; sometimes it is barely perceptible. The postmodern era corresponds to a postpositivist age, when certainties about the nature, content, and limits of reality have faded. Therefore, the barriers between the real and fictional or mimetic tend to fall. This is indeed a novelty, but a relative novelty. In spatial matters, let us recall that the ancient Greeks applied the same coefficient of reality (or unreality) to what we understand as geography and literature, and they did not distinguish between the two. This refers to the argument some critics make that any analysis based on linking the fictional representation to the referent is futile or misguided. Ultimately, this argument is admissible: by refusing to grant literature the role of the surveyor of the real, we only do justice to it, since we are saying that literature is *better* than that. In a nutshell, however, this argument is dubious. It assumes that the break between fiction and reality is straightforward, that fiction is divested of any representational power. But when we invoke the interaction between the two instances, this argument falls. Insofar as fiction is written in the world, it takes on the double faculty both to report reality and, at the logical extreme, to exert influence over reality, or, more precisely, over the representation of reality. Does reality exist outside of the variable, non-Euclidian geometry of its multiple representations? In this sense, adopting a geocentered approach amounts to arguing that literary representation is included in the world, in an enlarged reality, and in infinitely adjustable space that is in direct contact with a plurality of discourses. Geocriticism studies a concept that comes in many different forms (interface, connection, etc.), but forms that all lead the researcher to identify the interactive boundaries and to accord to them a nonmarginal status.

Parenthetically, I might say that geocriticism also brings together a series of representations of the Other, an Other to be embraced in its relation to the space within which it operates. Even if the researcher continued to focus strongly on the individual "consciousness imagining the other,"[7] there is no doubt that if the space is perceived and represented by more than one writer, it will be recentered (thus, geocentered). The spatial object of individual, subjective representation can then become the subject of the study. Several categories of referents are identifiable. The most immediate is the geographical reference deemed "real." Since the geocritical approach is geocentered and multifocal, it is essential that the artistic transcription is integrated into an image determined by the referent. The moment that the "writing" of a place is circumscribed by a single author, we return to the egocentered form of imagological analysis. That the representation of a given realeme would be isolated, and thus not representative, is all the more likely because the vast majority of places on this planet have been transcribed into texts more than once. There are some places seductive enough to have generated hundreds or thousands of artistic representations (e.g., New York, London, Africa, Japan, the Danube, the Caribbean, and on and on). On a different scale, the case of Santa Lucia di Siniscola, mentioned in Chapter 3, shows how the text abounds with relations to the realeme, even if its prestige is relatively limited. From a methodological perspective, the Sardinian example indicates that the first problem that geocritical enterprise must resolve lies in the scattering of sources. Collecting a sufficiently documentary base is sometimes hard. It is uncommon that artistic works are categorized according to the realemes they explore. Databases organized around spatial criteria are rare indeed. Indices that associate a work with a place are far less common than dictionaries of characters, for example. The Internet certainly helps, but a great deal of patience, and a certain amount of scholarship, will be indispensible in forming a corpus necessary for a fully geocritical analysis. To find out what real places André Gide represented in his books, reading a good monograph may suffice. However, it will prove less easy to put together a corpus of texts in which the action revolves around the Congo, Chad, and the Vatican. Allow me to close this parenthesis temporarily.

In their diversity, real referents abound: cities, islands, archipelagos, countries, mountains, rivers, lakes, seas, straits, peninsulas, deserts, continents, poles, and so forth. The variety of paradigms is considerable, such that geocriticism could devote all of its activity to any one of them. But the realeme is not always located in the sensory reality of the world, because the world is divided—at least in the universe of fiction—into a plurality of possible worlds in terms of representation. When transcribed in the literary text, the referent determines a particular world. If, in the traditional hypothesis, the referent is rooted in the *true* world, it also happens that the referent is outside the *real* world, somewhere in the text or in a series of texts. In other words, it becomes permissible to identify a referent in an intertextual chain that will be consolidated over time and across many different books (or paintings, or films, etc.). Examples abound. In *The Dictionary of Imaginary Places*, Manguel and Guadalupi make an inventory of several hundred places, but they forget two that are close to my own heart: Ruritania and Poldevia, imaginary places connoting the Balkans, examples of *interpolation*. Invented by British novelist Anthony Hope in *The Prisoner of Zenda*, Ruritania was then destined for a Hollywood career (thanks to three popular films). In 1929, in France, Ruritania became the model of "Poldevia" in an article by a journalist of Action Française, a hoax in poor taste aimed at discrediting several socialist and radical parliamentarians. A dozen years later, in wartime, Marcel Aymé took his lead from this fascist newspaper by situating one of his short stories in Poldevia, but then, after the Liberation, Poldevians made a Left turn with Queneau, Roubaud, and Perec, who all three imagined Poldevian characters. Poldevia does not exist in reality as described by a geography understood as an exact science, but it does exist in fictional texts. A referent has ended up forming a remarkably long intertextual chain. A geocentered approach is therefore conceivable, even with respect to the geocriticism of Poldevia, which could in various ways flesh out the interface between the reality and fiction of the Balkan referent, interpolated and concealed in the background of the text. It could also isolate the stereotypes that make it possible to reproduce a country in a ludic register.

Ruritania and Poldevia are not extraordinary cases, far from it. Under a somewhat different scheme of things, that of Plato's Atlantis, several referents may be found at the intersection of geology and mythology, of reality and fiction, more or less recognizable. One could therefore undertake a geocriticism of Atlantis. It would be more surprising to opt for a geocriticism of Lemuria, the mythical resurgence of a lost southern continent containing what is now Madagascar and the Mascarene Islands. As noted by Michel Beniamino,[8] Lemuria was imagined in the late nineteenth century by the Réunionnais writer Jules Hermann, before gaining the favor of the great Mauritian author Malcolm de Chazal, Boris Gamaleya (another Réunion poet), and several of their colleagues. We can go even further than Lemuria, if we choose, and allow ourselves to get lost in interstellar space. At the interface between the real and imaginary, derealized mythic elements can capture a poorly mapped (or even still virgin) space and are deployed in territories properly explored by science fiction. Going there is not all that different from going to the spaces of this world: some places are provided with a geographical referent that can be reduced to eventual representation, while others have been invented from whole cloth or derive in some cases from exclusively intertextual sources. A geocriticism of Mars or of the moon is certainly conceivable, although, to satisfy the criterion of multifocalization, we may have to wait for the discovery of the first texts written on green Martian paper or for early films shot aboard flying saucers. In any event, geocriticism is relevant whenever a geocentered and multifocalized approach is conceivable. This implies that certain thematic entities, even those without explicit toponymic referents, can enter the jurisdiction of the geocritic; for example, one could examine "the desert" or "the archipelago" without limiting oneself to a particular *named* desert or archipelago. Such analyses would necessarily be abstract, taking a more general turn. In a geocritical optic, they might serve as theoretical frameworks for studies of more specific geographical referents. In my view, however, the study of nongeographical places—intimate, domestic spaces, for example, so admirably described by Gaston Bachelard in *The Poetics of Space*—does not fall within the field of geocriticism. Geocriticism finds its natural applications in studying artistic representations of geographical referents, the oscillations of which have been described in the previous chapter.

An Interdisciplinary Approach

These considerations lead me back to the debate over interdisciplinarity and to the question of genre. In the "weakened" context of the postmodern, the impact of generic categories is lessened. Is the representation of human space radically different in a work of pure fiction from that presented in a travel narrative? Answering this question leads us to consider a particular aspect of the link between the referent and its representation, probably the least interesting aspect: the relative degree of verisimilitude of the representation—potentially high in strict reportage, medium in a travelogue, and low in a purely fictional story. Such gradations seems to me irrelevant. It is akin to the wheel of Virgil and the tripartite styles. If the intersection between representational verisimilitude and surreptitious fictionality is mobile, and if representational modes vary, then represented space is identical to itself, albeit in different phases of engagement with the processes affecting it. From the postmodern perspective, the border between genres conveying a given spatial representation remains unclear. As Pageaux points out, "the travel writer, by the very fact that he writes, becomes a storyteller [*affabuler*]."[9] Storytelling [*l'affabulation*] is coextensive with travel writing; it is coextensive with all writing. Recognized or not, it informs representation and posits the space that writing resimulates. Human space corresponds to the versatile ensemble of representations that are constructed and reconstructed, regardless of the nature of their genres. Transgeneric heterogeneity points to a more diffuse heterogeneity, one that relates to the taxonomy of knowledge, as seen in the division of disciplinary fields.

Conscious of the dangers of too rigid a compartmentalization, the scientific world, which ought to include the literary theorist as well, has sought to reduce the fragmentation of knowledge by developing interdisciplinary strategies. Interdisciplinarity can be understood in several ways, depending on circumstances as well as on one's audacity. Literary scholarship often views it in the narrow sense, which leads to the variations of aesthetic domains (e.g., links between literature and cinema, literature and photography, and so on). Thus understood, interdisciplinarity is at the center of a well-established comparative practice. But interdisciplinarity in literary studies can be approached differently, outside of and beyond affinities between aesthetic domains. The reflection will carry over to possible parallels between literature and social sciences, even (at its maximum extension) between literature and "exact" or "hard" sciences. The effects are numerous. For example, one could consider literary theory not a "soft" science but a flexible science. The excursus into other disciplines occupies a prominent place in comparative research. The discipline crossing is superficial when the researcher merely questions the links between literature and, for example, physics, limiting his research to a literary medium (or text) and a no less exclusively literary methodology. For instance, if the study is organized around the "theme" of physics in a novelistic or dramatic corpus, this is only slightly interdisciplinary. But aside from this, there is a conception of interdisciplinarity that deals with methodology at some times and with subject matter at others. In this case, literary studies either uses a theoretical framework that is not inherent to its discipline or uses sources outside of the field of literature, or both. What is the place and role of geocriticism here? The answer varies. At the first level of interdisciplinarity, geocritical analysis could follow a thematic approach, looking at the themes of geography and the geographer, the map and the mapmaker, the landscape and the surveyor, and so on. But, although it may lead to interesting results, this approach is not, strictly speaking, geocritical. Geocriticism explores two other paths that themselves lead beyond the purely literary.

The first of these may involve examining several forms of mimetic art in a single study of spatial representation. For example, cinematic representations of a given space might lie at the heart of a geocritical approach. A geocritical study of contemporary Lisbon would be incomplete without the films of Alain Tanner (*Dans la ville blanche*), Wim Wenders (*Lisbon Story*), or Manoel de Oliveira. But it is not only film that has a memorable effect, although it clearly establishes an idea of the place in the immediacy of the moving image. There are also photography, painting, computer graphics, and so forth. What would a geocriticism of Rome in the eighteenth century be without the *vedute* announcing the *Ruinenromantik*? What would a contemporary geocriticism of Venice be without photographs by Fulvio Roiter, who contributed to the carnivalization of the City of Doges? Or San Francisco without the hyperrealistic paintings of Robert Bechtle? The inventory is endless. Geocriticism augments (in part) and structures (a bit) the intersection between different arts that evoke material reality and the spatiotemporal coordinates used in creating an aesthetic representation.

The second path leads further into the field of interdisciplinarity, leading geocritics to reflect on both what methodologies and what sources to use. Geocriticism is based in the field of literary studies, more specifically comparative literature, but it is often driven by the desire to mobilize distinct but compatible methodologies. Imagology also takes that approach, as does sociopoetics (à la Alain Montandon), not to mention the often successful overlapping of general and comparative literature in cultural studies or gender studies. Sociology, anthropology, and psychology regularly enter into close proximity with literary theory. It is the same with geography, although the relationship is sometimes more problematic. In geocriticism, this connection is fundamental, however, as both the methodology developed in cultural geography and human space provide fertile soil for new readings. Many a geographer has had recourse to literary texts and to literary theory, and the literary scholar would benefit from research in geography, as we will discuss in the following sections. It will suffice here to mention the various and promising applications of *sensuous geography* in the areas of literature concerned with polysensoriality. As for philosophy, it supports geocritical reasoning each time it puts the world in a mobile and dynamic perspective that makes space an entity with a thousand faces, a perspective that literature can certainly appreciate.

Does geocriticism engage in extraliterary criticism, or, in any case, with categories outside of those traditionally associated with an interdisciplinary approach to literature? In other words, would geocriticism venture into textuality or iconicity where the aesthetic is subordinated to other performative criteria? I am referring, for example, to nonliterary sources for the textuality of space, including tourist guides and the advertising rhetoric of travel brochures. Nothing is wrong with this, unless one wishes to limit the literary field by what the Russian formalists called *literaturnost* (literariness). We perceive a distinction, however, explained by the presence of literary or artistic elements in the nonliterary text or nonartistic image that serves communicative purposes. It seems to me that here is sketched a boundary separating geocriticism from semiology or semiotics. If these two disciplines disclose that all texts and images have a phatic and performative function, a geocritical approach examines texts and images with respect to the ultimate goal, although it is not necessarily aesthetic, of depicting an artistic referent. How many Greek taverns have taken their name from *Zorba the Greek*, without explicitly referring to Alexis Zorba, the novel by Nikos Kazantzakis, or the film by Michael Cacoyannis? How many hotels and tourist facilities on the shores of the Mediterranean are placed under signs of Homer and Virgil? Nausicaa, Calypso, Dido, and Aeneas are veteran protagonists in new epics designed by tour guides, those small-footed gods of Olympus desecrated. But this trip is postponed. For now, it seems more urgent to discuss the methodology of geocriticism.

The different aspects of geocriticism are contained *in nuce* in the premises of spatiotemporality, transgressivity, and referentiality. The specificity of geocriticism lies in the attention it pays to a place. The study of the viewpoint of an author or of a series of authors, which inevitably posits a form of identity, will be superseded in favor of examining a multiplicity of heterogeneous points of view, which all converge in a given place, the primum mobile of the analysis. A multifocal dynamic would be required for this analysis. Without hesitation, I would say that multifocalization is the chief characteristic of geocriticism. The multiplication of points of view renders all the more visible the sensory perception, or sensual perception, that the authors have of space. When one writes, paints, or films, one inscribes the text into a scheme that is visual, olfactory, tactile, or auditory, a scheme whose extreme variability (as has already been noted by geographers and semiologists) is narrowly determined by the point of view. Since polysensoriality is thus a quality of all human spaces, it is up to the geocritic to take a fresh look, to listen attentively, and to be sensitive to the sensory vibrations of a text and other representational media. Multifocalization and polysensoriality can be considered in synchronic slices, but they will become more memorable as the space evolves over time, slowly at some times and quickly at others. The flux of space in time, which we have observed depends on its transgressivity, is another mainstay of geocritical investigation. Because space only exists in its temporal strata, geocriticism will have an archaeological—or better, stratigraphic—vocation. This diachronic delving, more or less deep, affects the relationship of the text to the referent: it is the re-presentation occurring a second time that aesthetically captures something that already exists. This "something" could be a realeme in its proper sense (the referent available from sensory reality), but it can also be an aesthetic referent (a text, still image, or film). In other words, the spatiotemporal stratigraphy in its aesthetic variation can be informed by the extension of an intertextual (or intericonic) chain. The imaginary Poldevia is an illustration of this principle, as are the novels of Italo Svevo in their literary representations of Trieste, a city that is already located on the map. Future developments will be articulated around the four cardinal points of the geocritical approach: multifocalization, polysensoriality, stratigraphy, and intertextuality.

Multifocalization

The gaze [*regard*] channels a perception that, according to Pierre Ouellet, corresponds to the "implementation of a spatializing and temporalizing imaginative activity."[10] The history of the gaze is the story of subjectivity, expressing the relationship of the individual to a world that resists objective determination. This is the story of the wonder that takes hold of the individual in the face of the Other; it is the story of the confrontations between the *hic et nunc* of a being immersed in a referential context and the *hic et nunc* outside the circle of the familiar, outside the perceptual field. The gaze, again according to Ouellet, triggers a "process of world making [*mondification*]."[11] It helps build a possible world, one of the many worlds that we coordinate in order to have a society. Is the gaze an overture? That is a question difficult or impossible to answer. Odysseus opened up a world of discovery, but was that what he wanted to do? If you believe François Hartog, it is dubious: "Odysseus, an unwilling traveler, dogged by Poseidon's hatred, was in the last analysis in quest of no Absolute; he was not even particularly curious about the world . . . All Odysseus, for his part, could dream of was getting back to what was familiar to him."[12] For Odysseus, the goal of navigation was homecoming. To the extent that we continue to agree with Hartog, who himself drew upon Emmanuel Levinas,[13] we must admit that the Greeks had two concerns: to occupy a center upon which the Other, if not avoided altogether, would not encroach; and to have other Greeks as interlocutors (and, in any case, those who could not understand the language were called "barbarians").

It is not my intention to write a history of the gaze. However, it must be noted that the criteria have changed little over the centuries. The gaze continues to fall on the Other, carrying astonishment, dismay, or indifference, and feeding a discourse exclusively used by the Same. Sometimes the voyeuristic gaze lingers on the spectacle of otherness, to gauge or to judge unworthy, and thus to claim a pretext for legitimating speech destined to reduce the Other to the Same. That is the gaze of the colonizer. It reinforces the traditional bipolarity. A subject, always the Same, observes an object, always the Other; a gazing culture focuses on a gazed-upon culture whose status as a "culture" is most often found to be minor or inferior. In literature, the adaptation of this most systematic form of cultural binarism operates in the travel narrative. A gaze falls on a space rendered exotic. This gaze is Western or Northern, since the dominant exoticism moves from north to south, from west to east. How many African writers voyaged to France or Great Britain during the first half of the twentieth century? How many French or British have traveled to Africa during this period? It is needless to engage in scholarly statistics, since the result is known beforehand. Gide, Conrad, or Duras (in *The Sailor from Gibraltar*) captured a portion of the Congo River. I know of no Congolese texts supporting a similar journey up the Loire or the Thames in the same period. Maybe I am misinformed. It is true that we do not even have written evidence of a Congolese traveler's journey up the Congo River at that time. The text was the exclusive property of one society—Western society—which arrogated to itself the monopoly of the transcribed gaze. This situation has evolved after the Second World War. One immediate consequence was the acceleration of the process of decolonization.

Other factors have contributed to disrupting the hierarchies of the gaze as well. The relativization of the relation between center and periphery has encouraged the affirmation of the female perspective and that of a large group of ethnic, religious, and sexual minorities. This affirmation, which in some cases was an emergence, resulted in multiculturalism and its profusion of voices and gazes, which were not necessarily new but were finally taken into account. In his manifesto, Guillermo Gómez-Peña articulates this movement: "Experimenting with the fringes between art and society, between legalidad and illegality, English and español, male and female, North and South, self and other; and subverting these relationships . . . to speak from the crevasse, desde acá, desde el medio. The border is the juncture, not the edge, and monoculturalism has been expelled to the margins."[14] Gómez-Peña is a *Spanglish* writer and performance artist (a self-styled "border artist") of the border between Mexico and the United States. This massive diversification, which one imagines is unprecedented in the history of ideas and cultures and which is audible in countless voices, led to an aesthetics of postmodernism, an authentic receptacle for counterhegemonic discourses and the place in the arts for third space.

The overcoming of bipolarism has been discussed at length. As bell hooks writes, "we begin the process of re-vision"[15] of the synoptic view that the long history of the West had imposed and based on misleading evidence. The synoptic, universal view reflected neither more nor less than the focal monopoly of the West. On behalf of an indispensable, multicultural reading of the world, writers have attacked what Gloria Anzalúa called the "tyranny of Western aesthetics"[16] or *ethnocentrism,* the term popularized beginning in the 1960s. There was a time not so long ago when the concept of ethnocentrism was unrecognizable to Europeans. In *Inventing America,* José Rabasa denounced the Eurocentrism of Mercator; the accusation was just, but in vain. The Dutch cartographer did not realize that one could consider the world from an angle different from that of a European. Also, the very word *European* was forged barely a century before his global mapmaking enterprise. It is sometimes possible, however, to reverse points of view. In *The Persians,* the earliest Greek tragedy whose text has been preserved, Aeschylus allows the Persians to narrate their defeat at Salamis. In truth, this permutation was artificial. The account of those vanquished at Salamis may as well have been presented by the spokesman of the Athenian victors, inasmuch as it reproduced the Persian speech and worldview with sometimes touching, but rather disconcerting, clumsiness. Ethnocentrism derives from the homologation of points of view. In a society in which mobility is minimal, a single perspective may be shared by a (large) majority of players, to the point of becoming "natural" and closing off any alternative view. This aspect has been made more visible in the face of accelerated popular migrations, which certainly began in the nineteenth century but have become more acute in the context of decolonization. Literature and other forms of mimetic art have dramatized this process. During the modernist period, which we generally agree ended with World War II, this alterity (the voice and view of the Other) is registered mainly in travel narratives. From the postwar period, and especially starting in the 1960s, the Other would speak to and from the heart of the previously dominant cultures. Men and women from the former colonies—or, more generally, from regions of the planet considered peripheral—could give free rein to *alternative* cultural expression, even under conditions (linguistic, generic, etc.) of "acculturation." Thus were born the works of a Salman Rushdie or a Hanif Kureishi in Great Britain, a Linda Lê or a Patrick Chamoiseau in France, or a Jakob Arjouni in Germany. The person who had been "gazed upon" for decades, even centuries, suddenly began to look at the "gazing" tradition, even on its own territory somewhere between deterritorialization and reterritorialization, launching a cultural revival.

However, the overcoming of cultural binarism is not exclusively a phenomenon that accompanies the process of decolonization and the movement of peoples. It was helped by the belated recognition of feminine discourse and that of sexual minorities. In an article proposing a feminist geocriticism of a particular quarter of Paris, Amy Wells raises the question of "a geo-*parler femme* that analyzes how geography can function as one of the codes used to create a female literary language."[17] The example chosen is the rue Jacob, the place inhabited in the 1930s by Djuna Barnes, Natalie Barney, Radclyffe Hall, and some of the outstanding novelists of the American diaspora in Paris, whose "act of writing establishes a female Parisian geography, which is often coded *femme* through female or lesbian sexual experiences or meanings."[18] The multiplication of points of view is also the result (or cause) of postmodern decanonization. While the hierarchy of point of view has been challenged by the end of the colonial era, the canonical scheme that gave precedence to Western productions has been altered by the postmodern aesthetic imposed upon parts of the world. We observe the simultaneous emergence of the postcolonial and the postmodern, which in some cases are combined. Placing themselves in Lyotard's wake, Bill Ashcroft, Gareth Griffiths, and Helen Tiffin have explained the conjunction by showing how the postmodern practice of deconstruction of the centralized, logocentric narrative shattered the Western image at the same moment that postcolonial forces were dismantling the center periphery binary that had supported the imperialist worldview.[19] In both cases, there has been questioning of the hierarchical relationship between the central reference point (dominant discourse) and the creative manifestations of the margin (counterhegemonic discourse). This redistribution has resulted in a significant diversification of views in a setting where, now that straightforward ethnocentrism no longer has legitimacy, the focus has ceased to be monopolized by only one group.

If we approach the issue from a different angle, that of phenomenology, one wonders about the nature and scope of the unique, monofocal gaze. According Eugen Fink, in his patient studies of the issue of *representation* (*Vergegenwärtigung*) and the image (*Bild*), "every position in the infinity open to the phenomenological problematic is by eidetic necessity a simplification (*Vereinseitigung*)."[20] Of course, *Vereinseitigung* is not only a simplification: it is a "unilateralization," a monofocal reduction. This reduction stems from the double impossibility of seeing space in its totality (this totality would be simply referred to as angle of view) and of experiencing the cohesion of the moment, which is accomplished "in a multiplicity of states of impression" and which, from a perspective of retention, corresponds to an "archi-impression."[21] Representation then is only a re-presentation—a result not only of the present moment but also of the place. With this view, one moves a good distance away from the absolute objectivity to which the ethnocentric gaze aspired. "There are almost as many worlds as eyes," writes Roger Munier,[22] poet and translator of Heidegger, in a verse quoted and commented upon by Ouellet. Without taking any chances, we could also say that there are as many worlds as there are narrations, because, as Rossana Bonadei recalls in an essay on the tourist's point of view, "The gaze is intertextual; it is built over time through various processes of differentiation and assimilation, and it brings together many texts that the mind and the imagination have joined to the space."[23]

These brief remarks on the essential incompleteness of the gaze show how an imagological or egocentered approach, precisely because it focuses on the subjectivity of the artist, is necessarily limited. Multifocalization is more meaningful in a geocritical, geocentered context. Derived from only a single source, the knowledge of a given space will be restricted, as the view of a single person, and thus less valuable. If confined to the study of a single text or a single author, geocriticism becomes lopsided. Outside of a network of perspective, we run the risk of generalization. But the goal is neither to present the psychology of a people nor to reinforce more or less tenacious stereotypes, but rather to banish them. Once one breaks away from the unitary work of a singular reticulated vision, the question of the corpus becomes crucial. It should first establish the threshold at which works acquire sufficient distance to apprehend the stereotypes with clarity. The calculation of this threshold of "representativeness" is obviously aleatory; it is not an objective arithmetic. The principle is simple: we will introduce a measure between the prestige of the observed or represented space and the number and variety of observers needed to cross this minimal threshold. Thus, to use an example from my own work, a wide-angle geocriticism of the Dalmatian islands is conceivable, though literary references are abundant only for the twentieth century.[24] However, there are those places that are themselves artistically mythic: Venice, Paris, London, New York, and Rome, just to name a few. To attempt to undertake a full-scale geocritical analysis of these hotspots would be madness. Thus it is essential to limit the corpus. To narrow the scope of the study, for example, one might add a temporal variable. In any event, it is clear that multifocalization requires a reticular arrangement of a certain number and a wide variety of viewpoints.

For many, reaching the "the threshold of representativeness" may just be determined on a case-by-case basis, ad libitum. For the sake of variety, one should respect the principle that, in the words of Paolo Zaccaria, "points of view do not exclude each other, but can coexist, cooperate, and be accomplices."[25] In *Figures III*, Gérard Genette conducted a classic study of the concept of point of view *within* the text, an approach similar to that described by Oswald Ducrot and Tzvetan Todorov in their *Encyclopedic Dictionary of the Sciences of Language*, which (like Genette's book) was published in 1972, at the height of the structuralist period: "*Point of view* refers to the relationship between narrator and represented universe. The category is thus tied to the representational arts (fiction, figurative painting, cinema; to a lesser degree theater, sculpture, architecture)."[26] Here, focalization is regarded in its narratological sense, as intrinsic to the (autoreferential) text—because, remember, in this environment, there is no outside of the text. If we reintroduce the extrinsic relation between the text and the context (heteroreferentiality), focalization can be viewed in different ways. For Genette, the problem of referentiality does not arise; one is therefore limited to plain text, described as *autotelic*, that has no relationship to a world outside the text's own representation. Because this issue of referentiality does intervene into geocritical analysis, the typology of focal categories is significantly more complicated, since one must first understand the point of view of the author who perceives the world subject to his or her own cultural inscriptions, and then one must identify the different modes of representation (re-presentation) of that point of view in the work. Therefore, one must question the link between authorial perception on the one hand and artistic representation on the other.

Different perspectives opened up by discourses that establish the relationship between the subject and the world have been explored in semiotics by Jacques Fontanille, who has theorized, among other things, a semiotics of passion. In this comprehensive theory, the division of language (into the *plane of content* and the *plane of expression*) is equivalent to the partition between the interior, *interoceptive* world and the exterior, *exteroceptive* world—the opposition between the two being resolved by the body that appears as an agent of *proprioceptive* reunion.[27] Moving between levels of perception and representation, psycholinguistics is also interested in the theory of point of view. By way of illustration, here is the schema proposed by Michel Metzeltin that examines the representation of Romanians (A) in their relations with other Europeans (B) through the example of journalistic statements:

1. A is presented to A in a certain way (interior self-representation).
2. A according to B is presented to A in a certain way (refracted self-representation).
3. A is presented to B in a certain way (exterior self-presentation).
4. A according to A is presented to B in a certain way (heteropresentation according to the presenter).
5. A according to B is presented to B some way (heteropresentation according to the one to whom it is presented).[28]

In many ways, this typology is seductive, but it seems to me only moderately operative in the context of geocriticism. Literary narrative, in contrast to some journalistic reports, only marginally grants "textuality an identifying function,"[29] which poses the question of the audience. If there is a presentation, it must be presented to someone, but to whom? The audience of a book is not always known. The model reader (or the implied reader) is usually an abstraction, notwithstanding Umberto Eco's sketch of one in *The Role of the Reader*. In fact, this restriction is itself flexible. As Gabriele Zanetto has announced, "The geography of Uruguay, for an Italian audience, will not—and could not!—be the same as the one offered to an Argentinean reader."[30] And that, every writer already knows.

In a geocritical sense, multifocalization is expressed in three basic variations. The point of view is relative to the situation of the observer with respect to the space of reference. The observer engages with this space through a number of relations ranging from those of intimacy or familiarity to those that are more or less absolutely foreign. This reflects the fact that the point of view alternates between endogenous, exogenous, or allogeneous characters. The endogenous point of view characterizes an autochthonic vision of space. Normally resistant to any exotic view, it limits itself to familiar space. For instance, this might describe the point of view of Mohammed Mrabet or Tahar Ben Jelloun in their representations of Tangier. The exogenous point of view, however, reflects the vision of the traveler; it exudes exoticism. Tangier is seen from the exogenous point of view of a Morand, of a Genet, and of all those American representatives of the Beat Generation (such as Lawrence Ferlinghetti, Jack Kerouac, and Allen Ginsberg) who, during the 1950s, made a stopover in the international city. Finally, the allogeneous point of view lies somewhere between the other two. It is characteristic of those who have settled into a place, becoming familiar with it, but still remaining foreigners in the eyes of the indigenous population. In Tangier, such is the case of Paul Bowles, a native New Yorker who established a split between the Atlantic and the Mediterranean throughout the second half of the twentieth century, from 1947 when he moved to Tangier until his death in 1999. Of the three types of focalization, the most widely discussed was always the exogenous point of view, which dominates the travel narrative (whether fictional or not), a genre with enduring appeal to literary theorists. A good many comparative analyses have been devoted to the genre, by imagology in particular; to mention only one example, Christine Montalbetti has analyzed the dangerous liaisons among travel, the world, and the library. One becomes interested here in the tropes of otherness, the lexicon of defamiliarization, the reproduction in the second degree (*mise en abyme*) of indigenous speech, and so on. The exogenous point of view is privileged by those who adopt the egocentered perspective of the author. In a geocritical study, the three points of view will be taken into account at the same level, in the play of their interactions.

This tripartite division could certainly be refined further. One could also broaden the theoretical examination of relations between, on the one hand, the various modes of focalization conceived as different levels of perception of the realeme (by the author) and, on the other hand, the discursive strategies that shape the representation of this realeme. In certain cases, the author's point of view is indeed shared by the narrator, but this assumption does not always obtain. The author has the freedom to overthrow his own point of view through a narrator or a character with an outside perspective. This situation occurs commonly in fictional narrative. If, in *Short Letter, Long Farewell*, the United States is represented from the exogenous point of view of an Austrian protagonist (thereby maintaining a clear link with the author, Handke), it is also represented from the endogenous point of view of a number of people, such as John Ford, whom the protagonist comes to find in California at the end of the novel. This splitting sometimes gives its dynamic to the narrative. We may remember Usbek and Rica, Montesquieu's famous Persians, who described eighteenth-century France from a totally exogenous point of view . . . all the better to convey the endogenous perspective of the Enlightenment writer. We also think of the endogenous focalization of the hero Michel Strogoff in depicting a Russia that is seen from the exogenous perspective of the author Jules Verne. The allogeneous point of view also varies. Agatha Christie demonstrates this, in making the Belgian detective, Hercule Poirot, a resident of Great Britain. On a much more massive scale, this happens to all art produced in a cultural situation of the in-between (or of accelerated deterritorialization); such art tends to transform the world into a purely liminal space, into what Zaccaria calls "a place of approximation of dualities conducive to the birth of a third."[31] From a postcolonial perspective, the allogeneous point of view embraces a stereophonic focalization, which promotes the emergence of third space.

Multifocalization is only one step in an overall argument, not an end in itself. The geocritical approach being geocentered, it is less a study of different types of perception than of the effects, in terms of representation, of the intersecting points of view. Multifocalization has a considerable impact on the spatial study of artistic representations. The aforementioned example of Sicily demonstrates both the extreme variety of viewpoints that can concentrate on one space and the rich potential for an analysis of the network of views. Like the territory, captured in a movement that makes, unmakes, and remakes it again without end, identity is plural, archipelagic. When fastened to an immutable landmark, identity is still only a myth, but a myth whose account is frozen, deprived of interest. When the territory seen in a multifocal perspective, it begins to move. Thus it allows the lymph of its concealed identity to flow. What does the network of points of view offer? As with the famous glass, half empty or half full, two responses are expected, responses that echo one another: multifocal reticulation enables a (peaceful) confrontation between *different* alterities, or a surplus of alterity in the heart of a common space. If otherness is gauged by the distance between an observer and the thing observed, the gap here is necessarily reduced as the observed object—a given space—is invested with multiple points of view, some of which are endogenous, others exogenous, and still others allogeneous. Employing an intersubjective subjectivity, it envisions the world as solid from the start. This is what Fink describes nicely in a work written in 1934, just when the Nazi regime was attempting to impose a pseudo-objectivist ideological perception upon the philosopher's homeland. But what is a "homeland" [*patrie*], if not the nondeterritorialized territory of the "fathers" [*pères*], a form of confused identity equivalent to the crystallization of a collective imaginary tradition, peddled over generations, that has paradoxically stopped evolving just in time to overlap exactly with the boundaries of a given space (the "territory")? As Fink explains, "The formation of the world is not an objectively comprehensible project, conceivable in objectivist categories, likened to the creative act of a 'world spirit' in which humans participate. The formation of the world is accessible only by the *most subjective* of all possible subjective attitudes, that which requires only that the predicative knowledge acquired in this hypersubjectivist attitude obtain an intersubjective validity of the *most rigorous* dignity."[32]

Nevertheless, the subjective point of view is not sufficient to render the world complete. It attests to a possible world—a world where (in Fink's elegant phrase) "our stars are even closer than cities only a few hours away by train, to the extent that these stars fall within our field of representation."[33] The confrontation of subjective points of view—endogenous, exogenous, and allogeneous—makes possible the extreme variability of discourse on the world, and moves away from all that tends to the singular: ideological or collective orthodoxies, which render the All into the Same and make "exemplary" the speech of a privileged subjectivity. Using a multifocal analysis of the system of representation of a place, one can understand that the two train stations are always closer than the starry heavens outside of our planet—both in art and in "real life." Artistic representation provides a lesson to the world. Of all the instances that capture the "real," it is without a doubt the most honest, because it alone does not indiscriminately posit its own objectivity, its own reality, or even its own quest for the truth. As Fink noted, "The new determinations formed through simulation [i.e., representation of the referent] are, for the ego's world of imagination, just as 'real' as those determinations received from the factual world. The imagination that resimulates is thus not a hybrid of posited and nonposited moments, but has the wholeness of a *possible* world."[34] In the geocritical context, which is governed by that existential oscillation (or transgressivity) that Fink and others have attested to, space floats and is open to astonishment. It *exists* only because it renews itself; it is renewed because, strictly speaking, it takes *place* in "the deployment of the astonishing question."[35] The Other is regarded in the regarding that one regards. Using geocriticism, one places more emphasis on the space than on the specific observer. This ensures that the textures of all focal networks constitute a kind of architext (perhaps between architecture and architexture) of a referential space, thus becoming a theater of representation, a place of spectacle translatable within the arts. By giving primacy to human space, a necessarily wondrous space, one can better assess the originality or conformity of different representations that arise. Geocriticism allows for the untangling, in part, of the author's own sensibility. The perspective of a work or a corpus articulated around the same spatial referent allows one to situate the expectations, reactions, and strategies of each writer. It allows one also to learn a valuable lesson about the space, and a *lesson* was originally a *lectio*, a "reading."

Polysensoriality

In 383, when Saint Augustine went to Milan, he met Ambrose, who had not yet become a patron of the city. In book 6, chapter 3, of his *Confessions*, Augustine described a circumstance that had attracted his attention. As he approached Ambrose, the latter was reading, but not out loud, as was customary: he read his book in silence. Was it to save his voice between sermons? To avoid having to answer difficult questions, which would interrupt his meditations? Augustine did not know. This episode is not a simple anecdote. The incident is one of those rare moments in the history of reading, a moment that in turn offers us a memorable lesson: "reading" is not the monopoly of the eyes; it also speaks to the ears. Seeing and hearing work in concert helps to discover meaning in the text. Not long ago, I mentioned the possibility of a "history of the gaze." Such a history would elaborate the long story of the world's conquest by vision over many years and describe the triumph of the visual over other forms of sensory perception. But the supremacy of the gaze, which in the early twenty-first century has become a virtual hegemony, was not inevitable. It is partly due to modernity. For many scholars, it is understood to have emerged during the Renaissance. With deference to the Gospels, some would say, like Saint Thomas, "seeing is believing." But they willingly forget that, as John reveals, the skeptical disciple certainly wanted to *see* the imprint of the nails on the hands of Christ, but he also needed to *touch* his pierced side (John 20:24–29).

In *Space and Place*, Yi-Fu Tuan has pointed out that when someone says "I see," that person comprehends (though not always very well). In this case, which applies to English, French, and many other languages, vision is synonymous with understanding. Yet, in another way, you can *hear* an argument or *listen to* reason. In French, the verb *savoir* (to know) maintains close ties with the word *saveur* (taste), and both words derive from Latin *sapere* (which means not only to know but also to have good taste). *Sapere* in turn relates to *scire* (to know, in Latin), as if to indicate that knowledge was acquired by tasting. Italian retains a vestige of this etymological evolution: when an individual knows, *egli sa* (third-person present tense of the verb *sapere*) . . . but ice cream can also *sa*, as in *il gelato sa di lampone* (the ice cream is raspberry-flavored; or perhaps hyperliterally, the ice cream knows the flavor of raspberry). We listen to reading; we are convinced by touching; we acquire the taste for knowledge; we are not content merely to look. The hierarchy of the senses, which has seemed to strengthen over time, is not culturally universal. In *Sensuous Geographies*, Paul Rodaway notes that the aboriginal Eskimos defined space more by sound than by sight: "Their world is of event rather than image, of dynamics and change rather than scenes and views."[36] The North Pole vibrates. Virulent in her denunciation of Western domination and its sensory control, bell hooks seems to affirm this: "The Australian aborigines say 'that smell of the white man is killing us.'"[37] Geographers and especially anthropologists could cite innumerable examples of this sort.

The view and its activation by the gaze are not the only centers of perception. The experience of an environment comes from all the senses. As Tuan notes, "Experience is a cover-all term for the various modes through which a person knows and constructs reality. These modes range from the more direct and passive senses of smell, taste, and touch, to the active visual perception and the indirect mode of symbolization."[38] Tuan's list does not mention hearing, but it is reasonable to assume that this is an involuntary omission, because the perception of our environment clearly involves all five senses . . . for now, let us forget about that hypothetical sixth sense that many books and films have embraced so enthusiastically. The dominance of the visual, which is actually more pronounced in discourse and metaphors than in perception, has been denounced by many cultural geographers specializing in sensuous geography. John Douglas Porteous summarizes the situation: "Notwithstanding the holistic nature of environmental experience, few researchers have attempted to interpret it in a holistic manner. Concentration on the non-visual senses is also rare. Few have investigated soundscape, and hardly any have chosen to encounter smellscape or the tactile-kinaesthetic qualities of environment. Taste remains a metaphor."[39] In fact, this hierarchy emerges directly from the language of geography that implies that certain senses are more active than others. Smell, touch, and taste would be intimate, passive, *bodily* senses, while sight and hearing are more remote and *mental*—although we should refrain from generalizing. In any event, all the senses convey perception insofar as they receive information (kinesthetic or biochemical sensation) and develop that information through a mental process (identification or association). Therefore, sensoriality allows the individual to conform to the world. It contributes to the structuring and definition of space. As Rodaway points out, "The senses are geographical in that they contribute to orientation in space, an awareness of spatial relationships and an appreciation of the specific qualities of different spaces, both currently experienced and removed in time."[40]

The relation to the world operating through the senses is variously understood. Either we may focus the discussion on a particular sense or we can apprehend this relationship in toto, in a polysensory way. The first hypothesis leads to the creation of a "sensory landscape," by turns either haptic, olfactory, auditory, or visual (or even involving taste, if one wishes). An early example of a nonvisual sensory landscape has been provided by Canadian composer and musicologist Raymond Murray Schafer. In *The Tuning of the World*, Schafer presented the theory of the *soundscape*, the ensemble of acoustic characteristics of a given place as noted by people who are both producers and listeners.[41] Subsequently, Schafer has undertaken a comparative study of different soundscapes, in Canada as well as in the rest of the world (in his World Soundscape Project). Schafer's ambitious work has influenced those interested in a "geography of the senses." Porteous has coined the term *smellscape* to describe the olfactory environment in which the individual evolves.[42] But the perception of the world is also understood through a polysensory approach that, according to Porteous, transforms the environment into an *allscape*: "We live in a multisensory world."[43] In this holistic perspective, we assess the relations that unite the five senses. Rodaway has identified a number of factors: *cooperation*, which expresses the synesthetic combination between several senses; the *hierarchy* between the senses; *sequences* of senses, which may vary within the same culture according to one's age (e.g., touching-hearing-seeing for the infant but seeing-hearing-touching for the adolescent) or which may vary from one culture to another according to differences in the perception of the environment; sensory *thresholds*, which are defined by levels of stimulation; and the *reciprocity* between the subject and the sensory environment.[44]

Polysensoriality is also a central concept in the semiotics of Fontanille, in which figurative syntax depends on synesthesia (or simultaneous perceptions) that provide figures for the sensible world. According to Fontanille, there are two types of synesthesia: synesthesia in a network, which is the "polysensory envelope of one's own body and/or of perceived objects," and synesthesia by (kinesthetic) movement that forms a "sensory bundle around a sensory-mobile experience."[45] This polysensory approach has implications for anthropology, psychology, and even marketing, for which sensory experience is involved in purchasing or using a product. Whether one selects one of the four *other* senses to challenge the hierarchy that places visual perception (the point of *view*) on top or one chooses a synesthetic approach that brings together two or several senses, polysensoriality influences the subject's representation of the environment. It is indeed an empire of the senses. As Porteous concludes, the "sensuous worlds of smell, sound, taste, and touch, as well as the visual sense, are closely integrated with the *paysage intérieur* of our minds."[46] At the interface of the *paysage intérieur* and a world open to the senses, perception provides representation of the second within the first. Depending on its own modes, artistic representation follows similar rules. The endogenous, exogenous, and allogeneous points of view find equivalents in the polysensory inveigling of the world, which is perfectly heterogeneous. In terms of representation, space is subject to the infinite variety of sensory perception. We sometimes encounter "landscapes" dominated by one sense, and sometimes the "landscapes" are synesthetic.

Sculpture creates a synesthetic landscape divided between the haptic and visual; music favors the auditory (as long as we forget that it is born in the *eyes* of the performers reading the sheet music); literature privileges the visual, because it is more common to describe what we see than what we feel, touch, hear, or taste. The discrimination between spatial approaches is primarily a function of the play of multiple looks. The view is not only an instrument of focus, a kind of sextant. As it catches the light, it registers the chromatic diversity of things and places. The visual landscape is a colorful landscape, a landscape to which subjectivity confers its dominant hue—akin to what one may add or remove from a given referent (such as Paul Éluard's sense that "the earth is blue like an orange," or Delaunay's red Eiffel Tower, etc.). But other sensory landscapes unfold, sometimes discreetly, in the text. Rodaway examines the olfactory geography in a few examples from the works of Aldous Huxley and Graham Greene.[47] After conceding the difficulty of creating a classification of odors, and thus of performing a "scientific" analysis of them, he notes that smells locate the subject not only in space but in time, because one retains a memory of smell (possibly associated with a specific location). This recalls that most famous memory of an odor, in which a gustatory geography may be said to exist in relation to a deferred temporality: Marcel, dipping his oh-so-Proustian little madeleine into a cup of tea, brings into the here and now the Combray from a few years back. Returning for a moment to the "olfactory landscape," we could discuss another novel whose plot is built around the smell of a hypertrophied hero, Jean-Baptiste Grenouille. In *Perfume*, Patrick Süskind constructs a Paris that no longer attracts the eye, but rather the nose, of the reader. Born into the world shortly before the French Revolution, "on the most putrid spot in the whole kingdom,"[48] Grenouille is a brilliant designer of fragrances. Shrinking from no crime to obtain the essences he samples for the manufacture of his perfumes, the protagonist travels the countryside, allowing the author and his narrator to filter space (urban in Paris, rural in Provence) through odor. When it is touch and sound that become the dominant senses, we arrive at a haptic or auditory geography. Haptic geographies are uncommon; they might emerge from the tactile impressions of a person struck blind (like Oedipus), or they might be erotic, as with hands touching the lover in the dark (like Psyche). The soundscape knows more numerous illustrations. It emerges every time that sounds determine the relationship of a character to his environment. The hubbub of the marketplace, musical notes, the impact of artillery fire, the sound of a voice or a kiss . . . these are all characteristics of the soundscape in novels, movies, and so on. In his version of the soundscape, Schafer distinguished between poorly identifiable *lo-fi* sounds (cacophonic) and easily recognizable *hi-fi* sounds (symphonic). In reality, all sensory perceptions could be organized in a range from euphoric to dysphoric. Certain novels coordinate several types of spatial perceptions, forming a vast polysensory landscape. This occurs in *Smilla's Sense of Snow* by Peter Høeg, in which Smilla, a specialist in cryology and the daughter of a Danish scientist and a Greenland Inuit, is able to assess the nature of the Arctic by both the color and consistency of snow. Smilla's perception of the environment is visual *and* haptic: "In some ways ice is so transparent. It carries its history on its surface."[49] And this surface is seen and touched. Moreover, the space becomes sonic when it is "heard" by a blind musician, who is able to recombine the sounds using his cassette player.

When examining the representation of space in a polysensory perspective, we are confronted, in most cases, by synesthesia, especially if the object of study is a complex and saturated space (such as a metropolis . . . or a glacier). As Marc Augé explains in reference to the sensitive and material existence of the city, it is "landscape, sky, shadows and lighting, movement; it is smell, odors varying with the seasons and the situation, places and activities—the smell of gasoline or motor oil, of ocean breezes, of ports and markets; it is noise, din, uproar or silence . . . This material dimension plays its role."[50] Since the publication of *Les fleurs du mal*, we all know that "perfumes, colors, and sounds respond to one another." For Baudelaire, synesthesia involved the perceptive field of the individual subject, but one could imagine a collective—or rather, an intersubjective—synesthesia. Human space is a sensory space whose nuances are defined by the group, and this group includes the literary community. A city feels good for some, bad for others. Rarely, it is seen as a homogeneous olfactory setting. Take the example of Alexandria in Egypt, which during the colonial period, like other cities that shared this fate, was divided into European districts and neighborhoods for "natives." For some characters, the European quarters were the nauseating ones. Marco, protagonist of a novel by Fausta Cialente, walks in the "melancholy and malodorous streets of the old European city."[51] However, when Darley, hero and narrator of Durrell's *Alexandria Quartet*, wanders into an Arab neighborhood, he breathes "the familiar smells of offal and drying mud."[52] But, referring to his childhood spent in an Arab neighborhood, Edwar al-Kharrat recalls how the "penetrating scent of native jasmine, and the smell of moist earth wafted to me."[53] It goes without saying that the implicit or explicit reference to the topoi of colonial literature (especially in that written from an exogenous point of view) and postcolonial literature (including those with endogenous perspectives) is informative and allows the reader to make judgments. It also informs a geocritical approach, where the specificity—and sometimes the singularity—of an odor smelled by a character or an author would provide some lessons about the nature of the representation. It cannot be insignificant that the Alexandrian districts mentioned are Cleopatra (mixed), Bacos (European), or Sidi Gaber (Arabic). It is also necessary to have a clue what Alexandria was like during the 1930s. Sensuous and physical geography would clearly be useful for literary study.

The perception of different sensory landscapes provides valuable information. The sounds that emanate from a place can be melodic or disharmonious. A city is noisy or cacophonous; in other cases, the soundscape will be considered symphonic or even operatic. Similarly, the color palette varies to some degree depending on the approach. Lisbon, *a cidade branca* (the white city), white and solar, would merit further comment. It is white in the title of the famous film by Alain Tanner. But on the literary banks of the Tagus, it is sometimes rainy and gray as Pessoa has painted it. The chromatic spectrum of the city is enriched, or depleted, in proportion to its literary representations. Of course, the analysis of the representations, when conducted using a polysensory approach, nourishes reflection on stereotypes and exoticism. It is a safe bet that the Africa of Conrad, Greene, Gide, and all other representatives of the exogenous perspective is not more fragrant, sonorous, colorful, and rich to the touch than it is to the endogenous writers. Depending on the observer, Africa is more green or less. At a seminar held at the University of Burundi, I asked students to tell me what they saw through the open window of the classroom. They saw nothing "special"; for me, I could clearly make out a beautiful red flower, which seemed incongruous in a landscape marred by an insidious civil war. My vision was tinged with exoticism. If I wrote a travel narrative about Burundi, I probably would have made a big deal of the "originality" of the local flora. If the students had described the same space, they probably would have left out any mention of the flowers, which would probably have been considered too trivial or banal for inclusion. With plants as with so many other things, sensory perception is a matter of perspective.

A Stratigraphic Vision

In relying on the point of view of a unique observer or a homogeneous set of observers, representation takes an apodictic turn and gives the impression of having hard evidence. But this impression is misleading. Any subject is already inscribed within a culture that associates focalization with a self-centered logic, whatever the intention of the observer. The degree of conformity of the representation is undecidable, because the perception of the referent itself is relative. It is circumscribed by the desire to *fix* the referent in a monologic narrative, which fosters the myth of the One in an environment open to the multiple. It would acquiesce to an extremely fragile convention: the established norm. But in a geocritical optic, what is interesting about the representation of a space lies at the crossroads of diverse views. Deterritorialization softens the rigidity of traditional standards; it causes the proliferation of focal centers and a global oscillation of the system of reference. The impact of the temporal factor on the reading of space also depends on the relativity of points of view. Each individual adheres to his or her own temporal regime or to one that is specific to a group or culture, although several parallel regimes, even competitors, are conceivable. This heterogeneity is expressed in the moment, because, on a planetary scale, the same instant assumes a different valence depending on who is alive at the time. The diversity of temporalities that we perceive synchronously in several different spaces, even in a single space, is also expressed in diachrony. Space is located at the intersection of the moment and duration; its apparent surface rests on the strata of compacted time arranged over an extended duration and reactivated at any time. This present time of space includes a past that flows according to a stratigraphic logic. Examining the impact of time on the perception of space is therefore another aspect of geocriticism.

Any representation leads to a reduction, because it is the product of a singular position-taking "in the open infinity of the phenomenological problematic," to use Fink's phrase.[54] In other words, it is a "unilateralization." According to Fink, who focuses on time, the past can be re-presented in its entirety, as it undergoes a selective process by memory. The representation, which is here a *presentification* (similar to Heidegger's *Jetzigen*), is the result of "a choice made according to the interests of significance" that underlies "the inconvertibility of the horizon of the past."[55] By its nature, the representation of time is destined to remain incomplete, because it could only partially "unveil a sedimented history."[56] Reducing space and its perception to a superficial dimension would be premature. Space, whose surface is illusory, becomes vertical in time, just as the syntagmatic phrase is written in a paradigmatic period of time.

Several theorists have addressed this issue in recent decades. Henri Lefebvre has argued that space, especially social and urban space, "emerged in all its diversity—and with a structure far more reminiscent of flaky *mille-feuille* pastry than of the homogeneous and isotropic space of classical (Euclidean/Cartesian) mathematics."[57] When he does not succumb to the temptation of the tasty layer cake, Lefebvre has also conceptualized this overlaying by invoking a spatiotemporal architectonic: "In space, what came earlier continues to underpin what follows . . . The task of *architectonics* is to describe, analyze and explain this persistence, which is often evoked in the metaphorical shorthand of strata, periods, sedimentary layers, and so on."[58] This architectonic attracts the combined attention of the geologist and the architect. Both act to probe the lower layer in order to imagine the top layer (or vice versa). In their examination of the stratification of space, Deleuze and Guattari write that different strata "are the thickening of the Body of the earth . . . accumulations, coagulations, sedimentations, folding."[59] Deleuze and Guattari have examined the "layers" of Lefebvre and named them "strata" in their own taxonomy. Each stratum, which is distinguished by its "unity of composition," is organized as a function of another stratum, which serves as a support (the *substratum*). This implies that one of its sides is always facing another stratum (the *interstratum*), but it also turns toward, not another stratum, but an "elsewhere" (the *metastratum*). Furthermore, according to a logic of transgressivity or deterritorialization, the strata maintain dynamic relations between them, transforming them into so many "intermediate states" whose variability is limited only by the threshold of identity or degree of the system's tolerance with respect to the deviation.

The metaphor of stratification includes all these variations. But it is not only useful for philosophy and geology. In the field of urban studies, Marcel Roncayolo has argued that "territorial constructions are primarily consolidated in time."[60] As with Lefebvre, Roncayolo notes that "there are different times of the city that are present at once." This presentification operates within the network of pathways, in the social composition of the roads, and so forth. At times when the heterogeneous is understood to disrupt the homogeneous, the coexistence of strata, considered anomic, could be the subject of virulent criticism. Roncayolo cites Louis-Sébastien Mercier's condemnation of the Paris of 1780 in his *Tableaux de Paris*. More than a century earlier, Boileau had complained of "embarrassment" for the capital in his *Satires*, just as Horace and Juvenal had done for Rome. As Roncayolo explains, the "idea of accumulating barely coherent historical strata, outside of a bit of respect for 'monuments,' is after all a new idea in the world. With this, no doubt, 'modernism' reaches its end."[61] It is true that the discourse of stratification has emerged at the precise moment that the modern flows into the postmodern. Thus a space is not *one* in a moment, just as "the city is never synchronous with itself."[62] The reduction of the heteroclite that corresponds to the present is unfair, albeit inevitable. Doubtless, we must simplify the relations between space and time in order to live. One nevertheless drills into strata situated in the diachronic depths, in an effort to produce an authentic stratigraphy.

If the present is an assemblage of instants or points of heterogeneous forces, they are autonomous and, as Hans Robert Jauss (inspired by Siegfried Kracauer) writes, "are de facto moments of entirely different time-curves, conditioned by the laws of their own 'special history.'"[63] Since the moments correspond to a differential logic, simultaneity is only an appearance of simultaneity. These observations also apply to the perception of space. As noted, in proportion to its degree of heterogeneity, human space (like the instant) is part of several temporal curves. Geocriticism emphasizes that the actuality of human spaces is disparate, that their present is subject to an ensemble of asynchronous rhythms that make their representation complex or, if ignored, overly simplistic. The asynchrony affecting human spaces is not a vague mental construct or an abstract postulate. It appears in the winding city streets and country roads. It accompanies the social evolution of the city. Asynchrony also affects subdivisions of space (such as city blocks), subdivisions that refer more to the idea of fragmented space than to that of composite time. For example, the accuracy of a representation of Barcelona will be measured by the observer's ability to articulate, in their diversity, the images of the various barrios. Barcelona is the (rather bourgeois) Eixample of Carmen Laforet or Eduardo Mendoza; the (populous) Barrio Chino of Francis Carco, Jean Genet, or André Pieyre de Mandiargues; the Rambla (a busy road and cultural center) of Claude Simon and Manuel Vázquez Montalbán; the Grácia of Mercè Rodoreda; or the Guinardó of Juan Marsé. As an undifferentiated ensemble, the barrios blend together in the visitor's sense of the city, losing their unique qualities. To explain this concept, we could borrow Jauss's beautiful astral metaphor. Just as "the seemingly present heavenly constellations move apart astronomically into points of the most different temporal distance,"[64] so too does space falsely unfold before the eyes of the visitor. The city, human space par excellence in the twentieth century and the beginning of the twenty-first, is a composite of multiple worlds. The city, like any human space, is an archipelago, both singular and plural. Geocritical analysis attempts to probe the strata that both undergird and record history, that give it its story. In a synchronic slice, the analysis addresses the strata's nonsimultaneity. One of the major tasks of geocriticism is to make the observer consider what he looks at or reproduces in all its complexity. In other words, the space must cease to appear obvious. What the observer perceives is an index of compossibility that denies the place's continuity. But in any case, if continuity is symbolized by a line, this one is a line of flight. Human space is a garden of forking paths—left, right, up, down—a rhizome.

As he describes the empire to Kublai Khan in Italo Calvino's *Invisible Cities*, Marco Polo is aware of the complex interweaving of time and space: "In vain, great-hearted Kublai, shall I attempt to describe Zaira, city of high bastions. I could tell you how many steps make up the streets rising like stairways, and the degree of the arcades' curves, and what kind of zinc scales cover the roofs; but I already know that this would tell you nothing. The city does not consist of this, but of relationships between the measurements of its space and the events of its past."[65] Marco Polo essentially tells Kublai Khan that the essence of a city (and of any space) does not correspond to its appearance, but is expressed at the intersection of space and time. Perhaps his best known novel, Ismail Kadaré's *Chronicle in Stone* sums up in its very title the project of the writer as observer of the city: to combine stony space and chronicled time, and thereby describe the artifacts of this intersection.[66] For Kadaré, this intersection is located in the town of Gjirokastër, in southern Albania. This city has a special feature: one can walk around it over the roofs and sometimes look down on the tips of minarets. In other words, depth seems to be surface. From the perspective in which Kadaré characterizes it, Gjirokastër is a city whose heights are reversed, a sort of anti–New York. For, whereas the skyscraper represents a vertiginous and risky future, the minaret stands for the eternal and the quotidian. New York tries to tear space from historical determinism. The artifact does not refer to history and to its present vestiges; it refers to what will be, what should be, what one wishes to be, and what one wishes had already been. But let us return to Marco Polo: "In every age someone, looking at Fedora as it was, imagined ways of making it the ideal city, but while he constructed his miniature model, Fedora was already no longer the same as before, and what had been until yesterday a possible future became only a toy in a glass globe."[67] The minaret, itself, is woven into the fabric of time and space in the city. Mediterranean cities are like that as well. In the Istanbul of *From Russia with Love*, James Bond tunnels through the city's underground to spy on Russian agents from below. And Beirut is a hole in space, into which one falls, as the narrator of Selim Nassib's *Fou de Beyrouth* discovers when a fissure opens up beneath him. He eventually finds an apt symbol for the changing city, an army of children scouring the ruins for stone to use in making a highway. Darley, Durrell's hero in *Clea*, suggests making an autopsy of rubble, as the city's ruins are abused, sacrificed to the teleological inevitability of the future. But, anyway, the ruins remind us of a city's diachronic identity, and hence of its depth.

There is also a depth of view, as Marco Polo remarks: "Beware of saying to them that sometimes different cities follow one another on the same site and under the same name, born and dying without knowing one another, without communication among themselves . . . It is pointless to ask whether the new ones are better or worse than the old, since there is no connection between them, just as the old post cards do not depict Maurilia as it was, but a different city which, by chance, was called Maurilia, like this one."[68] The postcard lacks thickness, like synchronic space. Diachrony is expressed in the strata underlying places. The two Maurilias, notwithstanding Calvino's remark, are not merely linked by spatial chance: the new Maurilia is coextensive with the former Maurilia; even their postcards interact. One can no longer evoke the stratigraphic dimension of space by considering only synchronic slices. Because of the weight of its history, space is compossibility, the concrescence of heterogeneous elements that make up its mass. Places can only be perceived in the multidimensional volume of space-time, space elevated to the level of time. The line of history that marks the depth of a place is then streaked with a series of horizontal lines that establish the false simultaneity of heterogeneous moments. If place is never confined to the present because of the winds of history, it does not display the same level of presence on its territory. Here and there, depth is brought to the surface. A Roman paving stone is kept within the confines of a postmodern media library in Limoges; according to architect Renzo Piano, the Pompidou Center was designed to be a spaceship rising from the middle of Le Marais. This "double coding" (as Charles Jencks calls it) deliberately associates the present with an aspect of the past or future to narrow the present, transforming the postmodern moment into a composite tempuscule. Here, the surface is broken up and the aesthetic of the fragment dominates urban space. Space is inherently asynchronous; synchrony is a ruse of history or an oversimplification on the part of the reader. According to the formula of Itamar Even-Zohar, it is "stratified heterogeneity."[69]

Space does not unfold in pure simultaneity due to the permanent reactivation of temporal layers that constitute and crisscross it. It also incorporates variations caused by the concatenation of diverse temporalities that regulate the rhythms of cultures. From one place to another, the perception of time and timeliness may differ. One's *present* does not necessarily correspond to another's. It has come up against what Ernst Bloch called the *Ungleichzeitigkeit*, a general nonsimultaneity that determines any development. In *The Dance of Life*, Edward T. Hall distinguishes between monochronic and polychronic time, whereby monochronic time is that of a system in which you do one thing at a time, while in a system of polychronic time, you perform several activities at once. Monochronic time would be inherent the American space, whereas polychronic time suits the Mediterranean zone. And, not surprisingly, when a representative of one of these systems moves into an area subject to the other, conflicts ensue. However, I believe that this distinction seems arbitrary. Fuelled by a stereotype, this distinction ends up strengthening that stereotype by locking it in place. Monochronic and polychronic time lend themselves to another type of analysis. Is monochrony a (hegemonic) vision that would impose a single temporality on the whole world? Is polychrony a vision that assigns a different temporality to each cultural area? In a monochronic system, perception of the present tends to synchrony, to monorhythm. If we attribute a polychronic valence to the world, we perceive at the same present in its asynchrony, and we see society as a "polyrhythmic body" (as Lefebvre puts it).[70] Asynchrony and polychrony are strongly linked, marking a perception of space oriented according to a temporal logic. Asynchrony introduces the reign of polychrony, which a closed culture attempts to occlude. The moment experienced by an individual does not have the same force as the same moment experienced by his neighbor. Like the illusion of local synchrony, universal monochrony is thus an illusion promoted by hegemonic forces that tend to impose a single, global temporal scheme.

Taking Europe as an example, we find that because of its heterogeneity, it is one of those polychronic spaces whose temporal depths and historical variations remind us of the starry sky of Jauss (or as evoked by the flag of the European Union). The Dutch novelist Cees Nooteboom reflected on this vision in a news conference at Groningen in October 1992, with reference to the arrow of Zeno. According to Zeno of Elea, a follower of Parmenides, space is infinitely divisible; therefore, the trajectory of an arrow is also infinitely divisible, so its target should never be reached. The same paradox extends to time. As the target, an actual present moment would be out of reach because the moments of the past on which it is based continue to pile up and never form an intelligible entity. Europe's actuality, a summit as inaccessible as the horizon, always emerges a little later. The past prevails. Further, Europeans do not all and always live in a common layer of the past. This paradox, which seems too abstract, may have practical and sometimes dramatic consequences for a common vision of space. Nooteboom gives two examples. He first mentions immigration, which brings together actors with different temporal standards: "Anyone traveling from the south to the north, or vice versa, often has the impression that it is possible, despite scientific laws, to travel through time. Asynchronous systems in a synchronous world, one's past is lost in another's future, and once more in that place, anachronism is divisive, and the material weapons of one epoch are tools of the mental universe to another."[71] Disregarding this asynchrony is a serious error, and ultimately a source of tension: "Those torn from their own epoch view themselves as hovering over an abyss, an existence impossible to endure, and they are threatened by our reciprocal anachronisms in a polychronic world. The one who is too far ahead of the history of the other becomes a danger to him . . . In the everyday synchronicity of the image, we live with visions of an asynchronous world."[72] Another example mentioned by Nooteboom confirms the threat that comes from an overhasty flattening of times: the then-current Yugoslav civil war. From this conflict comes a double temporal problem. In a sense, the apparent *present* of Yugoslavia in the early 1990s was an illusion, if we refer to the historical benchmarks of Western Europe. The Balkan wars of the early twentieth century, the Second World War, and even the famous battle of Kosovo fought in 1389 were still *present* in many minds (the present is also a *presence* in mind, however misguided at times). One could say that the excesses of historical memory generated the rancor that had never completely gone away: "Those who wanted to die and whose names are indeed dead are not lost in space, but in time, and the Europe of unification looks helpless before the Europe of bloody fragmentation."[73] Moreover, from the point of view of Western Europe, such a war was incompatible with the present era, which seemed to tend toward a comprehensive and global peace effort. It represented an aberration, preferably one to be avoided: "Precisely because it is an anachronism, Europe does not dare to intervene; it all belongs to a past that she has already left in tatters for the same reasons."[74] Nooteboom draws the moral of all this from two European battles (Sagunto, which pitted Carthaginians against Iberians, and Poitiers), which are transformed for the occasion into characters of a fable: "What is lacking is a historical consciousness, and one who wishes to live without memory always ends up among us."[75] This "among us," this inviting home, is the next battlefield. One must meditate on the Yugoslav–Albanian example that makes the Battle of Kosovo of 1389, for many, seem like a current event.

Ultimately, places respond to the criteria of constant deterritorialization, which gives them a paradoxical continuity by rendering them labile. It is extraordinary that the awareness of this vital fluttering occurs in a context of what many understand as the global village, a uniform planetary space of the ubiquitous communication society. This large-scale stasis presents a risk that Marco Polo, in his great wisdom, denounces: "But in vain I set out to visit the city: forced to remain motionless and always the same, in order to be more easily remembered, Zora has languished, disintegrated, disappeared. The earth has forgotten her."[76] The text feeds the memory of the place. Anyway, it is impossible to exhaust it. As one skirts the place, one approaches it. Any study of a space must take its geological or archaeological turns. From the clues we find and the relics we collect, we imagine some of the details of its history, a few fragments of its identity. By multiplying textual forays through a space and comparing the results obtained, we will know a little more about it. The fictional text brings out all the folds of time relating to a place. Or better, it imagines the form that a place can virtually adopt. It does not reflect only a past history, but anticipates what the city could be in a possible world that it haunts. Thereby, it ensures its survival in its own way. As Calvino points out, "The catalogue of forms is endless: until every shape has found its city, new cities will continue to be born. When the forms exhaust their variety and come apart, the end of cities begins."[77] When the city is no longer produced by the text, as in Calvino, it ceases to exist. Like Scheherazade as well? This applies to any place, urban or not. So, to pose a frightening question, What is this city but the paper on which I write, or that you read, at a given time?

The Fate of the Stereotype

The monolithic conception of space and its inhabitants is a breeding ground of the stereotype, whereby all definitions are made to square with a collectively fixed scheme. When space is reduced to a particular "territory," which embodies the spatialization of a political-institutional ensemble held to homogeneity, or to a "nation," which is a historicization of the ensemble, it is inevitably governed by stereotyping. The territory-nation seems to obey a *logic of belonging* that paradoxically legitimizes exclusion. Indeed, instead of stereotyping, one might be allowed to speak of *ethnotyping*, that is to say, the stereotypical representation of people categorized according to a series of xenotypes, cast in bronze for all time. Under this type of discourse or *doxa*, which piggybacks onto an immutable time, this space is set in a discursive register that is also the register of the stereotype. The latter, in fact, is born inasmuch as its proponents will "push into the past the fragmentary bits of truth that they melt into an image that is supposed to express the entire truth of a people," as Robert Frank has put it.[78] The static space of the state resorts to a similar logic, which is based on an institutionalized image developed by hegemonic, monofocal, and monochronic speech. Nationalism and ethnotyping often go together because the nationalist desire, manifest or not, sustains selected ethnotypes. The ethnotype reinforces a desirable self-identity (an ameliorative ethnotype) in opposition to neighboring entities, regarded as irrevocably *other* (a pejorative ethnotype). The stereotype gives an explicit reading of the Other just as it reveals the hidden nature of the Self. As Frank remarks, "the stereotype portrays an image of others, often exploited in terms of what we hope or what we fear for ourselves." Thus it does not present an image *in* itself, but an image *for* itself, an "image-pretext destined to be represented by itself."[79]

The stereotype is based on the permanent state (the striated space of the sedentary, Deleuze would have said) of the state. *Being* is elsewhere. It is in deterritorialization, in that which contests the necessarily singular space of identity imagined in the territory and the nation; it is also in the discourse that, instead of freezing everything in the *doxa*, embraces the paradox, the momentary exceeding of the One and the Other.[80] The navicular semantics of geocriticism could qualify the vague pseudo-objectivity of fixed representations. All representations have no other time than the instant; beyond the instant, the archimpression that is formed would become a stereotype. Like the ethnotype, the stereotype has a practical utility. Never innocent, never inoffensive, it is fundamentally pragmatic. It serves to strengthen the links between what Carl Schmitt called *Ordnung* and *Ortung*, between order and location. Geocriticism, for its part, seeks instead to establish a laboratory to study the phenomenon of *Entortung*, or delocalization. The question then would be whether it is possible to imagine a *Nomos raumlos*, "deterritorialized" and "despatialized." What appeared to Schmitt, an intellectual with close ties to Nazism, as the crisis of the European state derived precisely from its *total Mobilmachung*; but for geocriticism, *totale Mobilmachung*—when it brings with it transgressivity—is both the present condition and a challenge. In the factual world, everything is done to avoid splitting the coupling of *Ordnung* and *Ortung*, or, at least, to avoid doing away with it altogether. Perhaps that divorce is never mentioned, since *Entortung* is inseparable from the identity of human spaces. It *is* in duration and does not assert itself in the mere moment, and is therefore not a simple step in a movement. In other words, a fundamental and *foundational aporia* marks our destiny: we are condemned to live in a space whose representation strives to be unique and static (the identity of *stare*) when in reality it is inevitably shifting and plural, even in the short term (the permanent reidentification of *esse*). Insofar as literature, like any form of mimetic art, produces free representations, organic and nonorganic, it guarantees the compossibility of the universe, the movement between worlds. Never lose sight of the fact that representation is a re-presentation, therefore evolutionary and transgressive, and not a static image of a perpetual present.

It is undeniable that a geocritical analysis expanded to cover a whole nation comes with risks. Geocriticism can no longer be content to reach this one phase of the phenomenon of deterritorialization, and then commit its resources to it in the long term. Stereotyping is not confined to the stories we read; it also affects the commentator. To be truly safe from stereotyping, the critic should live outside the world, using some otherworldly metalanguage. He or she would have to become a decoding machine, without a soul and without mental states. The critic would in fact take the place of Laplace's demon, deterministic and grinning. The frantic quest for objectivity would lead inexorably to the installation of another stereotype, but this does not mean one cannot take precautions to limit the subjectivity (hence, the use of a large and varied corpus would be indispensible). The geocriticism of a place must form a *topos atopos*, integrating what Fink calls "the flux of imaginary variation of possible transformations."[81] It is also necessary to take advantage of fleeting lessons from the other mimetic arts to better understand the world, to capture—which does not mean the same as "to conquer"—human spaces in their movement, in their navicular essence. To do this, the critic must point to the role of a stereotype in any spatial representation and question the (permeable?) boundaries of otherness. For the *topos atopos* that gives a place its real dynamic is never a *topos koinos*, a "common place." Creative *atopia* is born in that place where rationalizing and universalizing types cease to operate, where one no longer holds as valid those generalizations produced in the flagrant and brittle logic of power that informs all standards.

Can one speak of the Other? The temptation is strong, even irresistible. It animates all voyagers who admire these "others" (or not), all of those who are curious, and also all of those who want to assert their superiority over the Other, if necessary. This temptation is often culpable. In his preface to the French translation of Edward Said's *Orientalism*, Tzvetan Todorov notes, with a not unfounded sense of bitterness, that the "history of discourse on the *other* is overwhelming. From time immemorial men have thought they were better than their neighbors; the only things that change are the flaws imputed to them."[82] These alleged flaws are scattered about the long history of stereotyping and ethnotyping. Can we then go beyond the stereotype? Can we move outside the "endotic limits of the stereotype" to "go out toward a world that draws the gaze away from the self, in exogenous, exotic spirit," in Ouellet's beautiful vow?[83] Yet it must be feasible. This is not what Marc Brosseau seems to believe, when he says that "otherness, by definition, is indefinable, because the definition would seek to refer to oneself."[84] In literary studies, as in other fields of humanities and in the social sciences, the analysis of otherness and of elsewhere is based on a binary opposition (sometimes related in an empathetic way) between the gazer and the gazed at, according to a principle of systematic and insurmountable difference. In the best case, the analysis places the interpreter in a third position with regard to looking and being looked at—a position that avoids the normative standard, or at least has a standard that is ideal, idealized, or somehow neutral. But, voilà, the display of neutrality is almost always a vindication of the center. Interpreting the role of the Other in its relations with a white intelligentsia that sets the rules of intercultural engagement, bell hooks protests, "I am waiting for them to stop talking about the 'Other,' to stop even describing how important it is to be able to speak about difference."[85]

It seems difficult to escape the *native* versus *alter-native* alternative in a monofocal and monochronic regime. A point of view dominates; a temporality prevails. The points of view will be partial, if not prejudiced; temporality tends to congeal. Whatever the cause, the representation will have the look of a stereotype. The representation, when not constantly re-presented, always refers to a "dated cultural model."[86] The metadiscourse that reflects the monofocal and monochronic narrative, the narrative that an author creates about a given place, is itself in a singular situation, in the true sense of the word. It will be a matter of gauging the relationship of the author to a place according to a virtual, and thus imprecise (or stereotypical?), encyclopedia with the aid of some global decoding device. Take the example of Pierre Loti's description of Istanbul in *Aziyadé*. What happens to criticism as a general rule? Although we cannot completely withdraw from showing the spatial referent in favor of studying the "literary" processes (a self-referential view of literature), the emphasis is still on the writer at the expense of the city. Some categorize Loti's novel as "Oriental" or

"Orientalist" fiction, of which there are many examples in the nineteenth century; others group this work in terms of the author's other productions, which also display his taste for the exotic. The specificity of Istanbul will be (more or less) ignored, to such a degree that the former capital of the Ottoman Empire will be primarily considered just another "Oriental" city. The specificity of its places will be erased, because Istanbul becomes, for Loti, an exotic medium, little different in its exoticism from Japan, Polynesia, Senegal, or China. Istanbul is just a metonym of Orientalism, a metonym of exoticism. Certainly, Rome is not in Rome. And Istanbul has not been in Istanbul for a long time. But as Ruth Amossy and Anne Herschberg Pierrot put it so well, "the analysis of stereotypes and clichés aims to demystify all that hinders interpersonal relationships, the free appreciation of reality, originality, and innovation."[87]

So can we succeed in placing Istanbul in Istanbul? Nothing is less sure, because after all the Greek etymology of the place would be *Istinpolis* "toward the city", and Roland Barthes spoke of Loti's Istanbul as a place "adrift."[88] Istanbul doubtless tends toward deterritorialization. But it is still always *somewhere*: in the narrative of fact and in countless stories of the world. It is not only in the tale of a writer, then, but in the rhizomatic canvas of stories—or lines of flight—that it inspires, near or far. Istanbul is what Loti depicts, just as it is the Istanbul of others. It is in the present moment, which soon becomes the past of other ones; it occupies the strata spread out over the decades and centuries. It is in the feelings it gives off and authors capture, each according to his or her own idiosyncrasies. It is, then, geocentered and not merely egocentered. Its representation proliferates depending on points of view, on discourses. It continues to inspire stereotypes, but, as they cross each other and explode the focal nodes that would limit our perspectives, they will reveal themselves as such. A geocritical metadiscourse should be able to situate each author in a network of precise references—here, this place, a place always oscillating between the realeme and the multiple representations that swirl around it. In this play of partial and virtually infinite references, there is no longer the Other, because it melts into a common place . . . but one that escapes the *topos koinos*, since the Other is now widespread. In the latter case, one concedes that each speaker of a place speaks at some distance with respect to the spatial context of its history, as if the place were hidden indefinitely before the narrative, as happens in *Invisible Cities*. We move "toward the city," *toward* the place to which we aspire, but never *in* place: the escape that is a beneficial effect of so many great stories, the escape that by its nature is a form of desire (*de-siderium*), is the sidereal attraction toward what is beyond. "Toward the city" is Istanbul, like the starry sky, like the object of desire, to be admired from a distance. It could be the One or the Other, but no matter: it will forever be the alter-native.

CHAPTER 5

Reading Spaces

Three Views of Paris

Beginning in 1967, Italo Calvino spent part of every year in Paris. He was interested in getting closer to the cultural life of what was once the City of Light. Wisely and, by his own admission, precariously balancing between the French capital and several major Italian cities (Rome, Milan, and Turin), Calvino had plenty of time to think about not only his intimate relationship to place but also the links between his work and space—the space that the work represented, that it refrained from representing, and that it emanated from. In a 1974 Italian–Swiss television interview, Calvino shared his perplexity: "For some years now I have had a house in Paris, where I spend part of the year, but hitherto this city has never appeared in the things I write. Maybe to write about Paris, I ought to leave, to distance myself from it, if it is true that all writing starts out from a lack or an absence."[1] But Calvino does not overcome his embarrassment; in his writings, Paris forever remained in limbo. In any case, the Italian writer indicates the source of the tension. In effect, what is the place of the text with respect to the (spatial) referent? And what is the place of the referent with respect to the text? For Calvino, it would seem that the work could not take off until the real place was hollowed out to allow enough room for an "inner landscape." This restriction does not imply any binary system, with a clear divide between reality and fiction. On the contrary, the link between text and place may well be inextricable. What, indeed, is a place like Paris? A real city, certainly, that we can credit Haussmann and a few others with creating, along with the plethora of Parisians by birth or adoption who have configured various Parisian places in their distinct ways. But Paris is also a city that one *thinks* and that one *builds* according to one's readings, without necessarily having traveled there. Calvino is no exception to the rule: "Before being a city of the real world, Paris for me, as for millions of other people in every country, has been a city that I have imagined through books, a city that you appropriate when you read."[2] Touchstones of this fantastic architecture include *The Three Musketeers*, *Les Misérables*, Baudelaire, all the painters, Balzac, Zola, and Proust, to cite a few. Each season of life corresponds to a writer or a painter, and sometimes imperceptible layers of representation accumulate. Paris is formed in the imagination of the author, and it unfolds its space even before one visits for the first time. For Calvino, a place is first of all an intertextual construction. "Or rather," as Calvino puts it, "a place has to become an inner landscape for the imagination to start to inhabit that place, to turn it into its theatre. Now Paris has already been the inner landscape of such a huge part of world literature, of so many books that we have all read, and that have counted in our lives."[3] The representation of places becomes even more complex. There is the "image" of Paris that conveys a common culture, that one retains even while sitting at home elsewhere; then there is the city "in itself," the "real" city. Calvino's reluctance to "write" the city is not based on anything to do with the realeme, but on the representation imposed by the *koinè*. The intertextual strata that make up the city are so dense that they intimidate the writer. And, for Calvino, what goes for Paris extends also to Rome. It happens that some places, intensely surveyed and mapped, turn into encyclopedias. Calvino sees in Paris a museum. The Louvre and the surrounding boroughs are seamlessly interwoven spaces. The city is a book, a space that one explores like a book, that speaks to the unconscious: "And at the same time we can read the city as the collective unconscious: the collective unconscious is a huge catalog, an enormous bestiary; we can interpret Paris as a book of dreams, an album of our unconscious, a catalog of horrors."[4] Therefore, certain perspectives are reversed. It is no longer the city that influences the literature, but literature that takes over and plays a concrete role.

In this same year, 1974, Georges Perec undertook a most formidable project: to match the text and the world by describing "what happens when nothing happens."[5] He could have camped out in the heart of the Sahara to meticulously put on paper *everything* that appeared before his eyes. Perhaps then he could have kept up with the rhythm of an exhaustive description, though, let us remember, it is not only visual: it would have had to transcribe the wind and the smell of sand, the taste of stone, and their asperities. But Perec instead chose to engage with the bustling Place Saint-Sulpice in "an attempt at exhausting a place in Paris,"[6] but he limited the experiment to the 48 hours or so, from the early morning of Friday, October 18 to midafternoon on Sunday, October 20. Although he was confined to one location at a specific time, the project was actually boundless. Yet enumerating the buses regularly passing by—the number 70, 86, 84, 63, and so on—would quickly become tedious. And what about the "hundreds of simultaneous actions," the "microevents" that occurred within the space of reference?[7] In addition, trying to contain the world in Place

Saint-Sulpice was a challenge to common sense because, as Perec recognized, when concentrating on one small detail at a time, one could just as easily imagine being in Bourges or Étampes, or even Vienna for that matter.

Twenty years later, Umberto Eco collected his Norton Lectures at Harvard University into *Six Walks in the Fictional Woods*, in which he comments upon Perec's experiment: "At two P.M. on October 20, he stops. It is quite impossible to tell everything that happens at a certain spot in the world, and when all is said and done, his own account is sixty pages long and can be read in half an hour. That is, if the reader doesn't savor it slowly for a couple of days, trying to imagine every scene described."[8] Few have done so. But in Eco's essay, it is not just about Perec. Like Calvino, Eco is interrogating his own links to Paris. Instead of limiting his thoughts to the strictly autobiographical and personal, Eco expands on the genesis of his second novel, *Foucault's Pendulum*, in which a number of characters stroll through the streets of the French capital. Unlike Calvino, Eco has never hesitated to use the referential Paris, which invariably returns in most of his novels. Contradicting his illustrious predecessor, Eco feels the need to recognize places before putting them on stage: "I like to have the scene I'm writing about in front of me while I narrate; it makes me more familiar with what's happening and helps me get inside the characters."[9] The construction of the place is no longer performed in absentia; the writer maintains an immediate and lived, almost carnal, relationship with the spaces that he then transcribes in his work. One of the key moments of *Foucault's Pendulum* is given a very precise date (the night of June 23–24, 1984), and Eco brings the same attention to detail in providing its location. As Eco describes the scene again in *Six Walks*, after a satanic ceremony at the Conservatoire des Arts et Métiers, Casaubon, one of the protagonists, "walks, as if possessed, along the entire length of rue Saint-Martin, crosses the rue aux Ours, passes the Centre Beaubourg, and arrives at the Saint-Merry Church. Afterward he continues along various streets, all of them named, until he gets to the place des Vosges."[10] In preparing to write chapter 115 of that novel, from which this episode is extracted, the author took great care. He began by taking his own nocturnal walk, following the trajectory that the fictional character, Casaubon, would take on that particular night in the novel; then Eco even took advantage of computer software that could show what the Parisian sky looked like on this crucial night in June. In sum, Eco had taken every precaution to ensure the alignment between the referent and its representation.

But since nobody is perfect, an incident had escaped him, and he received a query about it from an attentive reader, albeit one who may have been "affected by a sort of mild paranoia."[11] On this very night depicted in *Foucault's Pendulum*, shortly after midnight, a fire was raging at the intersection of the rue Réaumur and rue Saint-Martin. Was it possible that Casaubon had not seen it? Thus caught but also willing to play the game, the author replied that Casaubon had in fact seen the fire but had deliberately refrained from mentioning it for some mysterious, unknown reason. However, for the reader who has ventured into the woods of the novel and elsewhere in the company of a wolf like Eco, another explanation is advanced: "I maintain that my reader was exaggerating when he pretended that a fictional story should wholly match the actual world it refers to; but the problem is not quite as simple as that."[12] Not so simple, indeed. The connections between referent and representation are multifaceted and complex. The reaction triggered by the representation of place in *Foucault's Pendulum* is far from trivial. In addition to the remark of the man who went back and read too many newspapers, it is worth noting, as Eco does, the approach taken by two students at the École des Beaux Arts in Paris, who had photographed the "real" places "frequented" by Casaubon and other characters, including a particular tavern that Eco says he invented (though he undoubtedly based it upon the kinds of bars in that area). These photographs were not really reproductions, mere simulacra of a supposed referent: rather, they aimed to configure the site based on its layout in the novel. As Eco comments about this demiurgic project, "It's not that they had superimposed on their duty as model readers the concerns of the empirical reader who wants to verify that my novel describes the real Paris. On the contrary, they wanted to transform the 'real' Paris into a place in my book, and of all that they could have found in Paris, they chose only those aspects that corresponded to my descriptions. They used a novel to give form to that shapeless and immense universe which the real Paris is."[13] After finding that their project was really the opposite of Perec's (i.e., they emptied the city's places of nonnovelistic elements, whereas Perec tries to fill a textual place with elements), Eco adds, "Paris is far more complex than the locale described by Perec and the one described in my book."[14]

The postures that Calvino, Perec, and Eco have adopted with respect to Paris are distinct, but they all offer valuable lessons on the relationships between the writer and the city, between text and place. It seems too restrictive, or even just plain false, to deny the relationship between referential space and the fictional text, just as it would be naive to evaluate a text based on how well it mimetically copies the targeted space. The Parisian variations of the three authors confirm this. Three types of interconnection seem to emerge that give the text an active role. The impact of the text on the representation of the place may have increasing levels, from texts influencing the view of space, to places becoming themselves texts, to a genuine intertwining of text and place. Often the text precedes the place: Calvino, as well as Eco, come to Paris and *experience* Paris after having read the novels that have informed their inner landscape. The representation of Paris is for them a cross between their direct, polysensorial perceptions and the intertextual construction that makes up their separate personal encyclopedias. Within the Paris of Calvino and Eco, there are, like so many nesting dolls, the

Paris of Balzac, of Dumas, and of Utrillo. Geocriticism can reconstruct the intertextual trajectory that leads to this representation of space. The coefficient of impact would be even higher if, instead of perceiving the textual elements in a given space, one were to view the place as a text. Examples of this are admittedly fewer, but it has been repeated many times, as with Perec's panoptic *Tentative d'épuisement d'un lieu parisien*, which is an effort to translate two days of a Parisian place into sixty pages. The highest degree of relationship between referent and text remains the one that involves a genuine interaction between the two. It may indeed happen that the text rises above the place. In their charming ingenuousness, the Beaux-Arts students have simply pushed this logic one step further: if it is not possible to materially reconstruct a city according to a book, it is nevertheless possible to act on its representation on the basis of a work's mapping. The border between fiction and reality is permeable, and fiction can contribute to the development of the real.

Of Stone and Paper: Does the Text Precede the Place?

In the famous fairytale, Snow White's stepmother repeatedly asks her mirror who is the fairest in the land, until one day the mirror disappoints. In real life, beauty is not the main object of questions posed by stepmothers and stepfathers, and Snow White is often less pure than she appears in the Grimms's version. Sometimes one asks who is the most civilized; sometimes one asks who is the real owner of the kingdom. It is a refrain, obsessive and dangerous, which echoes in many kingdoms and regions of the world: Who's number one, him or me? Her or me? The desired answer invariably arrives: me. Its territorial history and definition has been examined since the beginning. In *Memories of Odysseus*, François Hartog has documented the efforts that the Greeks made to distinguish themselves from Egyptians and other peoples of Asia—efforts inevitably aimed at establishing that they were both better and older than their neighbors, which indicates the degree to which acknowledging earlier civilizations was a threat to Greek identity. Later, Rome does the same with Greece, notably attempting to secure Ulysses, the same Odysseus who was the quintessentially Hellenic spirit, as one of its own founding heroes. The phenomenon is universal: how to enslave one whose cultural prestige is believed to overshadow that of the new master? We can still find this hint in the Adriatic, as elsewhere in the world, in the late twentieth century. Albania and Serbia argue over the dubious honor of having been the first in the Balkan Peninsula. In Albania, one finds a national gesture in the heroic exploits of Teuta, the Illyrian queen who offered fierce resistance to the Romans. In Serbia, one is introduced to a number of cosmogonic heroes. And both make direct affiliations with the Greek epic, because it is better to rally behind an ancient tradition than to assert too vigorously one's ties to the Other. The work of Ismail Kadaré is full of this secular rivalry's echoes: a single thread leads from Odysseus and Aeschylus to modern Albania (and away from its Serbian neighbor, who becomes an impetuous latecomer).

Literature contributes to this enterprise, because sometimes it fans the flames of identity and inherits a task formerly performed by myth. We have seen the role played by Odysseus and Jason in ancient Greece. They had opened the way to the east (Jason and the Argonauts) and to the west (Odysseus and his companions). They also traced the path of the colonizer to the golden fields of the Caucasus and the future breadbasket of southern Italy, Magna Graecia. Literature has for a long time stayed a few steps ahead of geography. The book continues to be of capital importance in the era of transoceanic voyages that proliferated after Christopher Columbus. According to Benito Pelegrín, there is less a sense that "the explorers discovered geographical novelties than that they have rediscovered lands, landscapes formerly known, by us and them, but perhaps blurred by distance, or buried in the fog of collective memory."[15] The fabulous island of Antilia, which was invented by the Carthaginians after a possible Platonic detour, served as the etymon of the Antilles in the Caribbean; thus, a reversed Atlantis suddenly rises from the waters. These places and all the rest of the Americas emerged in the European imagination during these pivotal years. America is literally—literarily?—a European invention. According to Carlos Fuentes, "Columbus described an earthly paradise in his letters to Queen Isabella. But he believed, after all, that he had merely found the ancient world of Cathay and Cipango: the empires of China and Japan. Amerigo Vespucci, the Florentine explorer, was the first European to say that our continent was in actuality a New World. We deserve his name."[16] In this floating world, the utopian imagination had a prominent place. Whereas Thomas More's very name for *Utopia* declared it to be "nowhere" (*ou-topos*), writes Fuentes, "the European imagination promptly responded. Now there is such a place. It is America. America was not discovered, it was invented . . . It was invented by a European imagination and desire because it was needed."[17]

Moreover, utopia finds its way through the book, by the book, to a "no-place" par excellence that can evoke places just as well as it evokes phantoms with astonishingly real-world effects. In 1510, Garci Rodríguez de Montalvo's *The Exploits of Esplandian*, a continuation of *Amadis of Gaul*, was published, which, though popular in its time, is somewhat forgotten now. What does it have to do with us? It spoke of a certain island of California, ruled by Califia, Queen of the black Amazons, whose land was close to a terrestrial paradise. The conquistadors, who certainly had plenty of time to read while crossing the Atlantic, had remembered the names, Amazon and California. The latter, which Hernán Córtez quickly realized was a peninsula, not an island, nevertheless remained an island in the minds of many, long after the expeditions launched by Córtez in 1534 and 1535. On a famous 1719 map by Herman Moll representing North America, for instance, California continued to be separated from the mainland (and this error persisted in some maps until the end of the eighteenth century). *Scripta manent*: it was written as an island, so reality had better watch out, as facts give way to the fable. At the same time as these explorers ventured into the oceans, those who turned their eyes to the heavens, visiting the stars and reflecting on the respective positions of the sun and earth in the galaxy, also had to deal with a certain text, rather more prestigious than Garci Rodríguez de Montalvo's romance: the Bible. Giordano Bruno was burned at the stake, while both Galileo and Copernicus only narrowly escaped. As for those who conceived utopias to project beyond man's known world, they too took great risks. Thomas More was beheaded by the executioner of Henry VIII. In the same genre as *The Exploits of Esplandian*, Jacopo Sannazzaro's 1504 *Arcadia* eventually gave its name to Acadia (which had lost an *r* along the way) through the good offices of the Florentine explorer Verrazano, who is best remembered today as the name of a bridge in New York. "For a man of the Renaissance," writes Pelegrín, "it is thus literature, fiction, that testifies to the truth, that substantiates the true, and that makes the unlikely a reality."[18] The administrators of the first "American" colonies had more time to read, and were more cultured, than the conquistadors. According to Fuentes, among those "fired by the vision of the New World as Utopia" was "Vasco de Quiroga, a Franciscan bishop of Michoacán in western Mexico, who in the 1530s arrived with Thomas More's *Utopia* under his arm and promptly set about applying its rules to the communities of the Tarascan Indians."[19] Literature allows us to name this new and larger space, and to organize it according to a utopian ideal.

Nowadays, literature is perhaps less prestigious than in those heroic times, but it sometimes still moves a step ahead of reality. Calvino's experience, the fear of representing a Paris about which everything has already been said or written, is common to many writers. Some, like him, perhaps find themselves pained by it, while others use it to their advantage. This is the case of Michel Butor, a world traveler, who confesses, "When I travel in a country, I am going to read books concerning it, but it is especially to help me read the country itself."[20] The saturation of a place by the text is different from, or even opposed to, that which guided the intellectual fates of the Renaissance. As we have seen, the spatial surfeit leads to a still-empty space. The text no longer comes before the virgin land and uncharted seas: the text comes before a text, which in turn comes before another text, and so on in an endless chain in which the layers of paper pile upon one another with the beautiful regularity of geological and archaeological strata. The white spaces of the map are filled in as quickly as the white spaces on the page. Or, better, as the white spots disappeared from the maps, the white spaces on paper lost their innocence. But at the height of this proliferation, the text sometimes establishes human spaces. In *Répertoire V*, Butor offers a bold and fascinating hypothesis: "Archaeological research tells us that, everywhere on the planet, the first great modern cities arose at the same time as the invention of writing in the proper sense. So perhaps it is not that a large number of people in a given place cause an accumulation of texts, but the reverse. It is in the place where the text unfolds that people settle in such a way as to serve it."[21]

Claudio Magris observed that his hometown of Trieste was a city of paper, because "Svevo, Saba, and Slataper are not so much writers who are born in it and through it, but are writers who generate and create it, who give it a face that otherwise, in itself, would not exist in that form."[22] A practically blank space in the nineteenth century, Trieste has gradually become a written space in the extreme, to the point that Magris spoke of it as "literature squared." The text is no longer born of the city, but born of another text to which the city has been subjected. Literary criticism thus involves the extraction of roots. It would take nothing to show that the square of a literature raised to the power of the space that it frames would make this space a literary space squared. For this strange arithmetic to be acceptable, it must be understood that the space has first been subject to prestigious literary transpositions, because once space and literature blend together, it goes from arithmetic to variable geometry (which is mathematically strange, but credible in literature, as non-Euclidean a science as possible). This is the case for Trieste, whose representation and perhaps essence are marked by the work of Svevo. It is also the case for Dostoevsky's Saint Petersburg, Joyce's Dublin, Kafka's Prague, Bowles's Tangiers, and Pessoa's Lisbon. Here, human spaces and literature have become inseparable, and so also have the real and the imaginary.

The referent is no longer necessarily the one you think it is. In short, the writer becomes the author of the city. Dostoevsky and Kafka are cosmogonic heroes of the modern times; Joyce, Svevo, and Pessoa are invested with the highest powers, which they exert in and over their cities with authority. It is also not essential that a city have a single father or a single mother in literature. The literary genealogy of the major spatial hubs becomes lost in the fog, drowned in the mass of all those who have lived on paper. London, New York, Rome, Venice, Paris, and others are also filtered by the book. On the airplane that took him to Lisbon one winter day, Gianfranco Dioguardi, a journalist with *Il corriere della sera*, read Pessoa's *Book of Disquiet*. Arriving at the edge of the Tagus and on the strength of this reading, he was inclined, and perhaps destined, to consider "the city as a book to flip through before you read it."[23] Odysseus or Ulysses, the wily person, had founded Lisbon (Oulissipona) according to myth; Pessoa, which means "person" in Portuguese, had written Lisbon. It only remained to see how the city followed the line of the story, the melody of the verse. The jubilation of the flaneur, the reader in the making, is intense. Stefano Malatesta, another Italian journalist, for his part took a stroll down the Avenida da Liberdade, a major artery that runs through the heart of the Portuguese metropolis, alongside Antonio Tabucchi. He noticed, "on one of those white plastic walls a freshly painted little black figure, a silhouette that someone could have just affixed with a pad or a rubber stamp."[24] Tabucchi soon unraveled the mystery: Someone had drawn the outline of the Person. The chain never ends. In a visit to Lisbon, while on my own *flânerie* along the Avenida, I absently searched for the same figure, without seeing it, of course. The Person had reserved his rights to be erased. However . . . I ended up rediscovering his trace after all, there where most tourists would have been stunned to see it in the form of a bronze statue sitting at a table on the terrace of the A Brasileira café. This excessive presence would jostle against the circumspection of Pessoa, in perverting the reading or disturbing the reader with respect to the city whose image he had maintained in his head.[25] So much the better, no doubt, because if the writer is author of the city, he or she cannot be the tyrant. Baudelaire and Gracq had noticed that the form of a city changes more than a mortal's heart. But the form of a city changes faster also in the heart of a mortal, in his mind. This is what allows the literary process to begin.

It also happens that the shape of a city no longer exists only in the heart of a mortal. If the text sometimes—or always?—precedes the human space, it happens no less often after it survives the place. One could play with any number of literary examples that describe sites wiped off the map. After all, one of the oldest stories of Western civilization, the *Iliad*, depicts a city that has disappeared. The memorials to sunken cities are legion in literature, painting, and even film, with its much shorter history. Who is not now disturbed by the shadow cast by New York's twin towers in American cinema before September 11, 2001? Special mention could be made to homes, streets, and cities who suddenly change their configuration and whose autobiographer is the witness. Again, the inventory is vast. It includes Perec's *W; or, The Memory of Childhood*, in which the narrator relates with some nostalgia how his parents' house at 24 rue Vilin in Paris had been demolished along with three quarters of the street. Or take *The Snows of Yesteryear* by Gregor von Rezzori. The great writer from Bucovina (a former province of the Hapsburg Empire), had left the capital, Czernowitz, in the 1930s, traveling through Austria and Germany before settling in Tuscany. In the 1980s, Rezzori decided to return to Czernowitz to see what had changed in more than half a century. During the interval, Czernowitz had had time to become part of the Soviet Union, after being Austro-Hungarian and Romanian. Shortly afterward, it became part of Ukraine: Czernowitz, Cernăuţi, Tschernopol, Chernovtsy. Rezzori, who over the decades had meticulously prepared his depictions of the place, was confronted with the "present ugly reality" that now superseded it.[26] The writer had strayed into the diverse strata that constitute the complex representation of a place, as he was well aware: "So be it! It was indeed in the realm of the unbelievable and fabulous that my own Czernopol, the imagined counterpart to the factual Czernowitz, was located. The reality I had found in Chernovtsy threatened to destroy even this."[27] Where is reality? This nagging question, for Rezzori as for everyone else, keeps the text in place, the place in the text. Would it lie in the Dublin of Joyce's *Ulysses*? Eco thinks so, when he admits to being "one of those who has gone looking for the house in Eccles Street in Dublin where Leopold Bloom is supposed to have lived."[28] Others have gone in search of Sherlock Holmes's residence at 221B Baker Street in London. According to Eco, these are just pleasant activities, "episodes of literary fanship."[29] But in any event, the pilgrimage to somewhere in space (as with Perec or Rezzori) or somewhere that only exists in the text (as with the fans of Conan Doyle or Joyce) shows once again that the writer is the author of the city, the demiurge of places. The weight of intertextuality on the perception of a human space is considerable.

The Legibility of Places

The text precedes the place, and sometimes seems to anticipate its discovery. The way that the Antilles made their entry into European history shows how the ancient or medieval imagination could burst forth at any time into objective reality. Specifically, the imaginary seemed like a submerged iceberg of which the real was only the visible tip (even if that tip appeared only in the warm Caribbean). Maybe at the beginning of the Age of Discovery, there was already continuity between the real and the imaginary. Conversely, the text sometimes perpetuates a place in memory, in the image that it carries. In the Chernovtsy one now visits in Ukraine, there still exists the Czernowitz of Rezzori, and there remains on one of the streets a house that may have disappeared but that belongs to the author's family. The relationship of the text to the place is proleptic in some cases; in others, it is analeptic and steeped in strata that geocriticism must investigate. It sometimes happens that the text and the place overlap to the point that they end up merging. The place is then a text that is a place, or perhaps the text is a place that is a text. Reading a place and perceiving a text, the perception of what is read in a place, the multiple interweavings between the page and the stone or the earth—any combination is possible.

The association between the place and the text is close; it is particularly close between the city and the novel. "The city is a novel," writes Jean Roudaut, "The novel is an imaginary city."[30] Many writers would agree. Tokyo is one of those sites where all dimensions of reality and fantasy seem to converge. In *Répertoire V*, Butor devotes a chapter to "the city as text" in considering the Japanese megalopolis. Like Calvino, Butor is aware that human spaces never appear as blank pages: "If I arrive in a foreign city, Tokyo, for example, I am accompanied, received, and pursued by the text."[31] This prompts Butor to propose a somewhat geocritical project: "One could thus make for each culture a diagram of urban presence."[32] And that which applies to urban spaces could be extended throughout human space. Tokyo had earlier inspired analogous comments by Roland Barthes in *Empire of Signs*. Excited by the spectacle of Japan, Barthes had entered the mixed zone where text and city overlap, where what was once the city becomes text, while text in turn becomes the city: "The City is an ideogram: the Text continues."[33] The Text with a capital *T* seems situated at the intersection of various dimensions of reality. Trying to understand the physical environment here involves a complex exercise, which Barthes graciously agrees to perform: "I am, in that country, a reader, not a visitor."[34] Barthes had come to experience what Pierre Sansot, in his *Poétique de la ville*, calls the "legibility of the city."[35] In a sense, Barthes's project inaugurates his contribution to one of the major areas of literary theory of the 1970s: reading the city. This does not stop at the example of Tokyo, for the West also has its disorientating character, its disconcerting rhythms, and its ideograms, quite a few of which might be difficult to decipher, or could be judged beautiful or enigmatic. One does not just read spaces that are thought to be different from one's own. The quest for urban and spatial legibility is not marked by some new form of paradoxically postmodern exoticism, dedicated to reading the unreadable. Were one French, one would read Paris the same way as Tokyo or any place that is a text. Handke's opening words to *Alone*, "I shut my eyes and out of the black letters the city lights took shape,"[36] register the fact that black letters can illuminate human spaces. And it is in these spaces that the words are coiled. One must then, as Roudaut suggests, "consider the city as a text where, beneath a clear meaning, a thousand buried and murmuring words reside."[37]

Legibility is a characteristic of places, and not just for their use in fiction, cinema, or other arts. It is striking just how much the relations between text and place are the focus of the interdisciplinary field of spatiality studies. This connection gained force as soon as we began to understand that certain material spaces amounted to simulacra. The derealization of the world is incompatible with the perception of a solidly objective reality. Here, the terms of reality seem closer to those of fiction and the interpretative practices proper to fiction. We have seen that urban planners and architects are using the pages of Dickens (e.g., Kevin Lynch), or of Zola, Pratolini, and Vázquez Montalbán (Flavia Schiavo), to explicate the urban space of London, Paris, Florence, and Barcelona. Many geographers do the same, as they read fictional texts in order to expand their studies of representation of *real* spaces. A tradition is now emerging, and new directions taken in cultural geography reveal that it is no longer the book or other written discourses alone that carry the image of the city, but that the city itself is couched in a discursive framework that gives the place its materiality, that *takes place*, or that *makes* it a place.

In *Thirdspace*, Edward Soja has engaged in this reading using the example of Los Angeles, including the renovation program in Orange County. According to Soja, the first step on the path of derealization consists of effacing city limits, blurring the distinction between center and periphery. In geography and urban planning, this tendency has led in recent years to a proliferation of new terms—including outer cities, edge cities, technopole, technoburbs, silicon landscapes, postsuburbia, and the metroplex—so many "amorphous implosions of archaic suburbia," so much vocabulary to furnish a postmodern (posthuman?) poetics of the urban margins. For his part, Soja coins the term *exopolis* to describe these phenomena, before noting that they "are not only exo-cities, orbiting outside; they are ex-cities as well, no longer what the city used to be."[38] This *exopolis* is generated alongside other urban transformations, whereby the traditional city has become, in Los Angeles, a *flexcity* (postindustrial metropolis), a *cosmopolis* (a global and "glocal" world city), a *polaricity* (typified by increasing social inequalities), a *carceral city* (a prison or police polis), or a *simcity* (a hyperreal space of simulacra). These six neologisms correspond to the constitutive discourse of the postmodern megalopolis, of which Los Angeles is perhaps the paradigmatic example. The deconstruction of the traditional concept of urban space or place leads to a highly problematic relationship between what is termed "reality" and the discursive. It establishes space's fundamental status as a simulacrum where, in Jean Baudrillard's famous elaboration, reality is supplanted by a derealizing hyperreality. Here, according to Baudrillard, the map precedes the territory, the representation replaces the referent, which ultimately exists only in discourse—a discourse that could only be iconic. We may recall Franco Farinelli's interpretation of the megalopolis as spectacular, since it is clear that pure spectacle would be cut off from any objective reality. From this follows a long series of consequences that I will not go into here; instead, I will content myself to say that their effects are often perceived in a negative way, as it is assumed that the framework of uncertainty that characterizes the hyperreal also underwrites the crisis of representation in the last decades of the twentieth century. After a stay at the Bonaventure Hotel, again in Los Angeles, Fredric Jameson evoked the schizophrenia of the individual who attempts to map spaces in which the real and hyperreal no longer coincide. This complicates the subject's position in formerly familiar space, a space now lacking density and become radically antianthropomorphic.[39] Celeste Olalquiaga, in *Megalopolis: Contemporary Cultural Sensibilities*,[40] denounces an endemic, urban psychasthenia, whose symptoms are manifested in the split between the self and its environment. Soja, referring to Olalquiaga's analysis, observes that "bodies become likes cities in what she calls 'poetic condensation.' History is replaced by geography, stories by maps, memories by scenarios, with everything connected to 'the topography of computer screens and video monitors.'"[41] Postmodern urban space thus produces the complete subversion of the hierarchy governing the relations of space and time. The spatiotemporal ensemble now appears to be dominated by the spatial component; temporality itself dissolves in a context of diminished diachronic density.

However, as we know, the postmodern is a regime in which, like Figaro in his time, one has to laugh to keep from crying. Almost always, hyperrealism is playful, despite the deterioration of the environment that it embodies. It is a realm, in Jameson's phrase, of the "hysterical sublime," whose greatest, as well as most minute, feature is the simulacrum. In this context, the city becomes readable because it merges into a parodic discourse of text and image, the arrangement of the text or image produced by the map. The *place* in this now reduced range between the real and imaginary—a gap that can be filled, if one believes Soja, by the emergence of a "real-and-imagined" dimension—is born from the coalescence of two readings of the world that have traditionally been kept apart: the real and the imaginary. This new economy of the mind has reoriented postmodern cartography, and it has alleviated the torments created by too static a survey of the world. Michel Serres imagines an intriguing scenario: "Let us draw a map, real and imaginary, single and double, ideal and false, virtual and utopian, rational, analytic, of a world where the Alps are moved closer to the Himalayas, so that forms echo each other and the cries of those excluded are heard here and there."[42] In a world where the Himalayas and the Alps communicate across the great distances that separate them in the official atlases, the map slides into the sphere of plural readings, which is usually associated with the world of fiction. It expresses a possible world, encompassing both the real and the imaginary. Far from fixing things in place, it flirts with the provisional. As Serres notes again in his characteristic style, "the maps of places or roads are printed or written, made visible, on clay or marble, which wears out or is rubbed out on the fluid surface, with variable viscosity, where it evanesces, becoming invisible on the breaths of a volatile wind. How to capture, on the too solid pages of this atlas, these beautiful maps of clay?"[43]

Undoubtedly, it is not necessary to capture the representation of the entire world in order to read it. A fleeting glance will suffice. That is what Nuruddin Farah, the great Somali novelist, tries to put into practice in *Maps*. Raised in the Ogaden, a region long disputed by Ethiopia and Somalia and with its own tragic aspirations for independence, the young Askar is fascinated by maps, with which he lines the walls of his room. At the end of adolescence, now living in Mogadishu, Askar arouses the curiosity of his uncle Hilaal: "Tell me, Askar. Do you find truth in the maps you draw?" The young man is taken aback, so his uncle explains his thoughts more precisely: "Do you carve out of your soul the invented truth of the maps you draw? Or does the daily truth match, for you, the reality you draw and the maps others draw?" After taking time to reflect, Askar replies, "I hope, as dreamers do, that the dreamt dream will match the dreamt reality—that is, the invented truth of one's imagination. My maps invent nothing. They copy a given reality, they map out the roads a dreamer has walked, they identify a notional truth."[44] And this notional truth is, paradoxically, that of a dream. This example certainly speaks to the overall relationship between reality and the dream, between so-called objective reality and the imaginary, but from a postcolonial angle, it also illustrates the situation of Africa, which had been conceived according to the fantasies of the colonizer and whose representation varies depending on opposing points of view. As Farah's novel reveals, "There is a truth in maps. The Ogaden, as Somali, is truth. To the Ethiopian map-maker, the Ogaden, as Somali, is untruth."[45] In Africa, it remains to be seen whether a conversation between the Himalayas and the Alps will take place.

If the map is a means of interaction between the real and imaginary, between the realeme and a more or less faithful (but faithful according to what standard?) representation, the city—each location, in fact—enters a context in which everything is subject to reading. Examples abound, like those of Los Angeles, whose derealization has been explored by Jameson and Soja, or Tokyo, whose legibility struck Barthes and Butor. Many dissociating strategies underlie the space of the postmodern exopolis, strongly reinforced in the periphery. The city is inside out, upside down. After losing its center, after abetting its own processes of blurring, its essential marginalization, it today becomes analogous to the text, with deconstruction lying in wait . . . at least, where it is not already at work. Admittedly, as François Dagognet notes, "the city struggles against space and dispersion, which is why it piles up so much less than it encloses and organizes. More precisely, it does not cease to propose, like a mega-Book, summaries of itself; it redoubles and recenters its efforts to erase the misfortunes of a simple erasure."[46] But it cannot be satisfied with an indefinitely extended summary of itself. In doing so, it reasserts its singular identity, doomed to silence. If the city is a megabook, this megabook would be an open work that, like Borges's Aleph, feeds the dream of a space that contains all spaces, "the place where, without admixture or confusion, all the places of the world, seen from every angle, coexist."[47] This megabook could never be read to its conclusion, just as the space that contains all the spaces would be the object of an endless and inconceivable quest.

Reading the Text, Reading Space, and the New Realism

Space corresponds to a texture, because it is reticular down to its smallest folds. In the postmodern condition, the call for smooth space (see Deleuze) seems either nostalgic or incantatory, because striations are virtually everywhere. It is difficult to perceive the smooth in the dense layers of the world. Today, a return to the smooth seems like wishful thinking. Moreover, space is more than a texture. In Lefebvre's terms, space is architexture and architecture.[48] It is an intangible conglomerate that regulates the flows of society. In my view, mindful of the uncertain but constant oscillation between text and place, the coupling of architexture and architecture takes on a different meaning. Calvino makes the Paris that makes Calvino, Butor makes the Tokyo that makes Butor, Borges makes the Buenos Aires that makes Borges, and so on to infinity. The architexture–architecture dyad then gives way to a third, intertexture. Human space takes on an intertextual dimension as well. The story line is superimposed upon the road or the route. And like the line, this layout is an artifact of one or the other; by turns, if not in their entirety, all are real, imaginary, or real-and-imaginary, and they are subject to forces contradictory in themselves but similar in their effects; these forces tend to bring all three (real, imaginary, and real-and-imaginary) into closer proximity as they deconstruct them. Narrative is now freed from the linear progression that was traditionally reserved for it; space has become recalcitrant to the classical dialectic that radically opposed the center and the periphery. Narrative searches itself, as does space. Space becomes more complex and diversified, as does narrative. Human space and narrative tend to obey the common logic, analogous if not identical. Once again, the derealization of space leads to its fictionalization. Generalized fictionalization (the simulacrum of which Baudrillard speaks) necessarily leads literature and other forms of mimetic art into an original order, which requires a new approach to realism.

This new realism reflects a weakened reality, one that has become indistinguishable from fiction—the most striking paradigms of fictionalized reality are found in the theme park, the mall of every American town, or even the kaleidoscopic spectacle perpetually popping up on television screens. This postmodern realism engages in the representation of a world characterized by a rapid deterritorialization, a world eminently "transgressive." This realism thus has nothing to do with that of a Balzac or a Zola, since objective reality has learned to deal with blue oranges, with the multiplication of the unique, with everything that distances itself from the misleading evidence of an immediately perceptible referent. The perception of objectivity has learned to integrate the subjective and even the manifestly fictional. In this relaxed setting, the mimetic arts are able to participate more actively in the interpretation of a reality that closely approaches the fictional universe. After all, the Greeks did not have a word to characterize their literature in this way, instead wavering between *paideia* (education) and *mousike* (art of the Muses). The qualification between reality and fiction, which would have entailed their separation, made no sense in Greece because, as Carlos García Gual explains, "its literature was united with its mythology, and myths were united with the literature in a way that has no parallel in our world today."[49] No parallel? Indeed! What remains of the moat separating them, which, after the pioneering narratives of the Greeks, after the invention of the concept of "literature," had grown to the extent that it irrevocably cut off reality from fiction? A trench, at the very least . . . but no larger than the one we laugh at as we lightly step across it.[50]

As long as one adheres to this premise, is one entitled to apply the same approach to space as that previously reserved for literature, film, and so on? Can one imagine a *reading* of the city? If space and writing share a model, then it should be possible to read it, because ultimately all writing is readable. Evoking the Paris of Balzac, Marie-Claire Ropars-Wuilleumier has remarked, "Weaving texts, the city writes, inscribing cryptic traces that must be deciphered in order to reach the goal."[51] The text is in space, but space is also in the text. Interaction is the underlying principle. The reconciliation between the text and space was taken up by Butor in a discussion of "the city as a literary genre." Assuming that "the city can be regarded as a literary work," Butor reflects on the urban genre and reaches the following conclusion: "Within this great genre, one finds stylistic difference between Tokyo, Mexico City, New York, or Paris, as well as differences between the various neighborhoods of these cities!"[52] Butor is not just using genre as a metaphor; he is advocating a strong, "narratological" reading of the city and of space. It is true that he was not the first: one thinks of Kevin Lynch's pioneering work in urban geography, as well as Barthes's work in semiotics. In a lecture titled "Semiology and Urbanism" (originally given in Naples in 1967), Barthes discusses this discursive valence implicit in each city, and in each place: "The city is a discourse, and this discourse is actually a language: the city speaks to its inhabitants, we speak our city, the city where we are, simply by inhabiting it, by traversing it, by looking at it."[53] Inspired by reading Victor Hugo's *Notre-Dame de Paris*, in particular a chapter titled "This Will Kill That," in which Hugo measures the relative weights of the architectural monument and writing (and finds that the latter can kill the former), Barthes pushes this insight to its logical conclusion:

> And here we rediscover Hugo's old intuition: the city is a writing; the man who moves about the city, *i.e.*, the city's user (which is what we all are, users of the city), is a sort of reader who, according to his obligations and his movements, samples fragments of the utterance in order to actualize them in secret. When we move about in a city, we are all in the situation of the reader in Queneau's *100,000 Million Poems*, where we can find a different poem by changing a single verse; unknown to us, we are something like that avant-garde reader when we are in a city.[54]

Let us return briefly to Milan. Reading his book without uttering a word, Ambrose had once astonished Saint Augustine. He read as one would study a map: in silence. The book became a map. Perhaps the patron saint of Milan already intuited the close links between text and place, without which Augustine, immersed in that triple present of his own invention, would not have developed a new theory of time.

Can we go further than Barthes and Butor? Can we extend to the city an aesthetic of reception that would make the author an architect or an urban planner and make a townsperson a reader receiving a work? If the city, and hence any human space, were a megabook or a palimpsest consisting of layers of spatialized time, it seems conceivable that it could be approached with an aesthetic of reception. One could read a city in accordance with the reception theory of Hans Robert Jauss. Even if one does not follow him all the way to his conclusion, Jauss's seven theses regarding literary history are still applicable to the *reading* of spaces. Jauss's method takes into account seven criteria: (1) the process of realization of the text, (2) the horizon of expectation of the reader, (3) changes to that horizon that introduce and integrate innovation, (4) the history of the reception of works, (5) reorientation of the past under the effects of an innovative present, (6) the dialectic of the diachronic and synchronic, and (7) the social impact of reception. Just for the pleasure of bringing together (seemingly) incongruous things, let us explore the parallels for a moment.

Commenting on the process of realization, Jauss notes that the literary work "is much more like an orchestration that strikes ever new resonances among its readers and that frees the text from the material of the words and brings it to a contemporary existence."[55] Space is also an orchestration of this kind. Similarly, the space that one frequents supports a horizon of expectation, which constitutes a type of prior generic and thematic experience: space is metropolitan or rural, desertlike, or whatever; it may be marked by death or love, danger or pleasure, and so on. The third criterion for Jauss includes the concept of "aesthetic distance,"[56] which signifies innovation. This aesthetic distance arises from the difference between the preexisting horizon of expectation and the new work, but it is bound to decrease "to the extent that the original negativity of the work has become self-evident and has itself entered into the horizon of future aesthetic experience, as a henceforth familiar expectation."[57] It works the same with place, which in some cases contains an important aesthetic distance, a gap that can be absorbed into pure familiarity. Nothing is sadder than a new city turned old. The dialectic of innovation and sedimentation, which lies at the heart of Jauss's theory, underlies the history of reception, because the dialectical movement avoids the false notion of "the 'timelessly true' meaning of a literary work."[58] There is a constant tension between the work and the present time. What applies to reading literature applies equally to reading spaces.

From a geocritical point of view, this leads to a stratigraphic approach. Jauss's fifth thesis indicates that the emergence of a new work sometimes arrives from forgetting those ignored potentialities of a previous work. Thus Mallarmé's obscure lyricism prepared the ground for the return of the baroque poetry of Góngora. In other words, according to Jauss, the present may reorient the past, which, like objective meaning, is not given once and for all. Again, this notion is perfectly extendible to the reading of a space, whose past can be reactivated—and sometimes deliberately renewed—in the present. Postmodern architecture, especially via the principle of "double coding," has even made the reactivation of the past a pillar of its aesthetic. The Louvre in Paris, where I. M. Pei's glass pyramid lives alongside a sixteenth-century royal palace; the Sainsbury Wing (designed by Robert Venturi and Denise Scott Brown) of the National Gallery in London, where neoclassical pastiche brings together Corinthian colonnades and openings shaped like garage doors; Ricardo Bofill's Theatre d'Abraxas in Marne-la-Vallée, where a new city and a fake Palace of Versailles form a striking contrast—all illustrate the "presence of the past" aesthetic. Jauss's sixth criterion corresponds in part to the principle of asynchrony, which I tried to define in Chapter 4. Indeed, as Jauss notes, "a horizontal change in the historical process of 'literary evolution' need not be pursued only throughout the web of all the diachronic facts and filiations, but can also be established in the altered remains of the synchronic literary system and read out of further cross-sectional analyses." He adds that the "series of arbitrary points of intersection between diachrony and synchrony" allow the literary historian to "articulate the process-like character of 'literary evolution' in its formative moments of history as well as the caesurae between periods."[59] Like the text, the history of a given space is not entirely diachronic; its history may also be revealed in synchronic slices. The seventh thesis states that the "social function of literature manifests itself in its genuine possibility only where the literary experience of the reader enters into the horizon of expectations of his lived praxis, preforms his understanding of the world, and thereby also has an effect on his social behavior."[60] It goes without saying that the interaction between reading space and social behavior is significant; that is the very interaction that inspired the theories of Michel de Certeau and Torsten Hägerstrand on quotidian space, as well as the theories of Lefebvre and others.

The intimate dialogue between text and space is effective at the time when, in Dagognet's felicitous phrase, the poet creates less "a simple typography than a bold topography."[61] This dialogue has sometimes been incongruous, especially when it led to the confusion of identities between them. Both Lefebvre and Sansot have taken a stand against strictly overlapping the literary and the literal, or literature and a reality viewed as objective. For Lefebvre, "When codes worked up from literary texts are applied to spaces—to urban spaces, say—we remain, as may easily be shown, on the purely descriptive level. Any attempt to use such codes as a means of deciphering social space must surely reduce that space itself to the status of a *message*, and the inhabiting of it to the status of a *reading*."[62] In line with this reasoning, Lefebvre adds, "The problem is that any search for space in literary texts will find it everywhere and in every guise: enclosed, described, projected, dreamt of, speculated about. What texts can be considered special enough to provide the basis for a 'textual' analysis?"[63] In Lefebvre's view, space and literature are governed by different codes; the one—literature—is opaque to the other, or to put it more precisely, space is hermetic in literature and resists any reading in advance. The social dimension of space does not dawn on fiction; space is dispersed in the imagination, a proliferating, out-of-control, and de-scriptive machine.

Like Lefebvre, Sansot devotes part of his *Poétique de la ville* to casting doubt upon the potential of the text to interfere with reality. The text is the medium of a dream: "The city thus generates a poetics, for which we nevertheless have to take responsibility. But must we turn away from the construction site of the cities we live in? Is it possible to reconcile a practical and poetic city? The dream can be a barrier between men and the mechanisms that oppress them . . . The urban critic seeks, however, to transform reality."[64] Sansot appears to reduce the urban "poetic" to a mask we strap over the face of the "real" city, one that would hold an urban "practice." In this context, confusing the poetic and the practical would enhance the alienation experienced by *Homo urbanus*. Sansot asks, "Should we therefore demystify, instead of remythify, and differentiate between two kinds of imaginaries, inconsistent in their approach and their goals?" All "reverie" (Sansot's terminology, like his book's title, follows Bachelard's) is not sterile. It often carries with it "an outline of liberation while the alienation seemed extreme, a starting point for recapturing that which had been taken away and installed everywhere else."[65] This type of concession has opened a gap, which has engulfed not only post-Marxist and postmodern criticism but any criticism that wishes to pull fiction out of that hermetic ivory tower that has been traditionally erected on the beautiful landscape of the "real."

The objections of Lefebvre and Sansot, dating from the early 1970s, are neither isolated nor obsolete. However, they still rely on bases that I have tried to relativize. The poetics of the city (and of space) and the practice of the city (and of space) are not mutually exclusive. Poetics and practice are pledged to a common denominator: both revolve around a representation. Fiction is a representation of variable geometry, what Deleuze calls *orgiastic representation*: "When representation discovers the infinite within itself, it no longer appears as *organic* representation but as *orgiastic* representation: it discovers within itself the limits of the organized; tumult, restlessness and passion underneath the apparent calm. It rediscovers monstrosity."[66] Thus organic, reality is entirely circumscribed with a prestigious and dominant representation consecrated by the community. Books are meant to be read; at first glance, spaces are not meant to be read, and yet they are eminently readable, although heretofore, many viewed such reading as the "reduction" mentioned by Lefebvre. The imagination is not a factor of alienation. To the contrary, it is the monster that blazes the trail to infinity. Narrativity, albeit fictional, brings a greater knowledge of the essence of space, just as any other representation, discursive or not. According to Christine Montalbetti, "discourse does not express the world, but impresses, leaves its mark, and makes variable the interior and exterior balance of the city. Discourse is impervious to the world, but the world is permeable by discourse, which rearranges its shape; the world does not inform discourse, discourse transforms the world."[67] Accordingly, Montalbetti refuses to endorse the interaction between the library and the world, instead validating a one-way action by the library upon the world. Because the total break between the text and "real" space is now difficult to envisage, this has become the "incessant conversation between the written word and space," according to Marc Augé, who goes on to say that "the city exists in the imagination that it inspires and that is inspired by it, that it feeds and that feeds it, that it gives birth to and in which it is reborn in every moment."[68]

There is indeed an interaction. And this interaction manifests itself in massive intertextuality, for which it is the cause and effect. In its most usual definitions, intertextuality is seen as a process of continuity from one text to another based on a logic that allows for a single path within a textual system. A writing replies to another within the library, which becomes the basis for a differentiated repetition, legitimated by an autotelic, fully circular principle. Intertextuality was originally meant to clarify the arborescence of fictional production, the "discursive *alter-junctions*" (to use Julia Kristeva's phrase).[69] But intertextuality is not really a lonely walk through the woods of novels and other literary genres. Space, grasped through the representation that texts sustain, can be "read" like a text; the city, that paradigmatically human space, can be "read" like a novel. One reads space; one traverses a text; one reads a text as one traverses space. In this expanded view of textuality, which encompasses equally bookish architexture and spatial architecture, textuality eventually escapes the closed logic that confines the text within a textual "system" (another name, perhaps, for the ivory tower). The alter-junctions between the text and the space go beyond the radical otherness that separates the world and the library, reality and fiction, the referent and representation. This has already been identified by Montalbetti, who argues for an equivalence between writing and seeing the world: "The metaphor of the world as a book equates seeing and speaking, and thus restores a homonomy, an identity of laws, between the visual object and the writing that sought to capture it."[70] The intertextual dimension of the relationship between text and space is highlighted by Montalbetti as well, but it is truncated. The direction of this communication is one way, going from the library to the world; only space is a hyperlink, as we recall. This is a literary point of view. If one believes Marc Brosseau, who assiduously pays attention to the text even though he is a geographer, the interaction has its limits that mark the "real" world, because "the city *is not* a text," and therefore we should "not forget the metaphorical status of the text–place relationship, and seek to transpose literally modes of reading and analysis."[71] For Brosseau, the metaphor is didactic and heuristic. It carries interpretations but can go no further.

From a geocritical perspective, the two restrictions that Montalbetti and Brosseau point out require further comment. Is the relationship between text and space univocal? Are these alter-junctions purely metaphorical? As to the first question, we already know the answer: texts and spaces are thoroughly interconnected. Space informs the text that produces a fictional representation of a spatial referent. Conversely, and thus responding to Brosseau, the impact of the (fictional) text on a given space is obvious when one looks at the intertextual chain that associates spatial "reality" with fiction. The writer is the author of his city, and a given representation, even—especially?—a fictional one, eventually acts upon the realeme, affecting the way it is perceived. In a context of permanent movement, which Jauss subsumes under the term *innovation*, a new representation is born, a representation that integrates the fictional additions made by the writer or filmmaker in a world undergoing a process of derealization, which might be partly understood in a dialectical manner. It goes without saying that one of the major challenges for the geocritic is to engage with this looping mechanism by trying to understand and explain it (as best one can, because nothing is simple). One of the other issues facing geocriticism is no longer merely to identify the correlation between reality and fiction, between the world and the library, or to consider it as a metaphor, but to come up with a genuine working hypothesis. Since, in terms of representation, fiction is able to influence reality, it is conceivable that literature and other mimetic arts, on the basis of approaches they make possible, could have applications well outside of the fields to which they had traditionally been assigned. Would literary studies be "applicable" to areas outside of the library, or even outside the territories of fiction? In other words, could the study of literature help to decipher the world? I think so. I humbly concede that this credo is far from revolutionary: it has been shared by many people for a long time. I have referred several times to Butor's fifth *Répertoire*, but in his second, which dates back to 1964, he concludes his discussion of "the space of the novel" with these remarks: "Of course, it is first of all in the space of representations that the novel introduces its essential modification, but who can fail to see how information influences both routes and objects; how, in fact, beginning with an invention in a novel, objects can be effectively shifted, and the order of trajectories—journeys, voyages, passages, and paths—can be transformed?"[72] Supported by theoretical models that tend to reduce the gap between the referent and representation, geocriticism aims to explore the interface between these dimensions previously split apart, to bring into closer rapport the library and the world. The applicable fields for geocritical study are as numerous as one can imagine. But its domain, located at the crossroads of many disciplines, would include tourism, both the tourist industry and the dreamy tourism of fiction. Other areas could include urban planning and architecture, to name just a couple. In the end, its domain is coextensive with that of the imagination. Faced with this enormous project unfolding in literary studies, faced with the imaginary realm that one inhabits like a madhouse, it is impossible to really conclude. Let us then be content with a very provisional conclusion, albeit a *trompe-l'œil.*

In the infinite variation of cartographic discourses, reality finds its niche: sense and nonsense, territory and deterritorialization, the geography of the uncertain, and the geography of relationships too. In other words, it is the hesitant waltz of a space that lies just out of sight. All observers struggle to represent what unfolds before their eyes. All discourse is a transcript of a conceived spectacle. If there is a cleavage, it is between the representation orchestrated by the narrative and the present realeme. Literature is loose; it has room to maneuver. Other disciplines have less latitude; they attempt to reproduce as closely as possible a stretch of reality—one that they have chosen among many other possibilities. Thus one makes them alternatives, sanctioning a generic and partly epistemological rupture between literary production and "performative" productions (which participate in the "real" world), thus also invoking the autonomy of literature and literariness. Or else one believes that, subject to a principle of transgressivity, the threshold between reality and fiction can be crossed. Then one could try to address fictional narrative and performative narrative (as in tourist brochures, for instance) together, and one could consider their interactions. At a time when literary studies seeks pathways that could lead it out of the merely literary and bring it into line with the related "realities," I think geocriticism, insofar as it studies the literary stratifications of referential space, can play an important role, since geocriticism operates somewhere between the geography of the "real" and the geography of the "imaginary" . . . two quite similar geographies that may lead to others, which critics should try to develop and explore.

Notes

Preface

1. See, for example, Barney Warf and Santa Arias, *The Spatial Turn: Interdisciplinary Perspectives* (London: Routledge, 2008); see also, Peta Mitchell, *Cartographic Strategies of Postmodernity: The Figure of the Map in Contemporary Theory and Fiction* (London: Routledge, 2007).
2. Fredric Jameson, *Postmodernism; or, The Cultural Logic of Late Capitalism* (Durham: Duke University Press, 1991), 418; see also Edward Soja, *Postmodern Geographies: The Reassertion of Space in Critical Social Theory* (London: Verso, 1989).
3. See Bertrand Westphal, *Le rivage des mythes. Une géocritique méditerranéenne* (Limoges: Pulim, 2001).
4. See my review in *L'esprit créateur: The International Quarterly of French and Francophone Studies* 49.3 (Fall 2009): 134. On "literary cartography," see Robert T. Tally Jr., *Melville, Mapping and Globalization: Literary Cartography in the American Baroque Writer* (London: Continuum, 2009).
5. See Edward Soja, *Thirdspace: Journeys to Los Angeles and Other Real-and-Imagined Places* (Oxford: Blackwell, 1996).
6. Frank Kermode, *The Sense of an Ending: Studies in the Theory of Fiction* (Oxford: Oxford University Press, 1967), 3.
7. Among them, my edited collection (in progress), tentatively titled *Geocritical Explorations: Space, Place, and Mapping in Literary and Cultural Studies*, which contains a brief essay by Westphal and which may serve as a companion volume to *Geocriticism*.

Introduction

1. Yuri M. Lotman, *Universe of the Mind: A Semiotic Theory of Culture*, trans. Ann Shukman (Bloomington: Indiana University Press, 1990), 172.
2. Giuseppe Tardiola, *Atlante fantastico del medioevo* (Rome: Rubeis, 1990), 20.
3. Mikhail Bakhtin, *The Dialogic Imagination*, trans. Michael Holquist (Austin: University of Texas Press, 1981), 157.
4. Ibid., 207.
5. Michael J. Dear and Steven Flusty, eds., *The Spaces of Postmodernity: Readings in Human Geography* (Oxford: Blackwell, 2002), 5–6.
6. Ibid., 6.

7. Ibid., 254.
8. See Douglas Hofstadter, *Gödel, Escher, Bach: An Eternal Golden Braid* (New York: Vintage, 1989).
9. Hervé Regnauld, *L'espace, une vue de l'esprit?* (Rennes: Presses Universitaires de Rennes, 1998), 34.
10. Ibid., 115.
11. Yi-Fu Tuan, *Space and Place: The Perspective of Experience* (Minneapolis: University of Minnesota Press, 2002), 54.
12. Ibid., 83.
13. Ibid., 161.
14. Flavia Schiavo, *Parigi, Barcellona, Firenze: Forma e racconto* (Palermo: Sellerio, 2004), 77.
15. Maria de Fanis, *Geographie letterarie: Il senso del luogo nell'alto Adriatico* (Rome: Melteni, 2001), 21.
16. Hans Robert Jauss, *Aesthetic Experience and Literary Hermeneutics*, trans. Michael Shaw (Minneapolis: University of Minnesota Press, 1982), 288.
17. Ibid.
18. See Bertrand Westphal, "Pour une approche géocritique des textes," in *La géocritique mode d'emploi*, ed. Bertrand Westphal (Limoges: Presses Universitaires de Limoges, 2000), 9–40.
19. See Henri Lefebvre, *The Production of Space*, trans. Donald Nicholson-Smith (Oxford: Blackwell, 1991).

Chapter 1

1. Ilya Prigogine and Isabelle Stengers, *Order out of Chaos: Man's New Dialogue with Nature* (New York: Bantam, 1984), 75.
2. Ibid., 62.
3. Danilo Kiš, *Garden, Ashes*, trans. William J. Hannaher (New York: Harcourt Brace Jovanovich, 1975), 34.
4. Jean-Paul Auffray, *L'espace-temps* (Paris: Flammarion, 1996), 54.
5. Jean-François Lyotard, *The Postmodern Explained: Correspondence 1982–1985*, trans. Don Barry et al. (Minneapolis: University of Minnesota Press, 1993), 78.
6. Hans Meyerhoff, *Time in Literature* (Berkeley: University of California Press, 1955), 104.
7. Hermann Lübbe, "Der verkürtze Aufenthalt in der Gegenwart: Wandlungen des Geschichtsverständnisses," in *Postmoderne oder Der Kampf um die Zukunft*, ed. Peter Kemper (Frankfurt am Main: Fischer Taschenbuch Verlag, 1988), 145.
8. Homi Bhabha, *The Location of Culture* (London: Routledge, 1994), 1.
9. Ilya Prigogine and Isabelle Stengers, *La nouvelle alliance* (Paris: Gallimard, 1986), 366.
10. Alain Robbe-Grillet, *For a New Novel: Essays on Fiction*, trans. Richard Howard (Evanston, IL: Northwestern University Press, 1989), 22–23.
11. Paul Ricoeur, *Time and Narrative*, vol. 3, trans. Kathleen Blamey and David Pellauer (Chicago: University of Chicago Press, 1988), 31.
12. Georges Poulet, *Études sur le temps humain*, vol. 3 (Paris: Plon, 1989), 12.

13. Ibid., 40.
14. Maria Luisa Dalla Chiara Scabia, "Istanti e individui nelle logiche temporali," *Rivista di filosofia* 64 (1973): 99.
15. Ibid.
16. Gilles Deleuze, *The Fold: Leibniz and the Baroque*, trans. Tom Conley (Minneapolis: University of Minnesota Press, 1993), 77.
17. Gilles Deleuze and Félix Guattari, *A Thousand Plateaus*, trans. Brian Massumi (Minneapolis: University of Minnesota Press, 1987), 9.
18. Mikhail Bakhtin, *The Dialogic Imagination*, trans. Michael Holquist (Austin: University of Texas Press, 1981), 411.
19. Jorge Luis Borges, *Ficciones* (New York: Grove Press, 1962), 100.
20. Gilles Deleuze and Claire Parnet, *Dialogues*, trans. Hugh Tomlinson and Barbara Habberjam (New York: Columbia University Press, 1987), 102.
21. Prigogine and Stengers, *La nouvelle alliance*, 189.
22. Prigogine, *La nascita del tempo* (Milan: Bompiani, 1994), 42.
23. Ibid., 44.
24. Ibid., 71.
25. Yuri Andrukhovych and Andrzej Stasiuk, *Mon Europe* (Montricher: Les Éditions Noir sur Blanc, 2004), 150.
26. Pierre Ouellet, *Poétique du regard* (Limoges: Pulim, 2000), 337.
27. Brian McHale, *Postmodernist Fiction* (London: Routledge, 1987), 181.
28. Ibid., 58. See also, Roland Barthes, "Literature and Discontinuity," in *Critical Essays*, trans. Richard Howard (Evanston, IL: Northwestern University Press, 1972). In this essay, written just after the release of *Mobile*, Barthes defends Butor, who had received a barrage of criticism for arranging his text in the apparently arbitrary alphabetical order of U.S. state names: "Formally, alphabetical order has another virtue: by breaking, by rejecting the 'natural' affinities of the states, it obliges the discovery of other relations, quite as intelligent as the first, since the meaning of this whole combination of territories has come afterward, once they have been laid out on the splendid alphabetical list of the Constitution. In short, the order of the letters says that in the United States, there is no contiguity of spaces except in the abstract" (177).
29. Louky Bersianik, *Le pique-nique sur l'Acropole* (Montreal: Typo, 1992), 55.
30. Alina Reyes, *Behind Closed Doors*, trans. David Watson (New York: Grove, 1996), 1–2.
31. Marc Brosseau, *Des romans-géographes* (Paris: L'Harmattan, 1996), 79.
32. Joseph Brodsky, "Flight from Byzantium," in *Less Than One: Selected Essays* (New York: Farrar, Strauss, and Giroux, 1986), 435.
33. Fernand Braudel, *Les ambitions de l'histoire* (Paris: Le Livre de Poche, 1999), 59–60.
34. John Berger, "The Changing View of Man in the Portrait," in *Selected Essays*, ed. Geoff Dyer (New York: Pantheon, 2001), 102.
35. See Daniel Bell, *The Cultural Contradictions of Capitalism* (New York: Basic Books, 1976), 107–11.
36. Edward Soja, *Thirdspace: Journeys to Los Angeles and Other Real-and-Imagined Places* (Oxford: Blackwell, 1996), 169.
37. Deleuze and Parnet, *Dialogues*, 37, 23.

38. Marie-Claire Ropars-Wuilleumier, *Écrire l'espace* (Paris: Presses Universitaires de Vincennes, 2002), 8.
39. Georges Perec, *Species of Spaces and Other Pieces*, trans. John Sturrock (New York: Penguin, 1999), 51.
40. Ibid., 6.
41. Paul Virilio, "The Overexposed City," trans. Daniel Moshenberg, in *The Paul Virilio Reader*, ed. Steve Redhead (New York: Columbia University Press, 2004), 97.
42. Prigogine and Stengers, *Order out of Chaos*, 90. The quote is from Hegel, *The Philosophy of Nature*, § 261.
43. Ouellet, *Poétique du regard*, 333.
44. Ropars-Wuilleumier, *Écrire l'espace*, 237.
45. Bakhtin, *The Dialogic Imagination*, 84.
46. Ibid., 100.
47. Julian Holloway and James Kneale, "Mikhail Bakhtin: Dialogics of Space," in *Thinking Space*, ed. Mike Crang and Nigel Thrift (London: Routledge, 2000), 84.
48. Evelina Calvi, *Tempo e progetto: L'architettura come narrazione* (Milan: Guerrini, 1991), 22.
49. Braudel, *Les ambitions de l'histoire*, 102–3.
50. Daniel-Henri Pageaux, "De la géocritique à la géosymbolique: Regards sur un champ interdisciplinaire," in *La géocritique mode d'emploi*, ed. Bertrand Westphal (Limoges: Pulim, 2000), 129.
51. Emmanuelle Tricoire, "Géohistoire," in *EspacesTemps.net, Mensuelles* (June 18, 2003).
52. See David Harvey, *The Condition of Postmodernity* (Oxford: Blackwell, 1990), especially 211–25.
53. Ibid., 240.
54. Braudel, *Les ambitions de l'histoire*, 113.
55. Soja, *Thirdspace*, 47.
56. Jean Giono, *L'eau vive* (Paris: Gallimard, 1972), 205.
57. Hervé Regnauld, *L'espace, une vue de l'esprit?* (Rennes: Presses Universitaires de Rennes, 1998), 9.
58. Brosseau, *Des romans-géographes*, 17.
59. John K. Wright, "A Plea for the History of Geography," in *Human Nature in Geography*, ed. J. K. Wright (Cambridge, MA: Harvard University Press, 1966), 11–23.
60. Brosseau, *Des romans-géographes*, 31.
61. Ibid., 59–60.
62. Maria de Fanis, *Geografie letterarie: Il senso del luogo nell'alto Adriatico* (Rome: Meltini, 2001), 36.
63. Andrukhovych and Stasiuk, *Mon Europe*, 83.
64. Caren Kaplan, *Questions of Travel: Postmodern Discourses of Displacement* (Durham: Duke University Press, 1996), 144.
65. Flavia Schiavo, *Parigi, Barcellona, Firenze: Forma e racconto* (Palermo: Sellerio, 2004), 56, 67.
66. François Hartog, *The Mirror of Herodotus*, trans. Janet Lloyd (Berkeley: University of California Press, 1988), 344–45, emphasis added.
67. Ricoeur, *Time and Narrative*, 137.

Chapter 2

1. Pierre Auriol, *La fin du voyage* (Paris: Éditions Allia, 2004), 20.
2. Fernand Braudel, *Les ambitions de l'histoire* (Paris: Le Livre de Poche, 1999), 71.
3. Ilya Prigogine and Isabelle Stengers, *Order out of Chaos: Man's New Dialogue with Nature* (New York: Bantam, 1984), 313.
4. Michel Serres, *Atlas* (Paris: Flammarion, 1996), 64. [Serres's metaphor refers to the harlequin's clothing or coat, assembled from assorted bits and pieces, piled layer upon layer over the body, in a form of sartorial *bricolage*.]
5. Henri Lefebvre, *The Production of Space*, trans. Donald Nicholson-Smith (Oxford: Blackwell, 1991), 352.
6. Ibid., 411.
7. Ibid., 355–56.
8. Gilles Deleuze and Félix Guattari, *A Thousand Plateaus*, trans. Brian Massumi (Minneapolis: University of Minnesota Press, 1987), 370.
9. Ibid., 381.
10. Ibid., 371.
11. Ibid., 382.
12. Ibid., 479.
13. Ibid., 480.
14. Ibid., 482.
15. [English in the original.]
16. See Paola Zaccaria, *Mappe senza frontiere* (Bari: Palomar, 1999), 18.
17. Serres, *Atlas*, 12, 186.
18. Ibid., 130–31.
19. Ibid., 106.
20. Ibid., 141.
21. Dante, *Inferno*, trans. Mark Musa (New York: Penguin, 1984), canto 4, lines 70–72, p. 99.
22. Bernard Dupriez, *Gradus: Les procédés littéraires* (Paris: UGE, 1984), 237.
23. François Hartog, *The Mirror of Herodotus*, trans. Janet Lloyd (Berkeley: University of California Press, 1988), 331.
24. Ibid., 487.
25. Mark Bonta and John Protevi, *Deleuze and Geophilosophy* (Edinburgh: Edinburgh University Press, 2004), 82.
26. [A local expression in this region of France.]
27. Edward T. Hall, *The Dance of Life: The Other Dimension of Time* (Garden City, NY: Anchor, 1984), 3.
28. François Dagognet, *Le nombre et le lieu* (Paris: Vrin, 1984).
29. Deleuze and Guattari, *A Thousand Plateaus*, 323.
30. Bonta and Protevi, *Deleuze and Geophilosophy*, 17.
31. Itamar Even-Zohar, "Polysystem Studies," *Poetics Today* 11.1 (Spring 1990): 23.
32. Ibid., 24.
33. Michel Maffesoli, *Du nomadisme* (Paris: Le Livre de Poche, 1997), 73.
34. Jean Roudaut, *Les villes imaginaires dans la littérature française* (Paris: Hatier, 1990), 132.

35. Giorgio Agamben, *Stanzas: Word and Phantasm in Western Culture*, trans. Ronald L. Martinez (Minneapolis: University of Minnesota Press, 1993), xvii.
36. Julien Gracq, *The Shape of a City*, trans. Ingeborg M. Kohn (New York: Turtle Point, 2005), 27.
37. Even-Zohar, "Polysystem Studies," 11.
38. Ibid., 88.
39. Ibid., 13.
40. Ibid., 16.
41. Gloria Anzaldúa, *Borderlands/La Frontera: The New Mestiza* (San Francisco: Aunt Lute Books, 1999), 19.
42. Jacques Fontanille, "Formes tensives et passionelles du dialogue des sémiosphéres," in *La géocritique mode d'emploi*, ed. Bertrand Westphal (Limoges: Pulim, 2000), 119.
43. Yuri Lotman, *Universe of the Mind: A Semiotic Theory of Culture*, trans. Ann Shukman (Bloomington: Indiana University Press, 2000), 123.
44. Fontanille, "Formes tensives et passionelles du dialogue des sémiosphéres,"118.
45. Lotman, *Universe of the Mind*, 151.
46. Ibid., 162–63.
47. Ibid., 191.
48. Ibid., 203.
49. Deleuze and Guattari, *A Thousand Plateaus*, 369.
50. Ibid., 314.
51. Ibid., 322.
52. Ibid., 7.
53. Ibid., 505.
54. Gilles Deleuze and Félix Guattari, *What is Philosophy?*, trans. Hugh Tomlinson and Graham Burchell (New York: Columbia University Press, 1994), 109.
55. Ibid., 509
56. Caren Kaplan, *Questions of Travel: Postmodern Discourses of Displacement* (Durham, NC: Duke University Press, 1996), 90.
57. See Hartog, *The Mirror of Herodotus*, 121–25.
58. Maffesoli, *Du nomadisme*, 88–89.
59. Massimo Cacciari, *Geo-filosofia dell'Europa* (Milan: Adelphi, 1994).
60. See Carl Schmitt, *The Nomos of the Earth*, trans. G. L. Ulmen (New York: Telos Press, 2006), 345–46.
61. Deleuze and Guattari, *A Thousand Plateaus*, 380.
62. Luisa Bonesio, *Oltre il paesaggio* (Casalecchio: Arianna Editrice, 2002), 82.
63. Bonta and Protevi, *Deleuze and Geophilosophy*, 20.
64. Ilya Prigogine and Isabelle Stengers, *La nouvelle alliance* (Paris: Gallimard, 1986), 243.
65. Christian Jacob, *La description de la terre habitée de Denys d'Alexandrie* (Paris: Albin Michel, 1990), 21.
66. Christian Jacob, *Géographie et ethnographie en Grèce ancienne* (Paris: Armand Colin, 1991), 44.
67. Giuseppe Tardiola, *Atlante fantastico del medioevo* (Rome: Rubeis, 1990), 14.

68. Joseph Conrad, *Heart of Darkness*, ed. Ross C. Murfin (Boston: St. Bedford's, 1996), 22.
69. Jules Verne, *Robur the Conqueror*, in *Works of Jules Verne*, vol. 14, ed. Charles F. Horne (New York: F. Tyler Daniels, 1911), 92.
70. Auriol, *La fin du voyage*, 60.
71. Paul Rodaway, *Sensuous Geographies: Body, Sense, and Place* (London: Routledge, 1994), 134.
72. Franco Farinelli, *I segni del mondo: Immagine cartografica e discorso geografico in età moderna* (Firenze: La Nuova Italia, 2000), 9.
73. José Rabasa, *Inventing America: Spanish Historiography and the Formation of Eurocentrism* (Norman: University of Oklahoma Press, 1993), 202, 181.
74. Derek Walcott, *Tiepolo's Hound* (New York: Farrar, Straus and Giroux, 2001), 92.
75. Rabasa, *Inventing America*, 181.
76. Bi Kacou Parfait Diandué, *Topolectes 1* (Paris: Publibook, 2005), 44, 49.
77. See Rabasa, *Inventing America*, 186.
78. Farinelli, *I segni del mondo*, 70.
79. [Westphal's pun here involves the protagonist's name (Fisher) and the proximity between the French words for "fisher" or "fisherman" (*pêcheur*) and "sinner" (*pécheur*).]
80. Belén Gopegui, *L'échelle des cartes* , trans. Claude Bleton (Arles: Actes Sud, 1995), 98–99, 88.
81. Marie-Claire Ropars-Wuilleumier, *Écrire l'espace* (Paris: Presses Universitaires de Vincennes, 2002), 56.
82. Massimo Cacciari, *La città* (Villa Verucchio: Pazzini, 2004), 42–43.
83. Serres, *Atlas*, 51.
84. Zaccaria, *Mappe senza frontier*, 8.
85. Hall, *The Dance of Life*, 169–70.
86. See Gillian Rose, *Feminism and Geography: The Limits of Geographical Knowledge* (Minneapolis: University of Minnesota Press, 1993).
87. See Elizabeth Grosz, "Bodies-Cities," in *Sexuality and Space*, ed. Beatriz Colomina (Princeton, NJ: Princeton University Press, 1992), 241–54.
88. See Roberto Calasso, *The Marriage of Cadmus and Harmony*, trans. Tim Parks (New York: Penguin, 1994).
89. bell hooks, *Yearning: Race, Gender, and Cultural Politics* (Boston: South End Press, 1990), 48, 41.
90. Anzaldúa, *Borderlands/La Frontera*, 24.
91. Ngugi wa Thiong'o, *Petals of Blood* (New York: Penguin, 1991), 315.
92. Charles Bukowski, "Six Inches," in *The Most Beautiful Woman in Town* (San Francisco: City Lights, 2001), 24–34.
93. Steven Marcus, *The Other Victorians: A Study of Sexuality and Pornography in Mid-Nineteenth-Century England* (New York: Basic Books, 1966), 268.
94. Catherine Nash, "Remapping the Body/Land: New Cartographies of Identity, Gender, and Landscape in Ireland," in *Writing Women and Space: Colonial and Postcolonial Geographies*, ed. Allison Blunt and Gillian Rose (New York: Guildford, 1994), 234.
95. Ibid., 240.

96. Serres, *Atlas*, 24.
97. Ibid., 29, 28.
98. Anzaldúa, *Borderlands/La Frontera*, 25.
99. Ibid., 101–2.
100. Ibid., 25.
101. hooks, *Yearning*, 149.
102. Ibid.
103. Homi Bhabha, *The Location of Culture* (London: Routledge, 1994), 216.
104. Ibid., 225.
105. Ibid., 217.
106. Edward Soja, *Thirdspace: Journeys to Los Angeles and Other Real-and-Imagined Places* (Oxford: Blackwell, 1996), 56–57.
107. Ibid., 61.
108. Ibid., 70.
109. Frederick Luis Aldama, *Postethnic Narrative Criticism* (Austin: University of Texas Press, 2003), 90. [Like Soja, Aldama omits the space between modifier and "space" in distinguishing *firstspace* and *thirdspace* and so on.]
110. Ibid., 90–91.
111. Deleuze and Guattari, *What is Philosophy?*, 17.
112. Ibid., 18.
113. Serres, *Atlas*, 276.
114. Aldama, *Postethnic Narrative Criticism*, 108.
115. Serres, *Atlas*, 274.

Chapter 3

1. Mark Bonta and John Protevi, *Deleuze and Geophilosophy* (Edinburgh: Edinburgh University Press, 2004), 135.
2. Eugen Fink, *De la phénoménologie*, trans. Didier Franck (Paris: Minuit, 1974), 62.
3. Edward Soja, *Thirdspace: Journeys to Los Angeles and Other Real-and-Imagined Places* (Oxford: Blackwell, 1996), 8.
4. Henri Lefebvre, *The Production of Space*, trans. Donald Nicholson-Smith (Oxford: Blackwell, 1991), 85.
5. Ibid., 54.
6. Ibid., 251.
7. Jean Roudaut, *Les villes imaginaires dans la littérature française* (Paris: Hatier, 1990), 166.
8. Michel Serres, *Atlas* (Paris: Flammarion, 1996), 190.
9. Riccardo Bacchelli, *Poemi lirici* (Bologna: Zanichelli, 1914).
10. Massimo Cacciari, *L'arcipelago* (Milan: Adelphi, 1997), 71.
11. Apollonius of Rhodes, *Jason and the Golden Fleece: The Argonautica*, trans. Richard Hunter (Oxford: Oxford University Press, 1999), 50.
12. Ibid., 138.
13. Jean-Pierre Vernant, *The Universe, the Gods, and Men: Ancient Greek Myths*, trans. Linda Asher (New York: HarperCollins, 2001), 3.

14. Achilles Tatius, *Leucippe and Clitophon*, trans. Tim Whitmarsh (Oxford: Oxford University Press, 2001), 27.
15. Alain Ballabriga, *Les fictions d'Homère: L'invention mythologique et cosmographique dans l'Odyssée* (Paris: PUF, 1998), 109.
16. Christian Jacob, *La description de la terre habitée de Denys d'Alexandrie* (Paris: Albin Michel, 1990), 31.
17. Ibid., 51.
18. Ballabriga, *Les fictions d'Homère*, 8.
19. Raymond Chevallier, "Avant-propos," in *Littérature gréco-romaine et géographie historique* (Paris: Picard, 1974), 6, 8.
20. Valerio Massimo Manfredi, *Mare greco* (Milan: A. Mondadori, 1994), 60.
21. Ibid. 65.
22. François Hartog, *The Mirror of Herodotus*, trans. Janet Lloyd (Berkeley: University of California Press, 1988), 295.
23. Roudaut, *Les villes imaginaires*, 118–19.
24. Brian McHale, *Postmodernist Fiction* (London: Routledge, 1987), 16.
25. David R. Loy, "Saving Time: A Buddhist Perspective on the End," in *Timespace: Geographies of Temporality*, ed. John May and Nigel Thrift (New York: Routledge, 2001), 27.
26. McHale, *Postmodernist Fiction*, 27.
27. See, for example, Thomas G. Pavel, *Fictional Worlds* (Cambridge, MA: Harvard University Press, 1989).
28. Gilles Deleuze and Claire Parnet, *Dialogues II*, trans. Hugh Tomlinson and Barbara Habberjam (New York: Columbia University Press, 2007), 150–51.
29. Jonathan Culler, *On Deconstruction: Theory and Criticism after Structuralism* (Ithaca, NY: Cornell University Press, 1983), 181.
30. Peter Bürger, "Das Verschwinden der Bedeutung: Versuch einer postmodernen Lektüre von M. Tournier, B. Strauss and P. Handke," in *Postmoderne oder der Kampf um die Zukunft*, ed. Peter Kemper (Frankfurt am Main: Fischer, 1988), 307.
31. Pierre Ouellet, *Poétique du regard* (Limoges: Pulim, 2000), 256–57.
32. Lubomír Doležel, *Heterocosmica: Fiction and Possible Worlds* (Balitmore, MD: Johns Hopkins University Press, 1998), 114.
33. Doležel's example is Alain Robbe-Grillet's *La maison de rendez-vous*, in which the fragments of incompatible worlds are combined in contradictory ways.
34. Peter Middleton and Tim Woods, *Literatures of Memory: History, Time, and Space in Postwar Writing* (Manchester: Manchester University Press, 2001), 60, 78.
35. McHale, *Postmodernist Fiction*, 96.
36. Ibid., 28, 32.
37. Marc Augé, *L'impossible voyage: Le tourisme et ses images* (Paris: Rivages, 1997), 69.
38. Ibid., 71.
39. Ibid., 169.
40. Soja, *Thirdspace*, 274.
41. Ibid., 11.
42. McHale, *Postmodernist Fiction*, 219–20, McHale's ellipses. The quotation comes from Gerald Graff, *Literature against Itself: Literary Ideas in Modern Society* (Chicago: University of Chicago Press, 1979), 179–80.

43. See, for example, Hayden White, *Metahistory: The Historical Imagination in Nineteenth-Century Europe* (Baltimore, MD: Johns Hopkins University Press, 1973).
44. Soja, *Thirdspace*, 174. Soja's quotations are from Hayden White, *Tropics of Discourse* (Baltimore, MD: Johns Hopkins University Press, 1978), 98.
45. Michel Picard, *Lire le temps* (Paris: Minuit, 1989), 53.
46. Christine Montalbetti, *Le voyage, le monde et la bibliothèque* (Paris: Presses Universitaires de France, 1997), 1.
47. Ibid., 36.
48. Ibid., 66–67.
49. Ibid., 73.
50. Ibid., 86.
51. Ibid., 95.
52. Ibid., 72.
53. McHale, *Postmodernist Fiction*, 165.
54. Pavel, *Fictional Worlds*, 9.
55. See, for example, Doležel's "Fictionality and the Fields of Reference," *Poetics Today* 5 (1984): 227–51.
56. Pavel, *Fictional Worlds*, 11.
57. Umberto Eco, *The Role of the Reader: Explorations in the Semiotics of Texts* (Bloomington: Indiana University Press, 1979), 219.
58. Ibid., 221.
59. Doležel, *Heterocosmica*, 97.
60. Pavel, *Fictional Worlds*, 143.
61. See Nelson Goodman, *Ways of Worldmaking* (Indianapolis, IN: Hackett, 1978).
62. Andrea Carosso, "Introduction," in Thomas Pavel, *Mondi di invenzione* (Torino: Einaudi, 1992), ix.
63. Bertrand Russell, *Introduction to Mathematical Philosophy* (London: Allen & Unwin, 1956), 169.
64. Pavel, *Fictional Worlds*, 89.
65. See Charles Crittenden, *Unreality: The Metaphysics of Fictional Objects* (Ithaca, NY: Cornell University Press, 1991).
66. See David Lewis, *Counterfactuals* (Cambridge, MA: Harvard University Press, 1973) and *On the Plurality of Worlds* (Oxford: Blackwell, 1986).
67. Alessandro Zinna, *Les objets d'écriture et leurs interfaces* (Limoges: Université de Limoges, 2001), 176.
68. Ibid., 160.
69. Ibid., 164.
70. Gilles Deleuze, *The Fold: Leibniz and the Baroque*, trans. Tom Conley (Minneapolis: University of Minnesota Press, 1993), 137.
71. Russell, *Introduction to Mathematical Philosophy*, 169.
72. Jorge Luis Borges, *Ficciones* (New York: Grove Press, 1962), 25.
73. Pavel, *Fictional Worlds*, 29.
74. McHale, *Postmodernist Fiction*, 28.
75. See Earl Miner, "Common, Proper, and Improper Place," *Proceedings of the XIIth Congress of the International Comparative Literature Association*, vol. 3 (Munich: Iudicium Verlag, 1990).

76. Lennard Davis, *Resisting Novels: Ideology and Fiction* (New York: Methuen, 1987).
77. Italo Calvino, *Invisible Cities*, trans. William Weaver (New York: Harcourt, 1974).
78. Roudaut, *Les villes imaginaires*, 26.
79. See Saul Kripke, *Naming and Necessity* (Oxford: Blackwell, 1981).
80. Peter Handke, *Short Letter, Long Farewell*, trans. Ralph Manheim (New York: New York Review of Books, 2009), 100.
81. Paul Ricoeur, *Time and Narrative*, vol. 3, trans. Kathleen Blamey and David Pellauer (Chicago: University of Chicago Press, 1988), 191–92.
82. Pavel, *Fictional Worlds*, 45.
83. See, for example, Slavoj Žižek, *The Sublime Object of Ideology* (London: Verso, 1989), 159.
84. See McHale, *Postmodernist Fiction*, 45–58.
85. See, for example, Bertrand Westphal, "La Poldévie ou les Balkan près de chez vous," in *Neohelicon* 32.1 (2005): 7–16.
86. Sylviane Coyault, "Parcours géocritique d'un genre: Le récit poétique et ses espaces," in *La géocritique mode d'emploi*, ed. Bertrand Westphal (Limoges: Pulim, 2000), 45.
87. See Guy Davenport, *Da Vinci's Bicycle* (Baltimore, MD: Johns Hopkins University Press, 1979).
88. See Jean-Christophe Valtat, "Balkan près de chez vous, lieux transposés," in *La géocritique mode d'emploi*, ed. Westphal, 203–16.
89. Ronald Sukenick, *98.6: A Novel* (New York: Fiction Collective, 1975), 179.
90. Jean Grenier, *Islands: Lyrical Essays*, trans. Steve Light (Los Angeles: Green Integer, 2005), 91.
91. Georges Arnaud, *The Wages of Fear*, trans. anon. (New York: Farrar, Strauss, and Young, 1952), n.p.
92. Elio Vittorini, *Conversations in Sicily*, trans. Alane Salierno Mason (New York: New Directions, 2000), 1.
93. Robert Kroetsch, "Unhiding the Hidden: Recent Canadian Fiction," *Journal of Canadian Fiction* 3.3 (1974): 43.
94. See Soja, *Thirdspace*, 279.
95. Coyault, "Parcours géocritique d'un genre," 44.
96. Umberto Eco, *Sugli specchi e altri saggi* (Milan: Bompiani, 1985), 174.
97. Ibid., 175.

Chapter 4

1. Jean-Marc Moura, *L'Europe littéraire et l'ailleurs* (Paris: PUF, 1998), 35.
2. Daniel-Henri Pageaux, *La littérature générale et comparée* (Paris: A. Colin, 1994), 60.
3. Moura, *L'Europe littéraire et l'ailleurs*, 45.
4. Ibid., 40.
5. Lawrence Durrell, *Sicilian Carousel* (New York: Marlowe and Company, 1977), 74.
6. Yuri Andrukhovych and Andrzej Stasiuk, *Mon Europe* (Montricher: Les Éditions Noir sur Blanc, 2004), 108.
7. Moura, *L'Europe littéraire et l'ailleurs*, 41.

8. Michel Beniamino, "Une géographie mythique dans les Mascareignes: La Lémurie," in *Les mots de la terre: Géographie et littératures francophones*, ed. Antonella Emina (Rome: Bulzoni, 1998), 205–21.
9. Pageaux, *La littérature générale et compare*, 31.
10. Pierre Ouellet, *Poétique du regard* (Limoges: Pulim, 2000), 32.
11. Ibid., 32.
12. François Hartog, *Memories of Odysseus: Frontier Tales from Ancient Greece*, trans. Janet Lloyd (Chicago: University of Chicago Press, 2001), 9.
13. See Emmanuel Levinas, *Humanism of the Other*, trans. Nidra Poller (Urbana: University of Illinois Press, 2003).
14. Quoted in Edward Soja, *Thirdspace: Journeys to Los Angeles and Other Real-and-Imagined Places* (Oxford: Blackwell, 1996), 132–33, ellipses in original.
15. bell hooks, *Yearning: Race, Gender, and Cultural Politics* (Boston: South End Press, 1990), 145.
16. Gloria Anzaldúa, *Borderlands/La Frontera: The New Mestiza* (San Francisco: Aunt Lute, 1999), 90.
17. Amy Wells-Lynn, "The Intertextual, Sexually-Coded rue Jacob: A Geocritical Approach to Djuna Barnes, Natalie Barney, and Radclyffe Hall," *South Central Review* 22.3 (Fall 2005): 79.
18. Ibid., 80.
19. See Bill Ashcroft, Gareth Griffiths, and Helen Tiffin, eds. *The Postcolonial Studies Reader* (London: Routledge, 1995), especially 117.
20. Eugen Fink, *De la phénoménologie*, trans. Didier Franck (Paris: Minuit, 1974), 31.
21. Ibid., 37.
22. Roger Munier, *Opus Incertum I* (Paris: Deyrolle, 1995), 23.
23. Rossana Bonadei, "I luoghi mosaici degli sguardi," in *Lo squardo del turista e il racconto dei luoghi*, ed. Rossana Bonadei and Ugo Volli (Milan: Franco Angeli, 2003), 17.
24. See Bertrand Westphal, "Îles dalmates: L'odyssée des îles," in *L'œil de la Méditerranée* (La Tour d'Aigues: Éditions de l'Aube, 2005), 177–98.
25. Paolo Zaccaria, *Mappe senza frontiere* (Bari: Palomar, 1999), 102.
26. Oswald Ducrot and Tzvetan Todorov, *Encyclopedic Dictionary of the Sciences of Language*, trans. Catherine Porter (Baltimore, MD: Johns Hopkins University Press, 1979), 328.
27. See Jacques Fontanille, *The Semiotics of Discourse*, trans. Heidi Bostic (New York: Peter Lang, 2007), 11–12.
28. Michel Metzeltin, "L'imaginaire roumain de l'Occident: Questions de méthode et essais d'application," in *Imaginer l'Europe*, ed. Danièle Chauvin (Grenoble: Iris, 1998), 176.
29. Ibid.
30. Gabriele Zanetto, "Presentazione," in Maria de Fanis, *Geografie letterarie* (Rome: Meltini, 2001), 8.
31. Zaccaria, *Mappe senza frontiere* , 334.
32. Fink, *De la phénoménologie*, 195.
33. Ibid., 59.
34. Ibid., 62.

35. Ibid., 204.
36. Paul Rodaway, *Sensuous Geographies: Body, Sense, and Place* (London: Routledge, 1994), 24.
37. hooks, *Yearning*, 146.
38. Yi-Fu Tuan, *Space and Place: The Perspective of Experience* (Minneapolis: University of Minnesota Press, 2002), 8.
39. John Douglas Porteous, *Landscapes of the Mind: Worlds of Sense and Metaphor* (Toronto: University of Toronto Press, 1990), 6.
40. Rodaway, *Sensuous Geographies*, 37.
41. Raymond Murray Schafer, *The Tuning of the World: Toward a Theory of Soundscape Design* (New York: Random House, 1977).
42. See John Douglas Porteous, "Smellscape," *Progress in Human Geography* 9.3 (1985): 356–78.
43. Porteous, *Landscapes of the Mind*, 196.
44. See Rodaway, *Sensuous Geographies*, 36–37.
45. Jacques Fontanille, "Modes du sensible et syntaxe figurative," in *Nouveaux actes sémiotiques* 17–19 (1999): 1–67.
46. Porteous, *Landscapes of the Mind*, 197.
47. See Rodaway, *Sensuous Geographies*, chapter 4.
48. Peter Süskind, *Perfume: The Story of a Murderer*, trans. John E. Woods (New York: Vintage, 2001), 4.
49. Peter Høeg, *Smilla's Sense of Snow*, trans. Tiina Nunnally (New York: Delta, 1995), 418.
50. Marc Augé, *L'impossible voyage: Le tourisme et ses images* (Paris: Rivages, 1997), 150–51.
51. Fausta Cialente, *Cortile a Cleopatra* (Milan: A. Mondadori, 1973), 170.
52. Lawrence Durrell, *Clea* (New York: Penguin, 1991), 243.
53. Edwar al-Kharrat, *City of Saffron*, trans. Frances Liardet (London: Quartet, 1998), 20.
54. Fink, *De la phénoménologie*, 52.
55. Ibid., 53.
56. Ibid., 31.
57. Henri Lefebvre, *The Production of Space*, trans. Donald Nicholson-Smith (Oxford: Blackwell, 1991), 86.
58. Ibid., 229.
59. Gilles Deleuze and Félix Guattari, *A Thousand Plateaus*, trans. Brian Massumi (Minneapolis: University of Minnesota Press, 1987), 502.
60. Marcel Roncayolo, *La ville et ses territoires* (Paris: Gallimard, 1990), 20.
61. Ibid., 143.
62. Ibid.
63. Hans Robert Jauss, *Toward an Aesthetic of Reception*, trans. Timothy Bahti (Minneapolis: University of Minnesota Press, 1982), 36.
64. Ibid., 37–38.
65. Italo Calvino, *Invisible Cities*, trans. William Weaver (New York: Harcourt, 1974), 10.
66. Ismail Kadaré, *Chronicle in Stone: A Novel*, trans. anon (New York: Arcade, 2007).

67. Calvino, *Invisible Cities*, 32.
68. Ibid., 30–31.
69. Itamar Even-Zohar, *Polysystems Studies* [*Poetics Today* 11.1 (Spring 1990)], 87.
70. Lefebvre, *The Production of Space*, 206.
71. Cees Nooteboom, *L'enlèvement d'Europe*, trans. from the Dutch by Philippe Noble and Isabelle Rosselin (Paris: Maren Sell, 1994), 29–30.
72. Ibid., 41.
73. Ibid., 35.
74. Ibid., 35.
75. Ibid., 115.
76. Calvino, *Invisible Cities*, 16.
77. Ibid., 139.
78. Robert Frank, "Qu'est-ce qu'un stéréotype?" in *Une idée fausse est un fait vrai: Les stéréotypes nationaux en Europe*, ed. Jean-Noël Jeannerey (Paris: Éditions Odile Jacob, 2000), 19.
79. Ibid., 22.
80. On the relations of *doxa* to *paradox*, see, for example, Roland Barthes, *Roland Barthes by Roland Barthes*, trans. Richard Howard (New York: Farrar, Strauss, and Giroux, 1977), 71.
81. Fink, *De la phénoménologie*, 106.
82. Tzvetan Todorov, "Préface," in Edward W. Said, *L'Orientalisme*, trans. from the English by Catherine Malamoud (Paris: Seuil, 1980).
83. Ouellet, *Poétique du regard*, 207.
84. Marc Brosseau, *Des romans-géographes* (Paris: L'Harmattan, 1996), 75.
85. hooks, *Yearning*, 93.
86. Ruth Amossy and Anne Herschberg Pierrot, *Stéréotypes et clichés* (Paris: Nathan, 1997), 64.
87. Ibid., 118.
88. Roland Barthes, "Peter Loti: *Aziyadé*," in *New Critical Essays*, trans. Richard Howard (New York: Hill and Wang, 1980), 105–21.

Chapter 5

1. Italo Calvino, *Hermit in Paris: Autobiographical Writings*, trans. Martin McLaughlin (New York: Vintage, 2003), 167.
2. Ibid.
3. Ibid.
4. Ibid., 173.
5. Georges Perec, *Tentative d'épuisement d'un lieu parisien* (Paris: Christian Bourgois, 1975), 12.
6. [This is the title of the forthcoming English translation of Perec's book.]
7. Perec, *Tentative d'épuisement d'un lieu parisien*, 18.
8. Umberto Eco, *Six Walks in the Fictional Woods* (Cambridge, MA: Harvard University Press, 1994), 60.
9. Ibid., 76.
10. Ibid.

11. Ibid., 77.
12. Ibid.
13. Ibid., 87.
14. Ibid.
15. Benito Pelegrín, *Figurations de l'infini: L'âge baroque européen* (Paris: Seuil, 2000), 60.
16. Carlos Fuentes, *The Buried Mirror: Reflections on Spain and the New World* (New York: Mariner, 1999), 125.
17. Ibid., 124–25.
18. Pelegrín, *Figurations de l'infini*, 115.
19. Fuentes, *The Buried Mirror*, 134.
20. Michel Butor, with Christian Jacomino, *Frontiers*, trans. Elinor S. Miller (Birmingham, AL: Summa, 1989), 36.
21. Michel Butor, *Répertoire V* (Paris: Minuit, 1982), 36.
22. Angelo Ara and Claudio Magris, *Trieste: Un' identità di frontiere* (Torino: Einaudi, 1987), 16.
23. Gianfranco Dioguardi, "Lisbona fugge dalle acque," in *Il Corriere della Sera* (January 24, 1992).
24. Stefano Malatesta, "Lisbona: Benvenuta con i sogni di Pessoa," in *Panorama Mese* (November 1985).
25. [Westphal refers to the bronze statue of Pessoa, which sits as if another customer of the café in Lisbon.]
26. Gregor von Rezzori, *The Snows of Yesteryear*, trans. H. F. Broch de Rothermann (New York: New York Review of Books, 1989), 290.
27. Ibid.
28. Eco, *Six Walks in the Fictional Woods*, 84.
29. Ibid.
30. Jean Roudaut, *Les villes imaginaires dans la littérature française* (Paris: Hatier, 1990), 168.
31. Butor, *Répertoire V*, 33.
32. Ibid., 34.
33. Roland Barthes, *Empire of Signs*, trans. Richard Howard (New York: Hill and Wang, 1983), 31.
34. Ibid., 79.
35. Pierre Sansot, *La poétique de la ville* (Paris: Klincksieck, 1971), 67.
36. Peter Handke, *Alone*, trans. Ralph Manheim (New York: Macmillan, 2000), 3.
37. Roudaut, *Les villes imaginaires*, 10.
38. Edward Soja, *Thirdspace: Journeys to Los Angeles and Other Real-and-Imagined Places* (Oxford: Blackwell, 1996), 238–39.
39. See Fredric Jameson, *Postmodernism; or, The Cultural Logic of Late Capitalism* (Durham: Duke University Press, 1991).
40. See Celeste Olalquiaga, *Megalopolis: Contemporary Cultural Sensibilities* (Minneapolis: University of Minnesota Press, 1992).
41. Soja, *Thirdspace*, 240.
42. Michel Serres, *Atlas* (Paris: Flammarion, 1996), 263.
43. Ibid., 275.

44. Nuruddin Farah, *Maps* (New York: Arcade, 1999), 227–28.
45. Ibid., 229.
46. François Dagognet, *Le nombre et le lieu* (Paris: Vrin, 1984), 64.
47. Jorge Luis Borges, *The Aleph and Other Stories*, trans. Andrew Hurley (New York: Penguin, 2000), 127.
48. Henri Lefebvre, *The Production of Space*, trans. Donald Nicholson-Smith (Oxford: Blackwell, 1991), 118.
49. Carlos García Gual, *Mitos, viajes, héroes* (Madrid: Suma de letras, 2001), 30.
50. [Westphal makes a pun here, between the noun *rigole* (meaning trench or ditch) and the verb *rigoler* (to laugh or to poke fun).]
51. Marie-Claire Ropars-Wuilleumier, *Écrire l'espace* (Paris: Presses Universitaires de Vincennes, 2002), 136.
52. Butor, *Répertoire V*, 36.
53. Roland Barthes, "Semiology and Urbanism," in *The Semiotic Challenge*, trans. Richard Howard (New York: Hill and Wang, 1988), 195.
54. Ibid., 199.
55. Hans Robert Jauss, *Toward an Aesthetic of Reception*, trans. Timothy Bahti (Minneapolis: University of Minnesota Press, 1982), 21.
56. Ibid., 25.
57. Ibid.
58. Ibid., 29.
59. Ibid., 38–39.
60. Ibid., 39.
61. Dagognet, *Le nombre et le lieu*, 187.
62. Lefebvre, *The Production of Space*, 7.
63. Ibid., 15.
64. Sansot, *La poétique de la ville*, 418.
65. Ibid., 420.
66. Gilles Deleuze, *Difference and Repetition*, trans. Paul Patton (New York: Columbia University Press, 1994), 42.
67. Christine Montalbetti, *Le voyage, le monde, et la bibliothèque* (Paris: Presses Universitaires de France, 1997), 14.
68. Marc Augé, *L'impossible voyage: Le tourisme et ses images* (Paris: Rivages, 1997), 140, 142.
69. Julia Kristeva, *Sèméiotikè: Recherches pour une sémanalyse* (Paris: Seuil, 1978), 120.
70. Montalbetti, *Le voyage, le monde, et la bibliothèque*, 123.
71. Marc Brosseau, *Des romans-géographes* (Paris: L'Harmattan, 1996), 155.
72. Michel Butor, *Répertoire II* (Paris: Minuit, 1964), 50. [This appears in English as "The Space of the Novel," in *Inventory: Essays*, trans. Richard Howard (New York: Simon and Schuster, 1969), 38.]

Index